The B'nai B'rith History of the Jewish People

CREATORS OF THE JEWISH EXPERIENCE
IN ANCIENT AND MEDIEVAL TIMES

Edited with introductory notes by
Simon Noveck

Annotated bibliograph'
Reuven Kimelma

B'nai B'rith Books
Washington, D.C.

Jerusalem • London • Paris • Buenos Aires • East Sydney

Library of Congress Cataloging in Publication Data

Creators of the Jewish experience in ancient and medieval times.

Bibliography: p.   Includes index.
1. Rabbis—Biography. 2. Scholars, Jewish—Biography
3. Bible. O.T.—Biography. 4. Philosophers, Jewish—Biography
I. Noveck, Simon
BM750.C74 1985   296'.092'2 B   85-72300
ISBN 0-910250-02-2   ISBN 0-910250-03-0 (pbk.)

The B'nai B'rith History of the Jewish People
was first published during the years 1959–1964
as the B'nai B'rith Great Book Series.
The present edition, in five volumes,
has been selected to be part of the B'nai B'rith Judaica Library.
The Library is sponsored by the
B'nai B'rith International Commission on Adult Jewish Education
in an effort to promote a greater popular understanding
of Judaism and the Jewish tradition.
The volumes in the series are:
Creators of the Jewish Experience in Ancient and Medieval Times
Creators of the Jewish Experience in the Modern World
Concepts that Distinguish Judaism
Great Jewish Thinkers of the Twentieth Century
Contemporary Jewish Thought

Contents

Introduction

The towering achievement in publishing by the B'nai B'rith International Commission on Adult Jewish Education has been, to this date, the B'nai B'rith Great Book Series edited for four volumes by Simon Noveck and for the fifth by Abraham Ezra Millgram. These books, as Rabbi Noveck described, presented "the inner-content of Jewish tradition, the great personalities and thinkers, the ideas, beliefs and religious movements of Judaism." In short, they are a *History of the Jewish People*. The nearly fifty scholars, teachers, and rabbis who contributed original essays to these volumes were a preponderant majority of the great interpreters of Jewish civilization at mid-century. Twenty-five years after they began to appear, the freshness and vigor of each essay is undiminished.

The continuing demand for each of the volumes by colleges and universities, synagogues and day schools, is being met by this revised edition. The essays are presented as they originally appeared, though for greater clarity the volumes themselves have been retitled and the series renamed. It was my belief that this new edition would enjoy a greater utility if each of the essays were supplemented by annotated bibliographies that reviewed the literature relevant to the subjects of the essays. Three distinguished scholars and teachers have joined me in the preparation of these bibliographies: Steven T. Katz of Cornell University, Reuven Kimelman of Brandeis University and Arthur Kurzweil, the noted author and lecturer. Each of us benefitted as students from this series, and the opportunity to enhance its value has brought us much satisfaction.

The American journalist George Will recently wrote of the growing rootlessness of our lives, our failure to connect to our past and our neglect of our legacy of a shared and valuable civilization. He was addressing himself to the inadequacies of the American educational system as it teaches the essence of Western civilization, but his point applies with a special urgency to the demands of a sound Jewish education. He chose, quite fortuitously, a Biblical example to illustrate his argument:

> In 1940, a British officer on Dunkirk beach flashed to London a three-word message, "But if not..." It was instantly recognized as a quotation from the Book of Daniel, where Nebuchadnezzar commands Shadrach, Meshach and Abednego to worship the golden image or be thrust into the fiery furnace. They reply defiantly; "If our God whom we serve is able to deliver us, he will deliver us from the fiery furnace, and out of thy hand, O king. But if not, be it known unto thee, O king, that we will not serve thy gods, nor worship the golden image which thou hast set up."

The message from Dunkirk is stirring evidence of a community deriving cohesion, inspiration and courage from a shared history. The question this story raises is how many of us today could either receive or transmit such a message from the rich legacy of Jewish civilization?

B'nai B'rith International through its Commission on Adult Jewish Education is sponsoring the republication of these volumes in the belief that they can play a large role in stimulating a desire to learn about Judaism, Jewish history and Jewish civilization, and that of themselves they are superb examples of the living Jewish tradition.

The joy of being a Jew is not derived from books. It is a product of a rich family life wherein Judaism radiates a happiness and contentment that passes beyond the ability of language to describe. It is the product of partaking of the company of other Jews. Yet for the connectedness of one Jew to his religion and peoplehood there is a need for the passion to be grounded in understanding and knowledge. These essays can play an important part in awakening and satisfying a desire to learn and comprehend.

There is nothing obscure in these volumes. They have been written with an enviable clarity, and they will inform the non-Jewish reader as fully as the Jewish reader. In presenting these volumes to the public, B'nai B'rith looks forward to a full engagement of the ideas presented therein with the wisdom and curiosity of men and women everywhere.

The B'nai B'rith Commission on Adult Jewish Education continues to enjoy the support, advice and commitment of its founder Maurice A. Weinstein, and the then B'nai B'rith International President who worked diligently to establish the Commission's work at the center of the B'nai B'rith—Philip M. Klutznick.

This new edition has benefitted from the encouragement of B'nai B'rith International President Gerald Kraft and key members of the Board of Governors. Mr. Abe Kaplan, the immediate past chairman of the Commission, and Dr. A.J. Kravtin, the current chairman have been effectively energetic in promoting this work. Executive Vice President Dr. Daniel Thursz and Associate Director Rabbi Joel H. Meyers provide the leadership and environment necessary for a Jewish educational program of quality to flourish, and within the Commission my patient secretary Mrs. Edith Levine does the same. My collaborator on this project has been Mr. Robert Teitler, a devoted B'nai B'rith member and a creative publisher.

Michael Neiditch, Director
B'nai B'rith International Commission
on Adult Jewish Education

Washington, D.C.
July 24, 1985
5 Av 5785

Foreword

A difference of opinion exists among modern scholars and historians as to the influence of great men on the events and movements of history. There are those who feel that historical changes are due mainly to the underlying social and economic forces at work in a particular era. In their view, neither the fall of Rome, the rise of modern capitalism, the advent of World War I, the Russian Revolution, nor any other turning point in history can be directly attributed to the acts of individual men. These may at best precipitate events already in the making or hasten a process already under way. Other scholars, however, insist that strong leaders have a determining influence on the course of human affairs. If not for the teachings and activities of Paul, they point out, Christianity might never have emerged. The impact of the personality of Mohammed undoubtedly changed the whole history of the Near East and North Africa. Similarly, without Lenin there might have been no Communism in Russia today, and had Hitler not been allowed to gain power, millions of human beings might be alive today who perished during the Nazi period.

Whatever the pros and cons of this question, in Jewish history great personalities have often played important roles. Because of the nature of Jewish life which, especially since the destruction of the second Jewish state, has had largely a spiritual and cultural character, the prophets, sages, philosophers, and teachers of Judaism have exerted unusual influence. A knowledge of their deeds and thoughts can shed light on Jewish history and give us insight into the ideals of Judaism.

It is the purpose of this book and its sequel to present the life story and achievements of twenty-four such personalities who emerged during the more than three thousand years of Jewish history. This volume deals with heroes of the ancient and medieval periods, and a companion volume will consider twelve great figures of the past two hundred years. Though full-length biographies and sketches of several of these individuals are available, to our knowledge no book exists, both authentic in scholarship and popular in approach, which contains the biographies of outstanding Jews representing the entire sweep of Jewish history.

The present book begins with three towering biblical personalities: Moses, the great lawgiver and emancipator, through whose genius the foundations of the Jewish nation and faith were laid; David, the king, who united the warring tribes, freed Palestine from the domination of the Philistines, and created the kingdom of Israel; and Jeremiah, whose emphasis on the covenant relationship between man and God and on integrity and sincerity in human relationships make him one of the most relevant of the Hebrew prophets for our time. We then turn to Philo, the philosopher of Alexandrian Jewry, who tried to synthesize Judaism and Hellenism and who demonstrated for the first time that Jews could live creatively in two cultures. We then consider Akiba, outstanding rabbinic sage and one of the master builders of the Mishnah.

From the Middle Ages we have chosen Saadia Gaon, Judah Halevi, and Maimonides, the three most distinguished philosophers of Judaism of the Muslim era, whose views show the effect of a cross-fertilization of Judaism and the philosophies of their time. As a representative of Jewry in early Christian Europe we have selected Rashi, the famed biblical and Talmudic commentator of eleventh-century France. Then follows the dramatic story of Abravanel, statesman and scholar, who served as financial advisor to the sovereigns of four different countries in which he was forced to seek refuge. The volume closes with two eighteenth-century East European figures—the Baal Shem Tov, founder of *Hasidism*, with its emotional and joyous expression of religious piety, and the Vilna Gaon, who epitomizes the tradition of Jewish scholarship at its noblest.

Why have these particular men been selected for inclusion in this volume? In our judgment, each of the personalities who appears here has made a distinctive contribution to the development of the Jewish tradition and has been accepted by large segments of the Jewish people as an outstanding hero. Where a cluster of personalities arose in the same epoch, as during the prophetic and rabbinic periods, we have chosen the one whose message seemed to us most relevant for the modern world. An attempt has also been made to have as many different eras and countries represented as possible—Palestine, Hellenistic Jewry, Babylonia, Spanish Jewry's "Golden Age" and then its decline, medieval France, and eighteenth-century Poland and Lithuania.

While these men differed from one another in many ways—in personality, background, language, and in their approach to Judaism they all share certain basic character traits and reflect in their lives some of Judaism's great values. Except for the biblical era, when the Jews had a natural interest in their corporate destiny, the outstanding Jewish personalities were men of thought rather than action, concerned with problems of the mind rather than with political affairs. By and large, it has been the prophet, rabbi or teacher rather than the ruler or general whose leadership has guided the development of the Jewish people. For the most part the men in this book possessed a consuming love of learning for its own sake. Maimonides, in spite of a busy medical career, found time to study and write; Abravanel, though a finance minister, used every free moment to work on his commentaries; the Vilna Gaon gave up all other pursuits to probe the Torah and extract its deepest meanings.

Likewise, these men shared a passion for justice. Though they lived under different historical situations and often very trying circumstances, the concern for the underprivileged, the orphan, widow, slave, stranger, and laborer is a recurring note. This can be seen in the prophecies of Jeremiah, the legislation of Akiba, the *Code* of Maimonides, and the commentaries of Rashi, all of which reflect a deep concern for human rights.

Finally, all these men can be described as religious or spiritual personalities who shared the great beliefs of Jewish tradition—in God and His revelation, in the chosenness of the Jewish people, the coming of the Messiah, the doctrine of immortality. They all loved their people, identified with it, and were willing to sacrifice themselves for its welfare. Jeremiah endured loneliness, imprisonment, and the pain of being called a traitor, but continued with his prophetic mission. Maimonides and Abravanel accepted exile from their countries, and Akiba suffered the death of a martyr.

Because Jewish heroes have had these traits of character, a study of their lives, we believe, can be helpful to all who face ethical dilemmas in their personal lives, who must choose among conflicting loyalties in our complex society, or who are in search of a set of values.

This book can also serve as an introduction to the study of Jewish history and thought. While we cannot agree with Carlyle's famous thesis that history is in essence the biographies of its great men, yet it is true that biography simplifies history, reducing its complexities to the body of events, forces, and facts witnessed by one person. The lives of these men can give us insights into some of the major events in Jewish history—the Exodus from Egypt, the destruction of the First Temple, Bar Kokhba's tragic stand against the Romans, and the expulsion of the Jews from Spain—as well as an understanding of many aspects of the Jewish faith.

Every effort has therefore been made to make this book as useful a learning tool as possible. Though written by eleven contributors, all the essays have a common frame of reference. Most of the authors indicate at the very outset the significance and lasting contribution of the personality discussed, and make some reference to the character of the era in which he lived. The life story of each personality is then presented in some detail so the reader can become acquainted with the hero and feel a sense of identification with him. Unfortunately, sufficient biographical data is not always available, for in Jewish tradition there has been an aversion to biography, an avoidance of full-length portraiture. In the Bible the description of the personality is always subordinate to the story of the nation, and in the Talmud the individual life history is always relegated to the background. Also, during the Middle Ages no great emphasis was put on the personal details in the lives of the great scholars and personalities. Nevertheless, aside from Philo and Rashi, enough material is available to give us portraits of most of the men in this volume. The chronological sketch of each life is followed by a summary of the most significant work or achievements of the figure and an evaluation of his legacy for the modern world.

Introductions appear before each chapter or collection of chapters to orient the reader to the historical period involved, or to provide bridges from one era to the next. Since it has not been possible within the scope of this present volume to include representatives of every period of Jewish history, it is our hope that these brief introductions will help at least in part to fill in the inevitable gaps.

As far as possible, technical and philosophical terms have been kept to a minimum. Unfamiliar terms, subjects, or personalities have been explained in the Glossary, or in explanatory notes at the bottom of the page. An index has also been prepared.

It is our hope that the reader will become sufficiently interested in some of the personalities treated in this volume to pursue further reading. For that purpose, bibliographic guides to each personality have been provided at the end of the chapter.

A project of this scope cannot succeed without the cooperation of many persons in various capacities in the Jewish community. First and foremost go our thanks to the individual contributors who have graciously revised and in many instances rewritten their essays to fit into the frame of reference of this volume. Professor Oscar I. Janowsky of the College of the City of New York has read the essays from the point of view of an historian; Rabbi Harry Essrig of Grand Rapids, Michigan from the adult education point of view; and John Farrar, of Farrar, Straus and Cudahy, from the editorial point of view. I should also like to record my deep gratitude to Lily Edelman, who is serving as editorial associate for the entire B'nai B'rith Great Books project. She has participated in every stage of the planning and editing of this manuscript. There is no chapter in this book which has not benefited from her suggestions both as to content and style. In addition, she has assumed responsibility for readying the volume for the press.

The following have read several chapters of the manuscript and given us the benefit of their critical suggestions: Rabbis Myron Berman, Mordecai Chertoff, Ephraim Fischoff, Marvin J. Goldfine, Ludwig Nadelman, and Aaron Seidman; Dr. Max F. Baer, Dr. Louis L. Kaplan, and William C. Levy. Individual chapters were read by Isaac Franck, Rabbi Samuel Glasner, Dr. Moshe Greenberg, Dr. Edward W. Jelenko, Rabbi Jacob Kabakoff, Dr. Mordecai Kamrat, Dr. Joseph Kaster, Rabbi Seymour Siegal, Dr. Judah Stampfer, and Professor Samuel Sandmel.

My special appreciation goes to Maurice A. Weinstein, who has served with dedication as National Chairman of the Committee since the inception of the Department in 1954, and who, for several years prior to that time, was instrumental in encouraging adult education activities within B'nai B'rith. I am also grateful to Hyman and Rita Chipkin, Bernard Frank, and Harvey Platt, as well as to Rabbis Ira Eisenstein, Norman Frimer, Alfred Jospe, Arthur J. Lelyveld, Harold Weisberg, and Professor Marvin Fox for many acts of helpfulness and cooperation. None of the above, however, is to be held responsible in any way for the inadequacies in the conception or execution of the present volume. A word of thanks is also due to Joseph L. Rubin of the Roosevelt Four Freedoms Library of B'nai B'rith Women, to Lawrence Marwick and the staff of the Hebraic Section of the Library of Congress, and to Abraham Berger and the staff of the Jewish Division of the New York Public Library for their assistance.

I wish also to record my deep appreciation to the members of the Board of Governors of B'nai B'rith for their sponsorship of this publications program and for granting the editor complete freedom to plan and carry it out. Dr. Maurice Bisgyer, Joseph Sklover, and Bernard Simon have been particularly cooperative and helpful.

It is hard to express what the Great Books series owes to Philip M. Klutznick. Without his day-to-day interest in this and the forthcoming volumes, his constant emphasis both publicly and privately on the importance of adult education for the American Jew, and his personal encouragement and support, these books might never have seen the light of day.

Finally, it is fitting that a word of tribute be paid to the late Isadore Bennett of Charlotte, North Carolina, whose generous bequest to B'nai B'rith and to the Department of Adult Jewish Education has made possible the preparation of three volumes of this series.

SIMON NOVECK

Washington, D. C.

ANCIENT TIMES

The classical age of Judaism begins with Moses and extends until the completion of the Talmud in the fifth century of the Common Era. In addition to the Mosaic period, it includes the age of the prophets, the post-Exilic period when Judaism matured, and the Hellenistic and Rabbinic ages. While a Diaspora already existed during the days of the prophets, and increased in subsequent centuries, particularly under Hellenism, most of the activity of the Jewish people during these eras took place in Palestine. Here the foundations of the Jewish faith were laid, and the great ideas, beliefs, and practices developed upon which the Jewish people were to base their way of life during the following centuries.

Many great spiritual heroes arose during these creative years. "As soon as the sun of one righteous man set, the sun of another arose," a Talmudic sage wrote. In each of these ancient periods there appeared spiritual figures—prophets, teachers, sages—who helped shape Jewish life. We have chosen three from the biblical period, and one each from the Hellenistic and Rabbinic ages.

Because the first three are biblical personages, many of us are likely to approach them with a sense of reverence and awe. In Judaism, however, unlike other religions, there are no central figures who are enshrined and hallowed above all others. Islam, for example, is based primarily on the life and teachings of Mohammed as the prophet of Allah, while Christianity is inconceivable without the personality of Jesus. The major Christian holidays represent events in Jesus' life, and the New Testament consists in good part of accounts of his sayings and the deeds he performed. In Judaism, on the contrary, no one figure is indispensable. While Moses is regarded as preeminent among the prophets, neither the Jewish way of life nor the calendar of Jewish holidays is based on events in his life. Moreover, though he was the liberator who led the Jews from Egypt, his name is not even glorified in the Passover *Haggadah*. The rabbis say that had Moses not preceded him, Ezra would have been worthy of receiving the Torah from God at Sinai. Judaism is a people-centered rather than a hero-centered tradition.

Nevertheless, the personalities of the Bible have over the centuries become endowed with a special significance and moral grandeur. Each incident in their lives has been told and retold, and every aspect of their characters has been discussed so many times that they have acquired a special sanctity not ascribed to later heroes.

Did these men live and flourish in ancient Israel in the manner described by the Bible? Or are we to interpret the stories of their lives allegorically, as personifications of great ideals? Did the events in th · lives of Moses, David, and Jeremiah actually take place as recorded, or are these biblical accounts merely later folk embellishments? To what extent can the Bible be relied upon as a source for Jewish history?

Three views—all of which are still current—exist about the Bible and its heroes. From ancient times down to the middle of the eighteenth century, the first view prevailed which accepted the accounts of biblical heroes as the literal word of God, and therefore as unquestionably true and trustworthy. In this traditional view, Moses was the greatest of the prophets "whom the Lord knew face to face." He led the Jews out of Egypt, received the Commandments on their behalf, and wrote the five books which bear his name. David, too, had the gift of divine inspiration, and, in addition to conquering the Philistines and winning Jerusalem, wrote the Book of Psalms, including Psalm 134 ("By the Rivers of Babylon"), which he composed long before the Babylonian Exile. Traditionally, it was thought that Jeremiah was the author of the book bearing his name (with the help of Baruch) as well as of the Book of Lamentations.[1]

The Talmudic sages were, of course, aware of difficulties and discrepancies in the biblical text. Thus, some questioned whether Moses wrote the last eight verses of Deuteronomy describing his own death, or whether Joshua and Samuel were the sole authors of the books bearing their names. In the Middle Ages philosophers like Maimonides interpreted some of the miracles in the Bible in a rationalistic or allegorical manner, and exegetes like Ibn Ezra and Abravanel raised questions about the arrangement and authorship of certain of the books. But these criticisms were fragmentary and scattered; not one of these men denied the divine origin of the Torah or its historical accuracy. Josephus, the famous historian, summed up the traditional view when he described Scripture as the work of an unbroken line of prophets, who, by the grace of divine inspiration, obtained a knowledge of the events recorded. "It is not open to everybody to write the records," he wrote. "The prophets alone had this privilege, obtaining their knowledge of the most remote and ancient history through the inspiration which they owed to God."

About the middle of the eighteenth century, however, under the impact of the Age of Reason and the new scientific studies, scholars began to question the basic assumptions of the traditional approach and the historical validity of many of the events associated with the Bible and the date and authorship of its books.[2]

Jean Astruc, a French physician, originated what is now called higher biblical criticism,* and during the following century a series of scholars, mostly German Protestant in background, developed the theory. Its classic formulation came from Julius Wellhausen, who in 1878 published an epoch-making work, *Prolegomena to the History of Ancient Israel*, in which he claimed to have found the historical key to the interpretation of biblical literature.

What Wellhausen and his successors undertook to prove was that apparent repetitions, contradictions, and discrepancies in the Bible, and the use of different names for God in different sections indicate that the Bible was composed by many authors at various times. By studying these variations and repetitions, they were able to separate what they felt were various strata or documents and to determine approximately when they were composed. The conclusion of these biblical critics was that Judaism had passed through various stages until the days of the prophets, when it gradually developed the idea of ethical monotheism and the concept of a universal God. In the history of religion, they pointed out, ritual codes had generally emerged before ethical formulations, and they felt it was impossible

---

* Some regard Spinoza (1632-1677) as the father of biblical criticism. See Solomon Goldman, *Book of Books*, pp. 44-46, for a detailed discussion of Spinoza's contribution in this area.

for such lofty ethical conceptions as are found in the Bible to have developed so early in the history of the Jews, when Israel was still in a low state of culture. All that Moses at best could have given the Jews, they said, were a few religious principles, which were later worked out by the prophets and ascribed to him. As Ernest Renan put it: "Three-fourths of the rays of glory which encircle Moses should be credited to Jeremiah." [3] Some critics even doubted that the man Moses had ever existed; they were sure that the accounts of David and his exploits, and of Solomon and his vast building program were exaggerated and impossible at this early stage of Jewish history. Much of Jeremiah, they felt, was written by later hands, and, according to at least one outstanding scholar, the destruction of Jerusalem and the Babylonian Exile related by Jeremiah never actually took place.

In recent decades, this negative attitude toward the Bible and its heroes has gradually changed. As a result of increasing knowledge about the ancient Middle East, the decipherment of ancient languages and studies of ancient Semitic civilizations, and particularly through the dramatic discoveries of modern archeology during the past thirty years, the Bible is now regarded as basically a reliable and historic record of the past. Its descriptions of the origin of the Jewish people and the development of the Jewish faith reveal that the Bible had an "amazing historical memory" and a clear picture of its tribal and family origins.[4]

Excavations at Ur, the birthplace of Abraham in ancient Babylonia;[5] discoveries of thousands of clay texts at Mari on the upper Euphrates;[6] the discoveries in 1929 in the Syrian port of Ugarit of literary documents written in a language very close to biblical Hebrew and with identical phrases and idioms[7]—all these have thrown new light on the culture and conditions in ancient Mesopotamia and Palestine during the patriarchal age. When these are added to the Tell-el Amarna letters from the archives of Egyptian kings (found at the end of the nineteenth century), written by officials in Palestine and Syria,[8] and the Code of Hammurabi with its illustrations of ancient Babylonian law,[9] the background of the patriarchs becomes clarified and some of the events in their lives can be dated. According to William F. Albright, as a result of this accumulation of data, it becomes evident that "as a whole the picture in Genesis is historical, and there is no reason to doubt the general accuracy of the biographical details and the sketches of personality which make the patriarchs come alive." [10]

Similarly, as Harry Orlinsky explains, information is now available to relate the age of Moses to the general background of Egypt and other countries at that time. It is now known that Israelite law and institutions tend to be older and more continuous than was previously supposed. This earlier dating of biblical material leads to the conclusion that Moses played a highly original role in sifting and organizing Semitic and Hebrew concepts and practices. Thus, according to Albright, the Moses of tradition is "so consistent, so well attested by different Pentateuchal documents, and so congruent with knowledge of the Near East that his historicity is substantiated." [11]

An accumulation of data also indicates the accuracy of the biblical account of Jeremiah and his times. In 1935 a group of inscribed *ostraca* (fragments of pottery used as writing material) found on the site of the biblical fortress of Lachish, and identified as dating from the age of Jeremiah, turned out to be letters sent by a Jewish officer to the governor of Lachish, which referred to military problems caused by the Babylonian invasion, probably just before the fall of Jerusalem. These findings also contained a reference to "the words of the (prophet) who weakens the hands of the people"—an accusation identical with that made against Jeremiah[12] (Jeremiah 38:4).

Other aspects of the period of Jeremiah such as the first exile to Babylonia in 597 B.C.E. are completely confirmed from Babylonian records in language similar to that of Chronicles. An explicit reference to Gedaliah, governor of Judea until after the fall of Jerusalem, was found in the impression of a seal on which was the inscription "To Gedaliah who is over the House." On cuneiform tablets recovered in Babylon, Jehoiachin, the king of Judah who was taken captive to Babylon in 597, is described as "king of the land of Yahud," thus confirming the biblical story that after the exile Jehoiachin was restored to favor by the Babylonian king Evil-merodach.[12]

Because of these developments it is quite clear that the negative and skeptical attitude toward the Bible as a source of Jewish biography is no longer tenable. While many of the picturesque details in the lives of the heroes may not be accurate, and undoubtedly some of the events described may be embellishments of later generations, the Book of Books emerges as the best source available for a knowledge of ancient Israel.

With this in mind, the writers of the three essays that follow focus attention on Moses, David, and Jeremiah as historical figures whose words and deeds shaped the destiny of the Jewish people.

Moses

1 . *Moses*

[*c.1300 B.C.E.*]

HARRY M. ORLINSKY

A M O N G the great personalities in the long span of Jewish history, extending over a period of some four thousand years, Moses must invariably stand at the head. Already in biblical times, he had become so revered and so much a legend that when classical prophecy made its mark in Israel, more than half a millennium after Moses' time, he emerged as *the prophet* par excellence: "And there has not arisen a prophet since in Israel like Moses, whom the Lord knew face to face" (Deuteronomy 34:10).

Israel Comes to Egypt

At the turn of the third millennium, about 2000 B.C.E., a Hebrew* named Abraham, accompanied by his wife Sarah and their wordly goods, started out on a journey that was to take them from one end of the Fertile Crescent to the other, from Ur in southern Mesopotamia to the southwestern border of Canaan, at Egypt. Abraham and Sarah had left family and friends in Ur, and in Paddan-aram too, in northern Syria, to make this trek; and although they and their offspring maintained their family and cultural ties with the place of their origin for some time,

---

* While the terms "Hebrew(s)" and "Israel(ites)" are used interchangeably in this essay, the first is older than the second. It was during the period of the Judges (12th-11th centuries) that the term "Israelites" (Hebrew *bene yisra'el*, "children of Israel") came to replace the term "Hebrews," just as "Israelites" was later replaced by "Judeans" and "Jews" after the Exile in Babylonia. For further explanation, see Orlinsky, *Ancient Israel*, pp. 51-2.

Canaan was to be their permanent home, and that of their descendants.

In the course of time, in the days of Ishmael and Isaac, of Esau and Jacob, and of their children and grandchildren— among whom the twelve sons of Jacob and his daughter Dinah are best known—many more Hebrews were to be found in the land, some of them as immigrants from the Syrian part of the Fertile Crescent and from the Arabian steppes. The first half of the second millennium was an exciting period, characterized by mass movements. People were being attracted in the thousands from their more primitive abodes in the grasslands and highlands to the more settled, sophisticated, wealthy, and comfortable towns and villages not far distant.

But drought and famine, also, were a common phenomenon in many parts of western Asia, and could change the historical direction of a people. It was one such period of desolation that brought Jacob and his family, and thousands of non-Hebrews as well, to Egypt, the country of full granaries. The periodic overflow of the Nile River, today no less than in the past, gave life to the land and helped regulate it as an agricultural society.[1] Thus a thirteenth-century Egyptian document tells how the semi-nomadic inhabitants of Edom, south of Palestine, left their homes in time of drought to come to Egypt, "to keep themselves alive and to keep their cattle alive." And just as Abraham and Isaac in an earlier period had been compelled by famine to go south (Genesis 12 and 26), so too did Jacob in his time have to send his sons to Egypt to purchase grain.

Joseph, one of Jacob's sons, preceding his family to Egypt, had risen to high power, ranking next only to Pharaoh himself. When his father and brothers immigrated, they settled in the fertile Delta region of Goshen. This was the Eisodus, the "going into " Egypt.

The biblical tale concerns itself with the Hebrews alone. But in all probability the coming of the Hebrews to Egypt was part of a larger ethnic and military movement. During the first half of the second millennium Egypt had experienced an invasion and consequent degradation—reference to which was carefully, and, characteristically, avoided in its chronicles. A mixed group of Asiatics, apparently mostly Semites, and known generally as Hyksos (literally, "rulers of foreign countries"), appeared in the north, and in successive waves swarmed through Syria and Palestine. By about 1700 B.C.E. they had crossed the land bridge into Africa and conquered much of Egypt, a domination that was not to be completely broken until about 1550.

There appear to have been several points of contact between the Hyksos and the Hebrews during that century and a half. It is known, for example, that a certain Hyksos chieftain in Egypt bore the name Jacob-el (or perhaps: -har), which means "May El (or, Har—the mountain god) Give Protection." Another Hyksos leader was called Jacob-baal, "May Baal Protect." The verbal element Jacob, which means "protect," is identical with the name of the Hebrew patriarch who settled in Egypt.

Again, the historical kernel which resides in the dramatic story of Joseph's career in Egypt, of the coming to power of a Hebrew in the Egyptian royal court, could well have derived from the period of the Hyksos, when Semites, and in all likelihood Hebrews among them, were prominent among the new rulers of Egypt. It was not Egyptian habit to nourish the ambitions of strangers in their midst, and, furthermore, it would seem to be more than mere coincidence that in the Bible the Hebrews are said to have settled in the Delta, the very area which the Hyksos built up around their new capital, Avaris.[2]

Israel in Bondage; Birth of Moses

"And Joseph died, and all his brothers and all that generation," the Bible relates (Exodus 1:6-7), "and the Israelites were fruitful and prolific; they multiplied and increased very greatly, so that the land was filled with them. But a new king arose over Egypt, who did not know Joseph . . ." On the grounds that the Israelites were becoming too numerous and strong for the native government to handle, the new regime introduced a system of state slavery: "They set taskmasters over them to oppress them with forced labor; and they built for Pharaoh store cities, Pithom and Rameses" (v.11).*

* Biblical quotations in the essay, where they do not derive from the new, as yet unpublished Jewish Publication Society's Bible translation or from the Revised Standard Version of the Old Testament (Nelson), are the author's own versions.

At this point the findings of archeology come to our aid, helping us to paint a broader picture than the biblical writers had deemed necessary. When the Egyptians finally succeeded in overthrowing their Hyksos oppressors, they drove many of them from the land and enslaved the rest. The erstwhile free rulers became captives of the state, subject to forced labor. It is now known that two centuries later, about 1300 B.C.E., Seti I of Egypt, who had done much to reorganize the empire in Palestine and southern Syria, began the rebuilding of Avaris, the old Hyksos capital. His son and successor, Rameses II, continued the building project on a much vaster scale, changing the name of Avaris to Rameses. This same Pharaoh also did much rebuilding at other sites, notably at Pithom. Slave battalions worked at all these places, and there is little reason to doubt that Hebrews were among them.[3]

At this point, the biblical narrative introduces Moses. Pharaoh, the Bible relates, had given orders to drown in the Nile all Hebrew males at birth. But Moses' mother was able to hide her infant son for three months. At the end of that period, she placed the baby—who was of unusually striking appearance—in a waterproofed basket among the reeds by the bank of the Nile. A daughter of Pharaoh, coming down to the Nile to bathe, espied the basket. She sent a maid to fetch it, "and when she opened it, she saw that it was a child, a boy crying. She took pity on it, and said, 'This must be a Hebrew child'" (2:6).

Moses' sister, meanwhile, was stationed nearby watching for just such a development. She stepped forward and asked the Egyptian princess, "Shall I go and call you a Hebrew wet nurse to suckle the child for you?" And when the royal lady assented, she called her mother. When the child outgrew his mother's nursing and was brought back to the royal palace, the princess named him Moses (Hebrew *Moshe*): "because I drew him out (*meshitihu*) of the water" (v.10). So much for the biblical tradition.[4]

All peoples in antiquity were given to embellishing the circumstances of the birth of their great heroes, and so too did ancient Israel. A story similar to that of Moses was told of Sargon I (about 2300 B.C.E.), founder of the world's first empire, at Accad in Mesopotamia. The legend reads in part:

My (?) mother conceived me, in secret she bore me.
She set me in a basket of rushes, with bitumen she sealed my lid.
She cast me into the river which rose not over me.
The river bore me up and carried me to Akki, the drawer of
   water.
Akki, the drawer of water, lifted me out as he dipped his ewer.
Akki, the drawer of water, took me as his son and reared me.
Akki, the drawer of water, appointed me as his gardener.
While I was a gardener, Ishtar granted me her love.
And for four and (?) years I exercised kingship.
The black-headed people I ruled, I governed . . .[5]

While the biblical tale credits the princess with knowledge of
Hebrew, scholars have long recognized the Egyptian origin of
the common name-element Moses, meaning "offspring, born
of." The name "Moses" is no less authentically Egyptian than
such other contemporaneous biblical names as Miriam, Hophni,
Phinehas, Merari, and Puti-el. And these names, in turn, help to
authenticate the Egyptian locale of the biblical account of the
principal heroes and events involved in this phase of Israel's career.

Midian: The Call of Moses

All that we really know for certain, therefore, is that Moses
was born in Egypt. How he spent his formative years no one
knows. The Bible, having brought Moses into the royal family as
the princess' adopted son, took him out of it in the very next
verse (2:10-11), telling us nothing whatever about his youth.

Grown to manhood—in all probability in the same environment as that of his enslaved Hebrew brethren—Moses was
aware and conscious of his Hebraic origin, and ready to avenge
the affliction of his people. His first positive act, understandable
under the circumstances even if committed impulsively, was to
strike down "an Egyptian whom he saw strike down one of his
Hebrew kinsmen" (v.11).

Moses had to flee the land, for he had been seen—by two Hebrew slaves—beating the Egyptian. He went to the land of
Midian, generally located south of Edom, in Arabia. There he
met the seven daughters of Jethro, a Midianite priest, and married one of them, Zipporah.

This was the turning point of Moses' career, and that of biblical Israel. While tending the flocks of his father-in-law, Moses experienced his first contact with the God of his fathers. "When he came to Horeb, the mountain of God," the Bible reads (3:1 ff.), "an angel of the Lord appeared to him in a flaming fire out of a bush. He looked and, lo, the bush was aflame with fire, yet the bush was not consumed. And Moses said: 'I must turn aside and see this marvelous sight: why the bush does not burn up.' "

At this point the Lord revealed Himself to Moses: "I am the God of your father(s) . . . I have marked well the plight of My people in Egypt . . . I have come down to rescue them from the Egyptians, and to bring them out of that land to a good and spacious land, to a land flowing with milk and honey, to the region of the Canaanites . . . Come, therefore, I will send you to Pharaoh, and you shall free My people the Israelites from Egypt."

In this period, God's actions—and sometimes God Himself— were associated by the Hebrews with natural phenomena like fires, lightning, thunderstorms, mountains, and volcanoes. They believed that He manifested Himself and His will not merely by direct speech and in dreams, but also through these natural agents. Imbued as Moses was with the spirit of liberation and the desire to free his people at a time when the possibility of re- demption was more favorable than before, it is understandable that he would see in natural phenomena, especially when they occurred unexpectedly or in unusual form, a theophany—that is, a visible appearance of God.

But Moses seems out of character in the dialogue that ensued. Rather than accept readily this mission from God to His peo- ple, he tried to find reasons why he should not become a spokes- man for God (3:11-4:13). "Who am I?" Moses asked, "that I should go to Pharaoh and that I should bring forth the Israelites from Egypt? . . . What if they do not believe me or heed my voice, but say, 'The Lord did not appear to you?' . . . Please, O Lord, I have never been a man of words . . . for I am slow of speech and slow of tongue . . . Please, O Lord, send whom- ever else You will!" And Moses consented to go only after the Lord had assured him that his brother Aaron would be his spokesman.

In proper perspective, however, this biblically recorded conversation makes good sense. It was an ancient convention for one who felt himself chosen by God for a special mission to find reason for not responding at once and with eagerness to the call. Hesitancy, lack of confidence, fear of the consequences—these were conventionally attributed to God's chosen one when the call came. While Moses may have had a speech defect, and may also have felt some qualms about the enormity of the task, the biblical statement should not prevent us from recognizing in him a strong desire to lead his people out of slavery; for otherwise he would not have experienced the vision in the first place.

The Egyptian World in Moses' Time

What manner of civilization did Egypt constitute in this period so crucial to Israel? What were its material, artistic, and spiritual achievements?

The Near East, that quadrangle of land lying between the Mediterranean, Caspian and Red Seas, and the Persian Gulf, and connecting—at Israel and Sinai—Asia and Africa, is the birthplace of civilization. Egypt had long been one of the great powers in that part of the world. Indeed, during most of the third and second millennia B.C.E., Egypt was the principal power at the southwestern end of the Fertile Crescent, corresponding to the dominating regime at the northeastern end—Sumer, Babylonia, the Hittites, or Assyria.

The conquest at the hands of the Hyksos was Egypt's first full-scale and long-term experience as a subject people. Egyptian culture sank so low that this period has been described as "The Great Humiliation" (see note 2).

After the gradual expulsion of the Hyksos, the Egyptians began to devote their energies primarily to the reconquest of the neighboring regions, the rebuilding of the land, its army, shipping service, civil service, and temples. That accomplished, a decision had to be reached whether to venture into expanding imperialism or to remain essentially a localized economy. Queen Hatshepsut represented the latter view, her nephew Thutmose III the former. Ultimately, imperialism prevailed. And by the time that Thutmose had achieved his notable conquests (c. 1450 B.C.E.) Egypt was once more the greatest power in Western Asia. The revival that followed was on such a grand scale that the ensuing period of the New Kingdom, especially during the Eighteenth and Nineteenth Dynasties (down to shortly after 1200), has been called the Golden Age, and was the subject of a recent book suggestively titled *When Egypt Ruled the East.*[6]

Ikhnaton and Atonism

During the reign of Amenhotep IV (c. 1380-1360), a fundamental split developed between the royal house and its supporters, on the one hand, and, on the other, the powerful priestly interests of the god Amon at Thebes. The latter group was apparently keenly interested in continued imperialist expansion and consolidation. The royal regime moved its headquarters from Thebes to a new site about three hundred miles to the north, and laid primary emphasis on another diety, Aton, the round disk of the sun. The king himself changed his name to Ikhnaton (Akhen-Aton, "He Who is Serviceable to [or, "It Goes Well with] the Aton"), and named the new capital Akhet-Aton ("The Place of the Effective Glory of the Aton"), modern Tell el-Amarna. Art became more naturalistic than ever before. Women began to play a more prominent role in public life. Something of a democratization of social life was manifest in the public informality of the king, his wife, and their six daughters.[7]

The virtually exclusive worship of Aton by the royal household has led a number of scholars to assert that Ikhnaton was a monotheist, the first in the world. Some scholars, going even further, placed Moses in Ikhnaton's period, and claimed that he obtained his knowledge of monotheism, directly or ultimately, from Ikhnaton.[8] Sigmund Freud, in *Moses and Monotheism* (1939), made Moses an important Egyptian official in Ikhnaton's court who became a protector of the Hebrews, converted them to Ikhnaton's "monotheistic" religion, and led them out of Egypt. According to Freud, those passages in the Pentateuch that stood in contradiction to this theory were to be dismissed as invention and distortion; thus it was really Moses, not Abraham, who introduced the custom of circumcision among the Hebrews. This study of Moses by Freud is now regarded by many as a naive venture, constituting in reality a more important source of information for the analysis of Freud himself than of Moses.

According to more reliable treatments of the subject, however, it is clear today that Moses derived nothing from Ikhnaton's reign or outlook. Recent study has made it more than dubious that Ikhnaton was really a monotheist, or that his views circulated outside his royal court or subsequent to his death. What had been regarded by some as monotheism, the recognition and worship of Aton alone, has on closer study turned out to be a form of syncretism, a process by which several distinct gods came to be merged with a single deity so that all their functions were attributed to him. Ikhnaton, it is true, initiated a violent attack upon the god Amon, hacking the name out of inscriptions; at the same time, however, the many other less powerful and important gods were rarely disturbed. Indeed, the entire matter becomes clear when it is realized that Atonism was basically not a religious—let alone monotheistic—but an economic and political revolt against the powerful Amon interests.[9]

Another important factor differentiated Moses' beliefs from those of Ikhnaton. Already in the preceding, patriarchal period, there had come into being among the Hebrews a concept of deity which, while not monotheistic in our sense of the term, was yet not polytheistic either. In a sense, the patriarchs may be said to have practiced monotheism, but without defining it. While they probably did not think of denying the existence of other gods, the patriarchs attached themselves to one God and worshipped Him alone. With Him, they entered voluntarily into a covenant which was binding forever, never to be broken under penalty of severe punishment and, theoretically at least, of complete rejection. In sponsoring monotheism, Moses was therefore not actually introducing a new concept to the Hebrews. He had a familiar, developable Hebraic idea of monotheism with which to work. Even the covenant of Sinai represented not so much a change in kind as a change in degree from the old way of binding oneself to the deity. Moses and the Hebrews, therefore, had little need of Egyptian assistance—which was not forthcoming anyway—in this direction.[10]

The Age of Rameses II

Thanks largely to the findings of archeology during the past few decades, evidence has been accumulating from various sources to indicate that the career of Moses is probably to be sought not in the reign of Ikhnaton but about a century later, in the decades following 1300 B.C.E., during the long reign of Rameses II (c. 1290-1224). It is quite certain that Israel was in Canaan in some force around 1250; excavations at several sites point to the Israelites as conquering Canaanite settlements at about that time. Indeed, around 1230 B.C.E., King Merneptah of Egypt celebrated his victory over numerous foes in an alleged campaign in Western Asia. And the Pharaoh boasted:

> Israel is laid waste, its seed is not,
> Palestine is become a widow for Egypt.[11]

If we add a few decades to 1250 to allow for the wilderness wandering under Moses, we arrive at a date well within the reign of Rameses II. It also seems clear that the store cities, Pithom and Rameses, said in the Bible to have been built by the Hebrews in bondage, were erected in the days of this same Rameses. All in all, one cannot be far wrong in dating Moses about 1300, and the Exodus during the thirteenth century.[12]

Rameses II could well be the vainglorious Pharaoh whose heart softened and hardened by turn. Rameses was the king-god who walked into a Hittite trap at Kadesh on the Orontes River in Syria, and then turned his feat in escaping from the ambush into a great personal triumph. On his return to Egypt, he outdid all his predecessors—and, it turned out, all his successors too—in covering the wall space in the temples with carved representations of his remarkable "victory." Steindorff-Seele describes him bluntly as the "greatest of Egyptian boasters." [13] The biblical Pharaoh of the bondage could scarcely be described better!

The Exodus

This was the Egypt to which Moses returned after his vision of God in Midian. His brother Aaron joined him, and the two together began the difficult and arduous task of persuading and organizing their fellow Israelites to leave their land of bondage. According to one version in the Bible, Aaron performed for them the signs that the Lord had commanded: he caused his staff to turn into a serpent and then into a staff again; he brought leprosy upon his hand and then cured it; and, finally, he poured on the dry ground some water from the Nile so that it became blood. "And the people believed," the Bible asserts (4:31), "when they heard that the Lord had taken note of the Israelites and that He had seen their plight; and they bowed in homage." But another version has it that when Moses told the Israelites what the Lord had told him, "they would not listen to Moses, their spirits crushed by cruel bondage" (6:9).[14]

Pharaoh could hardly have been expected to consent to the release of so many thousands of unpaid workers. The biblical interpretation is different: God could readily have made Pharaoh free his captive Israelites; but He wanted to demonstrate for all time His power and glory. "The Lord said to Moses: Go to Pharaoh. For I have hardened his heart and the hearts of his courtiers, in order that I may display these My signs among them, and that you may recount in the hearing of your sons and your sons' sons how I made a mockery of the Egyptians and how I displayed My signs among them, that you may know that I am the Lord" (10:1-2).

And thus there began a series of ten events that have been retold by countless generations—the ten plagues. In the case of the first nine, neither blood nor frogs nor lice, neither insects nor pestilence nor boils, neither hail nor locusts nor darkness could stay Pharaoh from the swift completion of his appointed round. The tenth plague, however, brought matters to a head. "In the middle of the night the Lord struck down all the firstborn in the land of Egypt, from the firstborn of Pharaoh who sat on the throne to the firstborn of the captive who was in the dungeon, and all the firstborn of animals" (12:29). Pharaoh and his courtiers did not wait until morning. They arose in the night and summoned Moses and Aaron: "Depart from among my people, you and the Israelites with you! Go, worship the Lord as you said! Take also your flocks and your herds, as you said, and be gone! And may you," the divine Pharaoh pleaded with these two men, "bring a blessing upon me also."

For those who do not believe in miracles, the biblical account is understandable in natural terms. Scholars have long recognized that most of these plagues are natural phenomena that have afflicted Egypt throughout the ages. The Nile has long been known to acquire a reddish color. Frogs have on occasion plagued the country, their decomposition resulting in a vast multiplication of lice, insects, and pestilence. And what moderns explain as natural phenomena in aggravated form, the biblical writers accounted for in terms of God's direct and supernatural intervention in behalf of His people.

It seems clear that in the midst of some such upheaval, Moses and those slaves, non-Hebrew as well as Hebrew, who were courageous or desperate enough to follow him, made a dash for liberty. Their aim was to escape Egyptian territory to freedom. This they achieved. Thus Moses found himself at the head of an undisciplined collection of people—the Bible refers to the non-Hebrews as the "mixed multitude" and "rabble" (Exodus 12:38; Numbers 11:4)—numbering several thousand.*

Deliverance at the "Red" Sea

Moses' leadership was tested at once. Normally, he should have led the Hebrews directly to Canaan, the land that they believed God had promised the patriarchs to give to their descendants—and where, incidentally, some Hebrews had remained when the others went down to Egypt. But no. "God did not lead them by way of the land of the Philistines," we are told (Exodus 13:17), "although it was nearer; for God said, 'The people may have a change of heart when they see war, and return to Egypt.' " In other words, the Philistines were settled in Canaan when the biblical account of the Exodus was being written down, but not yet when the Exodus took place. Moses realized full well that he dare not make directly for Canaan lest his people run head on into several Egyptian fortresses and garrisons en route. This road, so important for economic and military reasons, was always closely guarded. Instead, Moses led the Israel-

---

* According to the census lists in Numbers 1 and 26, said to have been taken right after the Exodus and at the end of the forty years of wandering respectively, the number of male Israelites who left Egypt under Moses, not including the Levites (or the wives, children, and cattle), came to just over 600,000. This figure can scarcely be taken seriously, for sundry and sufficient reasons. It is not unlikely that these lists originally belonged to a later period, perhaps that of David. In any case, scholars generally tend to guess at the number of people involved in the Exodus and Wandering at about 5,000.

ites roundabout, south and east, by way of the wilderness at the Red Sea—more correctly, Reed (or, Marsh) Sea.*

After a short period of wandering, the Hebrews found themselves up against the Reed Sea. In the meantime, an Egyptian force had set out—the biblical narrator states that in order to recapture the fugitive slaves Pharaoh himself "hitched up his chariot and took his men with him: he took six hundred of his picked chariots, and the rest of the chariots of Egypt, with reserves in all of them . . ." (14:5-9)—and they overtook the Hebrews encamped by the Sea.

At this point, tradition recounts, when panic and the urge to surrender to the Egyptians overcame many of the Israelites, Moses stepped forth and said, "Have no fear! . . . The Lord will battle for you, and you hold your peace!" (14:13-14). The following morning the curtain came down on the final scene of Israel's first great act in the drama of man's attempt to achieve and maintain freedom. A strong east wind backed up the waters of the sea, "and the Israelites went into the sea on dry land, the waters forming a wall for them on their right and on their left. When the Egyptians came in pursuit after them into the sea . . . The waters turned back and covered the chariots and the horsemen of Pharaoh's entire host that had followed them into the sea; not one of them remained" (vv.22-26).

The Song of Triumph

Then Moses, assisted by his sister Miriam and the Israelites, sang this song to the Lord (15:1 ff.):

> I will sing to the Lord, for He has triumphed gloriously;
> Horse and driver He has hurled into the sea. . . .
> The deeps covered them;
> They went down into the depths like a stone.
> Thy right hand, O Lord glorious in power,
> Thy right hand, O Lord, shatters the foe! . . .
> The foe said,
> "I will pursue, I will overtake,

---

* The biblical term *yam suph* has been incorrectly translated "Red Sea." A clear discussion of this, as well as of the route of the Exodus, may be found in G. E. Wright-F. V. Filson, *Westminster Historical Atlas to the Bible* (revised edition, 1956), 38-9; or Wright, *Biblical Archaeology*, 60 ff.

I will divide the spoil;
My desire shall have its fill of them.
I will bare my sword;
My hand shall subdue them."
You did blow with Your wind, the sea covered them;
They sank like lead in the majestic waters.
Who is like You, O Lord, among the mighty,
Who is like You, majestic in holiness,
Awesome in splendor, working wonders! . . .
The Lord will reign for ever and ever!

Though Moses' song is ancient, it is scarcely his, for only one who had lived in Canaan and knew Canaanite poetic composition—from which ancient Hebrew poesy derived—could have written it. Exactly what transpired at the Reed Sea can no longer be determined. We do know that it was invaders from the east Mediterranean, known as Sea Peoples—among whom the Philistines are the best known—who were largely reponsible for the collapse of Egypt after about 1200. "The relentless surge of wave after wave of Sea Peoples," it has been noted (Wilson, 245), "shows one great folk-wandering . . . The Sea Peoples alone did not deal the vital blow to Egypt's proud position in the southeastern Mediterranean world, but they were one strong factor among many in sapping Egyptian power and shrivelling Egyptian spirit." One may wonder whether the biblical song of Israel's triumph at the Sea of Reeds, composed after the Philistines had become neighbors of the Israelites in Canaan, does not reflect something of the later battles between the Sea Peoples and the Egyptians.

To biblical Israel the Exodus became the greatest event in her history. If only for his leadership in the Exodus, Moses would have become immortal in Jewish history. The Israelites interpreted this single act as demonstrating that God had chosen them as His own. Time and again in the Bible the Exodus is referred to as the physical proof of God's selection of Israel out of all the peoples of the world. Thus, when the Judeans were in the Babylonian Exile (first half of the sixth century B.C.E.), the Isaiah of the Exile could comfort and urge on his fellow exiles with the argument of God's first Exodus, and the new Exodus, soon to transpire (Isaiah 43:18 ff.). So it has been throughout the centuries, in the Diaspora, down to the several exoduses in our own time into the State of Israel from tyrannical countries in Europe, Asia, and Africa.

Passover, Matzot, and the Haggadah

Several later aspects of Israelite life in Canaan came to be associated with the Exodus. Such purely agricultural practices as sacrificing a lamb in the springtime, eating unleavened bread (probably in connection with the barley harvest), and dedicating everything firstborn—practices known in agricultural society from of old—came to be associated with Israel's coming forth from the Egyptian bondage. These nature festivals thus became historical feasts. And in time—especially when the Jewish people found itself exiled by Rome and again in need of an exodus—the Passover feast became the most popular occasion in Jewish religious life.

An essential part of the feast was the retelling (*Seder Haggadah*) of the Exodus and its by-products in accordance, of course, with the biblical account. The haste with which the Israelites had to leave was made responsible for the *matzot:* "And they baked unleavened cakes of the dough that they had taken out of Egypt, for it was not leavened, since they had been driven out of Egypt and could not tarry" (12:39); therefore, "seven days you shall eat unleavened bread (*massot*) . . . And you shall tell (*we-higgadta;* whence the term *Haggadah*) your son on that day, 'It is because of what the Lord wrought for me when I went free from Egypt' " (13:6-8).[15]

Journey to Sinai

The career of Moses was really hammered out in the generation-long wandering in the wilderness of Sinai. The period of his mature life coincided with the older generation of Israelites that was to die, and with the younger one that was raised in the stimulating but harsh environment of Sinai's rugged terrain. Only the determined and hardy could withstand—and thus in a way thrive on—the many trials. This phase of Israel's history affords an excellent example of challenge and response in man's struggle with his environment.

After traveling three days in the wilderness of Shur, the Israelites were without any water; and when they came to Marah (Hebrew for "bitter"), they found its water bitter. But by casting a log into the water, the Bible asserts, Moses made it sweet. Not long afterwards the Israelites found themselves without food in the midst of the wilderness of Sin, between Elim and Sinai, and they cried out in anguish, "Would that we had died by the hand of the Lord in the land of Egypt, when we sat by the fleshpots, when we ate our fill of bread! For you have brought us out into this wilderness to starve this whole congregation to death" (16:3).

This was the occasion for God to provide the people with "manna": "In the morning there was a fall of dew about the camp; and when the fall of dew lifted, behold, something fine and flaky upon the face of the wilderness, fine as frost upon the ground. The Israelites saw it and said to one another, 'What is it?'—for they did not know what it was. And Moses said to them, 'It is the bread which the Lord has given you to eat' . . . The House of Israel named it manna; it was like coriander seed, white, and it tasted like wafers in honey" (16:14-31).

On another occasion, the "rabble" (Hebrew *asafsuf*) urged the Israelites on: "and they said, 'O that we had meat to eat! We remember the fish we ate in Egypt free; the cucumbers, melons, leeks, onions, and garlic. Now our strength is dried up, and we have nothing before us but manna!" (Numbers 11:4-6). In response, the Lord brought on enough quail to keep the people busy capturing them for two days and a night. But when the people began to gorge themselves with quail, the Lord became angry and struck many of them down for their lust (vv. 31-35).

At Kadesh, in the wilderness of Sin, the people were once again overcome by thirst: "This is no place for grain, or figs, or vines, or pomegranates; and there is no water to drink" (Numbers 20:5). Moses struck a rock—though the Lord had instructed him merely to speak to it—and it gave forth water for the people and their cattle.*

Here again, what the ancients considered to be God's intervention in their behalf—sometimes by a miraculous act and

---

* Scholars generally agree that the Books of Exodus and Numbers have probably preserved varying versions of the same event. Thus Exodus 16:13 and Numbers 11:31-35 deal with the quail; Exodus 17:1-7 and Numbers 20:1-13 deal with obtaining water from a rock by striking it.

sometimes by the miraculous timing of an act of nature—the modern scholar would explain more naturally. Quail fly over the vicinity of Sinai in large numbers every fall in their migration from Europe to Africa and Arabia. The limestone rock in Sinai has been known—and Moses may have known this from his previous sojourn in Midian—to give forth water when struck, the broken surface exposing the soft and porous rock underneath. And the manna was almost certainly the honey-like substance found on the tamarisk: ". . . manna production is a biological phenomenon of the dry deserts and steppes. The liquid honeydew excretion of a number of cicadas, plant lice, and scale insects speedily solidifies by rapid evaporation. From remote times the resulting sticky and often times granular masses have been collected and called manna." [16]

The Route of the Wilderness Wandering

To reach the Reed Sea, Moses led his people from Rameses to Succoth, "and they encamped at Etham, at the edge of the wilderness . . . Then the Lord said to Moses, 'Tell the Israelites to turn back and encamp before Pi-hahiroth, between Migdol and the sea, before Baal-zephon; you shall encamp facing it, by the sea' " (Exodus 13:20; 14:1-2).

This part of the Israelite itinerary can now be traced with fair certainty; previously, many thought it scarcely historical. Succoth has been identified with modern Tell el-Maskhutah (excavated since 1883, when numerous inscriptions were found), and Tell Defneh (Greek Daphne) is believed to be the modern site of ancient Baal-zephon.[17]

The route taken to Mt. Sinai, however, is not as certain, and the identification of Mt. Sinai itself is disputed. Tradition has long placed the holy mountain at the southern end of the peninsula of Sinai. Others, however, locate it farther east, across the Gulf of Aqaba, in Midian. Still others place it in the north-central part of Sinai. Had the Israelis been permitted to remain longer in Sinai after their campaign in 1956, a team of scholars might have been able to determine the site of the famed mountain. As of now, there is insufficient reason to give up the traditional location, except that what is conventionally called "Mt.

Sinai" may in reality be a range of mountains rather than a single peak.

Moses and Jethro

Even before the great event at Mt. Sinai, Moses was playing something of the role of arbiter and lawmaker. When differences of opinion arose, when disputes and recriminations resulted, even when simple inquiries had to be made, he acted as arbiter. Fortunately for Moses, Jethro, his Midianite father-in-law, came to the camp to see his daughter Zipporah and the grandchildren, and to congratulate Moses and Israel. "Blessed be the Lord," Jethro said, "who delivered you from the Egyptians and from Pharaoh . . . Now I know that the Lord is greater than all gods . . ." (18:10-11).

But when he saw how "Moses sat as magistrate among the people, while the people stood about Moses from morning until evening," Jethro advised his son-in-law as follows: "The thing you are doing is not good: you will surely wear yourself out, both you and this people with you, for the task is too heavy for you; you cannot do it alone. Now listen to me. I will give you counsel—and God be with you! . . . And Moses heeded his father-in-law," we are told, "and did all that he had said. Moses chose capable men out of all Israel, and appointed them heads over the people—chiefs of thousands, hundreds, fifties, and tens. And they exercised authority over the people at all times: the difficult matters they brought to Moses, and all the minor matters they decided themselves" (18:17-26).

There can be little doubt of the essential authenticity of this tradition. It is not likely that anyone would fabricate an Israelite dependence upon anything Midianite—the Midianites later became mortal enemies of Israel—especially one that involved Moses in relation to the administration of law. Then again, there is independent reason for recognizing an early and close relationship between some Midianites and the Israelites, e.g., by way of Hobab the Kenite, of the family of Moses' father-in-law (Numbers 10:29-32; Judges 4:11). Indeed, some scholars believe that the Lord, God of Israel, was originally the God of the Midianites (or Kenites), and that Moses adopted Him as God only after marrying into Jethro's family; this theory, however, is quite hypothetical.

Mt. Sinai: The Covenant

Israel was now ready for the corollary of the Exodus, the solemn establishment of the theocracy at Sinai on the basis of the "Book of the Covenant" (*sefer ha-brit*, Exodus 24:7), which consisted of the Ten Commandments and a code of laws (chaps. 20-23). The two events together—for Exodus and Sinai are really inseparable—formed the basis of the national covenant (*brit*) between God and Israel, a pact around which the entire Hebrew Bible was to revolve. It is impossible to comprehend the biblical view of Israel's career without recognizing the central role of the covenant; the entire rabbinic view of Judaism derives wholly and directly from it. Indeed, early Christianity found it necessary to alter this covenant between Israel and God by proclaiming a New Covenant (or, Testament) that was to replace the Old, one which Jesus was to mediate and which was to involve all the nations of the world (Matthew 28:18 ff.; Hebrews 8:6 ff.).

The great event at Sinai, befitting its status as The Revelation, is majestically and vividly described in the Bible. It is true that much of the biblical account is the product of a later period; thus many of the laws derive from the experiences of a settled community long occupied in agriculture. On the other hand, since they associated God with awesome aspects of nature, it was natural for Moses and Israel to choose a setting like Sinai, amidst desert thunder and lightning, for the consummation of the act of covenant. Whether the Ten Commandments were introduced by Moses to Israel for the first time at Sinai, or were simply formally confirmed on that occasion—the fact seems to be that Sinai was a real event at Israel's coming into nationhood.

For three days the Israelites purified themselves. On the third day, "Mount Sinai was all smoking, for the Lord had come down upon it in fire . . . and the whole mountain trembled violently. The blare of the horn grew louder and louder. As Moses spoke, God would answer him in thunder . . ." (Ex. 19:18 ff.).

In this setting, "God spoke all these words, saying: 'I the Lord am your God who brought you out of the land of Egypt, the house of bondage. You shall have no other gods beside Me . . .' " (20:1 ff.) Then came the other nine commandments:

> You shall not make for yourself a sculptured image . . .
> You shall not swear falsely by the name of the Lord your God . . .
> Remember the Sabbath day and keep it holy . . .
> Honor your father and your mother . . .
> You shall not murder . . .
> You shall not commit adultery . . .
> You shall not steal . . .
> You shall not bear false witness . . .
> You shall not covet . . . anything that is your neighbor's.*

Accompanied by thunder and flashes, the blare of the horn and the smoking of the mountain, the people heard these words and agreed solemnly to the conditions of the covenant. The Israelites and their descendants voluntarily bound themselves exclusively to one God, who, in turn, obligated Himself forever to Israel. It was unthinkable that God, the incomparable, would fail to protect a law-abiding Israel and make it prosper; had He not already demonstrated by His acts His interest in Israel? But if Israel failed to heed God's commandments, then He could punish and even destroy her.

Yet over and above the letter of the law, another element was recognized in the covenant, namely, God's love for Israel and His devotion (ḥesed, traditionally rendered "lovingkindness") to her. It was believed that no matter how grievously Israel sinned and how undeserving she might be of God's protection, God would never cast her off completely. This concept is the core not only of the Written Law (the Bible), but also of the Oral Law (the Talmud, consisting of the Mishnah and the Gemarah) and of the liturgy.

The concept of covenant was not novel. Earlier, each patriarch had entered into a covenant with God. Abraham had entered into a mutually exclusive agreement with "the God of Abraham," whereby Abraham was to recognize and worship no

---

* This version of the Decalogue is that of Exodus. The Book of Deuteronomy (5:6 ff.) offers a somewhat different version; cf. Driver, *Introduction to the Literature of the Old Testament*, 33-35.

other deity but God, and God was to watch over the welfare of Abraham and his family. When Isaac renewed the pact, God became "the kinsman (*paḥad*) of Isaac." For Jacob, God was "the champion (*'abir*) of Jacob." [18]

This concept of covenant between two parties, it is now known, derived from earlier western Asia, where the covenant involved two equal rulers or a powerful ruler and a vassal. As in the case of the patriarchs, and later in the Mosaic period, the two parties of the covenant were bound by an oath, sometimes consisting specifically of blessings and curses; no legal means of enforcement was involved.

Significantly, however, only the patriarchs and their descendants are known to have entered into a covenant with a deity. They alone, it would seem, adopted a single god; but why they should have done so, in the midst of a polytheistic world, has not yet been determined.

In the wilderness, what had been a personal covenant involving God and an individual patriarch became for the first time a national covenant, one that brought together God and an entire people. As a result of the Exodus and Sinai, Israel came into being as a nation covenanted with God. The central figure and mediator in this epochal event was Moses.[19]

The Law

As part of the covenant, Moses proceeded to set before the Israelites some of the laws by which they were to live. Law, from the very outset, has constituted a necessary and useful brake against oppression of the weak on the part of the strong. Indeed, law marks the beginning, and the basis, of the trend toward a democratic society.

Western Asia, and Mesopotamia in particular, was the birthplace of law on earth. Three lawbooks, two written in Sumerian and one in Babylonian, have recently been discovered; preceding by about two to three hundred years Hammurabi's famous Code of about 1700 B.C.E., these are the oldest known lawbooks, and they antedate the earliest known codification of Roman law by more than fifteen hundred years.[20]

Law in the ancient Near East—Egypt produced no lawbooks because the god-king was himself the source of law and authority²¹ —reached its peak in the Bible. The constitution of ancient Israel was frequently called "the Torah of Moses" by the biblical writers. And while scholars today recognize several later strata, post-Mosaic layers of law, in the Torah, Moses came to be acknowledged as Israel's lawgiver, recipient of the Torah directly from God Himself.*

The collection of instructions (*torot*) that Moses is said to have set forth (Exodus 20:23-30; 38), regulating the social and religious life of the people, was called "The Book (or: Record, Document, Writ) of the Covenant." A better term could scarcely be found. Biblical law dealt with the individual's relationship to his neighbor—as an individual and as a member of society—and to God; all three parties, the individual, the state, and God, shared importance in the Mosaic code or covenant. Man's life, limbs, cattle, and fields (20:23 ff.) must be guarded and respected, according to the terms of the code, no less than the details of the Tabernacle (or, Tent of Meeting), the Ark, and the sacrifices (25:1 ff.). Social and religious responsibility were the two complementary aspects of the covenant, a view never lost sight of in biblical tradition. Thus the prophet Isaiah asserted (Isaiah 1:2-4, 10-23) that no matter how many sacrifices and prayers the Israelites offer to the Lord, He will reject them all if the worshipper has failed in the commandments pertaining to man and society.

The Tabernacle and the Ark

Closely connected with the event at Sinai are the Ark and the Tabernacle (Hebrew *mishkan*). In the former, the acacia chest, Moses is said to have placed the two tablets of stone on which the Ten Commandments were recorded; the latter was the movable shrine around which the political and religious life of the wandering Israelites revolved.

There can be little doubt that these institutions are the product of a nomadic or semi-nomadic society, even if later priestly writers embellished the original account considerably. Acacia wood—cedar, cyprus, or olive was later used in Canaan—ram-

---

* All lawbooks in western Asia were said by their compilers or royal patrons to have emanated from the gods and been given to the rulers as a trust to uphold.

skins, lambskins, cloth of goat's hair, and the like are all manifestations of nomadic existence. Again, while little is really known about many aspects of life among the nomads in antiquity, e.g., the religious—they left virtually no records—we do know that among some nomadic, pre-Mohammedan Arabs portable shrines (sacred tents) were employed.

The Tabernacle was to become later, after the conquest of Canaan, the "Tent of the Lord" at Shiloh, and it was ultimately replaced by the Temple that David planned and Solomon built. In the case of the Ark, Solomon placed it in the Holy of Holies in the Temple, and—except for a single unclear reference during the reign of King Josiah about two hundred years later (II Chronicles 35:3)—was heard of no more. It is clear that the Tent and the Ark were ancient institutions that played a more significant role in the wilderness wandering than they did in conquered Canaan.[22]

Desert Sojourn: Grumblings and Uprisings

Having received the covenant at Sinai, the Israelites were now ready to prepare themselves to enter the Promised Land. But problems still remained. At Rephidim, on the way to Mt. Sinai, the Amalekites, semi-nomadic desert folk, came and fought with Israel. Moses appointed a promising young man, Joshua, to lead a picked group of men in battle. In keeping with the manner in which the Bible interpreted history—combining the miraculous with the natural—Israel was victorious because God came to the aid of Moses, who kept his hands erect—with the aid of his brother Aaron and Hur of the tribe of Judah—until the sun set, thus ensuring the defeat of hated Amalek (Exodus 17:8-15).

At Hazeroth (Numbers 12), Miriam criticized her brother for having married an Ethiopian woman. Moses said nothing in defense. "The man Moses," the text reads, "was very humble, more than any other person on earth." But the Lord was vexed by this criticism. He summoned Moses, Aaron, and Miriam, but spoke only to the last two: ". . . My servant Moses is entrusted with all My house. With him I speak mouth to mouth . . . Why then were you not afraid to speak against My servant Moses!" Then the Lord struck Miriam with leprosy, from which she was cured only after Aaron persuaded Moses to appeal to the Lord in her behalf.

This attempt on the part of Aaron and Miriam to reduce the total power and authority of Moses failed. But other revolts broke out against Moses (Numbers 16-17). A Levite named Korah, heading some two hundred and fifty chieftains, not all of them Levites, "assembled against Moses and Aaron and said to them, 'You have assumed too much! For the entire community, every one of them, is holy, and the Lord is in their midst. Why then do you exalt yourselves above the congregation of the Lord?' " (16:1 ff.). In defense, Moses bade them offer fire and incense to the Lord at the sanctuary, "and the man whom the Lord will choose shall be the holy one." As a consequence, "a fire went forth from the Lord and consumed the two hundred and fifty men offering up the incense."

At the same time, Dathan, Abiram, and On, all three of the tribe of Reuben, led another segment of the people in rebellion against Moses: "Is it a small thing that you have brought us up from a land flowing with milk and honey, to kill us in the wilderness, that you must also make yourself a ruler over us . . . ?" (vv. 13-14). Unlike the ecclesiastical revolt of Korah and his group, this was a rebellion of laymen against the civil authority which Moses claimed. Their punishment and end were dreadful.

The climax of the revolt and its collapse came the next day. "The entire Israelite community murmured against Moses and Aaron, saying, 'You have killed the people of the Lord!' " (17:6 ff.) The Lord then took matters into His own hands. He caused a plague to break out among the people, killing many of them (14,700 according to v. 14). Had not Moses intervened hastily, with an atonement offering of incense, the biblical text asserts, the people would have perished to the last man.

That many elements among the people at one time or another opposed Moses is certain; it is hardly likely that anyone gratuitously created in a later period such hostile sentiment against Israel's outstanding Founding Father. But what can never be clear is to what extent the opposition to Moses was justified under the circumstances. Later writers naturally tended to put Moses in the right, and use the divine acts as evidence against the guilty ones. If some of Moses' critics had actually been the victims of an epidemic, an earthquake, a fire, or a skin disease at about the time that they voiced their discontent, these occurrences were readily interpreted as indications and proof of God's view. It is more likely, however, that the biblical pattern of history-writing, in defending Moses, simply made use here of well-known natural phenomena.

Death in the Wilderness:
Punishment for Disobedience and Lack of Confidence

In the second year of the Exodus, Moses took the first positive action in regard to the conquest of Canaan by sending spies from the wilderness of Paran to the Promised Land (Numbers 13-14). "See what kind of country it is," they were instructed by Moses, "whether the kind of people that dwells in it is strong or weak, few or numerous; whether the cities are open or fortified."

The report that the majority of the spies brought back was far from favorable. True, the land "flows with milk and honey," they said, "but the people that inhabits the land is powerful, and the cities are fortified mightily . . . It is a land that devours its inhabitants . . ." And a final touch: we saw such giants there that we appeared in their eyes like grasshoppers.

Caleb, son of Jephunneh, however, supported by Joshua, son of Nun, gave a dissenting report. "If the Lord delights in us," they exhorted the people, "He will bring us into this land . . . Only do not rebel against the Lord, and do not fear the people of the land . . . The Lord is with us, do not fear them!" Caleb and Joshua were about to be stoned by the people when the Lord intervened (14:6-10).

To what extent this story is true cannot be determined.* But it was made, or, as some scholars would say, created to serve as the reason that so few of the erstwhile slaves in Egypt lived long enough to enter Canaan. The assumption is that had the people rejected the pessimistic view of the majority of the spies in fa-

---

* It has long been recognized that the biblical text is made up of two versions of the story, and the older one did not include Joshua at all (see Driver, *Introduction*, 62-3).

vor of the confident outlook of the minority, relying utterly
upon the power and protection of God, they would shortly have
marched into Canaan and conquered it. Instead, God decided,
except for such as Caleb and Joshua, only the children would
live to reach Canaan; all the older folk, those who had been
twenty years and over when the first census was taken, were going to die in the wilderness. Hence the forty years of wandering.*

If the facts preserved in the Bible are essentially true, then one
may posit simply that the forty years—which is sometimes only
a round number used in the Bible to indicate a generation—of
wandering were made necessary by the urgent need to train and
discipline the horde of slaves for the conquest of Canaan. Disaster clearly stared them in the face were an all-out invasion of the
land undertaken prematurely.

Moses, too, and Aaron did not enter the Promised Land. The
Bible gives two reasons, both in keeping with its religious interpretation of history: they, too, like the people, were disobedient
and lacked confidence in God. In the older version (Deuteronomy 1:37),[23] Moses was excluded from Canaan along with the
people because of their reaction to the pessimistic report of the
spies (Numbers 13:20). According to the later version, when
the people were overcome by thirst at Kadesh, in the thirty-
seventh year of the Exodus, God had ordered Moses to take his
staff, assemble the people, and "tell the rock before their eyes
to yield its water" (Numbers 20:1-13). Instead, Moses used the
staff to strike the rock. Whereupon the Lord told Moses and
Aaron, "Because you did not believe in Me, by sanctifying Me
in the eyes of the Israelites, therefore you shall not bring this
congregation into the land that I give them." Why Moses is said
to have struck the rock, instead of speaking to it as commanded,
is for the folklorist to interpret; but if he had spoken to the rock,
then the biblical writer would have had to look for another explanation.

Shortly afterwards Aaron died, on the top of Mt. Hor, on the
border of Edom.

---

* A few scholars would reduce the total period of wandering to but a few years:
cf., e.g., H. H. Rowley, *From Joseph to Joshua* (Oxford University Press,
1950); nowhere else will so full a bibliography on the subject be found.

On the Eve of the Conquest of Canaan: Moses' Death

The people were now approaching inhabited territory. They had reached the land of Edom. Moses sent messengers to Edom's king for permission to go through his land. "We will not pass through field or vineyard," they assured the Edomite government (20:14 ff.), "neither will we drink water from a well . . ." But the king refused permission, and the Israelites had, once again, to take a roundabout route.

Farther north, in Transjordan, the people approached the territory of Moab, then dominated by the Amorites under King Sihon, who also refused to grant transit permission. Instead, Sihon attacked Israel; for his pains he and his forces were defeated, and the territory was occupied by the victors (21:21-32). North of Moab, in the territory of Bashan, King Og, too, attacked Israel and was vanquished.

At long last the Israelites found themselves at the border of Canaan (22:1). And Moses had now reached the point of neither return nor advance. His mission was accomplished. He had played the central role in effecting the Exodus from Egypt, in achieving the crossing of the wildernesses in the peninsula of Sinai, and in preparing the Israelites, as a more-or-less united group bound by a national covenant to a single deity, for the conquest of Canaan. Even the vexing problem of successorship had been solved; no opposition seems to have arisen—among a people that was given so frequently to opposition—to Moses' selection of Joshua of the tribe of Ephraim as his successor.

After attributing to Moses a long review of his career just ended and a preview of his people's career about to begin (chapters 1-32), culminating in his famous blessing (33), the Book of Deuteronomy (34) tells us that "Moses went up from the steppes of Moab to Mount Nebo, the top of Pisgah, which is opposite Jericho," from which the Lord showed him Israel's land. After which "Moses the servant of the Lord died there in the land of Moab. And He buried him (or he was buried) in the valley of Moab opposite Beth-peor; but no man knows the site of his grave to this day. Moses was 120 years old when he died; his eyes were not dim, nor his natural force abated."

Jewish sources have embellished the story of Moses' death. Early legends differed as to whether Moses had experienced an unusual manner of dying or had simply not died at all. From the biblical text itself it is not clear whether God or someone else had buried Moses. The Septuagint (Old Greek) translation reads "they buried him." Philo, the Alexandrian Jewish philosopher of the first century, in his essay on "The Life of Moses," wrote: "He was entombed not by mortal hands, but by immortal powers . . ." And Josephus, the Jewish historian and Philo's younger contemporary in Judea, asserted: "While, after having taken leave of the people, he was going to embrace Eleazar and Joshua on Mount Nebo, a cloud suddenly stood over him, and he disappeared, though he wrote in Scripture that he died, which was done from fear that people might say that because of his extraordinary virtue he had been turned into a divinity."

The Man and His Legacy

For the modern Jew, who may or may not accept the legends that have sprung up around Moses,* the patriarch remains the prime mover in the actions and decisions that led to the founding of Israel as a nation. Even if it is not possible to delimit precisely his role, he alone was the leading personality and subjective factor among the objective conditions that made possible the Exodus from Egypt. In the wilderness of Sinai, not in Egypt, Israel was forged, hammered into the shape of nationhood amid appalling hardship. The weak and the weary perished, leaving the young and strong to drift yet another mile toward the Land of Promise, the ancestral home.

The struggle for power within the group that Moses led from Egypt was violent. Every faction in this group, religious and civil, including members of his own family, challenged the authority and wisdom of Moses. Only a man of iron will, patience, compassion for his people, and—above all—unlimited faith in his goal could have endured this endless bickering, scheming, and backsliding.

---

* No biblical character has been able to compete with Moses in sheer quantity of legend in post-biblical times. In Louis Ginzberg's monumental collection of *The Legends of the Jews*, the material on Moses fills more than one-third of the pages (611 out of 1728). Moses also played a prominent role in Christian and Muslim literature.

Moses comes through this struggle as a very human personality, revealing both positive and negative qualities. Several independent incidents would indicate that Moses had quite a temper. His act of beating an Egyptian to death for striking down a
Hebrew is a case in point. When Dathan and Aviram accused
Moses of authoritarianism, "Moses became incensed and he said
to the Lord, 'Do not favor their offering! I have not taken a single
ass from them, neither have I harmed a single one of them'"
(Numbers 16:15). On several occasions he is also said to have betrayed indecision. At the "Red" Sea, with Pharaoh's superior
forces approaching, the Israelites cried out to the Lord. "But the
Lord said to Moses, 'Why do you cry out to Me? Tell the Israelites to go forward . . . !'" (Exodus 14:15 ff.). At Marah, too
(15:22-25), and at Rephidim (17:1), when the people thirsted
for water, Moses "cried out to the Lord."

It was indeed a difficult struggle, and about a generation—the
traditional "forty years" of wandering—had to elapse before
Moses could weld the heterogeneous, inexperienced, and uncul-
tured mass together into something of a unified force and social
group.

Besides founding the nation, Moses taught the concept of
monotheism to his people. It used to be generally thought in
scholarly circles, as has already been pointed out, that monotheism did not come to Israel until the period of the prophets
(eighth century), and that Israel had little substantial origin or
existence during the second millennium B.C.E. The patriarchs
were frequently regarded as the figment of a much later writer's
imagination. And those who credited them with something of an
existence usually attributed to them the beliefs and practices of
polytheism. Thanks to archeology, few scholars today would
deny at least some historicity to the patriarchs; even fewer
would refuse to grant some substance to the career of Israel in
Egypt and to Moses.

There can now be little doubt that the patriarchs recognized
the concept of covenant, each patriarch making his pact with
God. It was under Moses that the covenant was made between a
total nation and God.

This concept and act of covenant involving Israel and the
deity was an integral part of a second concept, that of monotheism. It is impossible to postulate the covenant between the two

without belief in the One. The biblical tradition is clear and consistent that Moses was the individual most responsible for emphasizing and cementing Israel's alliance with God. This is precisely what the very first of the Ten Commandments asserts: "I the Lord am your God who brought you out of the land of Egypt, the house of bondage. You shall have no other gods beside Me . . . !"

It has long been recognized that Moses is not the author of the Torah. This is a far cry, however, from denying to Moses all responsibility for helping lay the basis of Israel's legal system.

Judaism came to recognize the Talmud, the Oral Law, as no less authoritative than the Written Law, from which it derived. And just as Moses was credited with receiving the Written Law from God on Sinai, so did he become the ultimate authority also of the Unwritten Law.

Thus, Moses, the lawgiver, was the midwife of the Israelite nation. In the extraordinary career of Jews and Judaism, his figure and personality stands out as brilliantly today as it did some thirty-two and a half centuries ago.

FOR FURTHER READING

FROMM, Erich, *You Shall Be As God's* (New York: Holt, Rinehart & Winston, 1966).

GAGER, John, *Moses in Greco-Roman Paganism* (Nashville: Abingdon Press, 1972). A comprehensive picture of Greco-Roman literature.

LEVENSON, Jon D., *Sinai and Zion: An Entry Into the Jewish Bible* (Minneapolis: Seabury Press, 1985).

"Moses," in *Encyclopedia Judaica*, Volume 12, pp. 371–411 (Jerusalem: 1972). A survey of Moses in Biblical, Hellenistic, rabbinic, medieval and modern Jewish literature along with presentations of Moses in Christian tradition, Islam and in the arts.

SILVER, Daniel, Jeremy, *Images of Moses* (New York: Basic Books, 1982). A study of the idealization of Moses as an insight into the Jewish heroic idea.

The Torah (Philadelphia: Jewish Publication Society, 1962).

WALZER, Michael, *Exodus and Revolution* (New York: Basic Books, 1985).

David the King

After the death of Moses, the leadership of the tribes fell to Joshua, under whose command the Israelites invaded Canaan and entrenched themselves in the hill country of the Promised Land. Egypt, which had dominated Canaan for the previous three centuries, was at this time in a period of anarchy. Not until a generation later was Egypt able to recover its Asiatic empire, and then only nominally. This breathing spell helped the Israelites to gain a foothold in the new land. But the struggle for its possession continued long after the death of Joshua.

The Israelites found a highly developed society and culture in Canaan, whose fortifications, buildings, and other material techniques were far superior to anything they themselves were able to develop until the time of David. In religion, also, the Canaanites had developed an elaborate system of temples and shrines, a pantheon of gods, and elaborate rituals intended to insure the fertility of the soil. Inevitably many Israelites adapted Canaanite practices, and the new Mosaic faith was put to a crucial test during the first centuries in the new land.

Aside from this challenge, the Hebrews also faced the problem of physical survival in Canaan. Having no capital city or central sanctuary in the early days to unite them, the tribes warred among themselves. "In those days there was no king in Israel; every man did that which was right in his own eyes" (Judges 21:25). Periodically during the next few centuries the Israelites were attacked by Midianites, Ammonites, and Moabites from beyond the Jordan.

From time to time "judges" arose who inspired the Israelites to defend themselves. These military heroes were believed to be endowed by some special outpouring of the spirit of God, which made them superior in valor and wisdom. Among the outstanding judges were Deborah, who effected a temporary coalition of almost all the tribes against the Canaanite menace in the north; Gideon, who overwhelmed the Midianite raiders by stratagem; and Jepthah, a famous outlaw of Gilead whose aid was enlisted to crush the Ammonites. But no one of the judges succeeded in uniting the tribes or in giving them religious leadership to withstand the challenge of the surrounding cults.

The most formidable of all the enemies during the period of the Judges were the Philistines, a sea people from Crete and Asia Minor, who, repelled by Egypt, settled on the coastal plain of Canaan. Superior in military art and possessing iron weapons, they pressed up from the plain into the hills and inflicted great losses on the Israelites. For a time Samson, a Nazarite of the tribe of Dan, fought against them; but while he performed deeds of personal prowess, he did not have the ability to lead others. The Philistine attacks soon turned into a systematic war of conquest; Shiloh was destroyed, and the Ark, which had been placed there, was captured by the enemy.

The Philistines might have made themselves permanent masters in Canaan were it not for Samuel, the most influential leader since Moses. Making Ramah the center of his activities in place of Shiloh, Samuel made a regular circuit to Bethel, Gilgal, and other towns, reminding the Israelites of the covenant they had made with God and urging them to follow the laws of Moses. When Saul of the tribe of Benjamin successfully helped the tribes in Transjordan to withstand an attack of the Ammonites, Samuel approved his appointment as king, thus hoping to provide the country with a strong unified government. Under Saul's leadership the Philistines were temporarily expelled from most of the areas of Jewish settlement, but their shadow still lay over the land. While at first Saul inspired confidence, it soon became apparent that Israel's first king was not equipped either with the temperament or the ability to unify the tribes and insure peace. It was time for another personality who could consolidate the nation and strengthen the Mosaic faith. The leader who came to the fore was the Judean shepherd David.

2 . *David the King*

[c.1000 B.C.E.]

MORTIMER J. COHEN

E A C H generation has shaped an image of David to appeal to
its own mind and heart and its own needs.* This image is based
in part on history, and partly on the hopes and yearnings of the
Jewish people. The "real" David who lived and ruled the Jewish nation around the year 1000 B.C.E. was an outstanding general, statesman, and diplomat, the architect of the Jewish nation, who completed the work of Moses.

David molded the Jewish people into a nation, giving it a capital, a court, and a government that could make itself felt. He
was also the royal champion of Israel's religion. He made the
city of Jerusalem the fortress of a faith, the sanctuary, and the
home of Israel's God. In addition, David is regarded as the poet-
patron of Jewish psalmody and Jewish music. Though he did
not write the whole of the Psalter, he undoubtedly wrote some
of the psalms,[1] a number of which have become part of the
liturgy in synagogue worship.

Like all creative personalities, David is greater than his actual
achievements. He emerges as the ideal king who lived and ruled
in Israel's "Golden Age." To catch glimpses of the "real" David
we must try to disentangle as best we can, with the aid of modern biblical scholarship, the changing images of David which

---

* The chief source for the life of David is found in the Books of Samuel and
the first Book of Kings. Another source is the account in the first Book of
Chronicles, chapters 11 to 29. But when examined carefully, the material in
Chronicles appears to have been taken from Samuel and Kings, and David has
been remade into a more religious figure. Other references to David in the
Bible do not add any new material beyond what the main sources furnish.

are reflected in the Bible and in other documents of Jewish history.

Judean Shepherd

David was born in Bethlehem of the tribe of Judah during the reign of Saul, first king of Israel. We know almost nothing of Jesse, his father, except that he must have been a man of some affluence since he owned flocks and herds. The rabbis, however, fill the empty gaps ingeniously. "David, the 'elect of God,'" they say in the Talmud, "came of distinguished ancestors. He was a descendant of Miriam, the sister of Moses, and so the strain of royal aristocracy (his great-grandmother, Ruth, was a Moabite princess) was reinforced by the priestly aristocracy (Miriam, Moses, and Aaron were of the priestly class). David's great-grandfather, Boaz, was one and the same person with Ibzan, the judge of Bethlehem. His grandfather's whole life was a continuous service of God, whence his name Obed, 'the servant,' and his father Jesse was one of the greatest scholars of his time." [2]

Why, of all occupations, did David choose to be a shepherd? "It was his shepherd life," the rabbis say, "that prepared him for his later exalted position. With gentle consideration he led the flocks entrusted to him. The young lambs he guided to pastures of tender grass; the patches of less juicy herbs he reserved for the sheep; and the full-grown sturdy rams were given the tough weeds for food. Then God said: 'David knows how to tend sheep, therefore he shall be the shepherd of My flock Israel.' " [3]

Evidently David was known for his musical ability, for he was summoned to alleviate with his music the disturbed feelings of King Saul. "And it came to pass, when the (evil) spirit from God was upon Saul, that David took the harp, and played with his hand; so Saul found relief, and it was well with him, and the evil spirit departed from him" (I Samuel 16:23). He won the friendship of Saul's son, Jonathan, heir-apparent to the throne, and the hand of Saul's daughter, Michal.

David is pictured as a man of supreme courage and strength. Even before he met Goliath the Philistine, a young man described David in these significant words: "Behold, I have seen a son of Jesse the Beth-lehemite, that is skillful in playing, and a mighty man of valor, and a man of war, and prudent in affairs, and a comely person, and the Lord is with him" (I Samuel 16:18).

Hardly had he become "armor-bearer" to King Saul than he was catapulted to fame through his victorious fight against the Philistine giant Goliath. Knowing that he could not face his enemy in direct combat, David resorted to other than ordinary weapons, "five smooth stones out of the brook." Above all, he entered into mortal struggle with a defiant half-prayer upon his lips: "Thou comest to me with a sword, and with a spear, and with a javelin; but I come to thee in the name of the Lord of hosts, the God of the armies of Israel, whom thou hast taunted" (I Samuel 17:45). He was a warrior of brilliant stratagems fortified with a deep religious faith. Even if this passage at arms with Goliath is merely a legend, he emerges from it as the volunteer champion of Israel.

When King Saul had earlier questioned David's ability to stand up to Goliath, David had confidently answered: "Thy servant kept his father's sheep; and when there came a lion, or a bear, and took a lamb out of the flock, I went out after him, and smote him, and delivered it out of his mouth; and when he arose against me, I caught him by his beard, and smote him, and slew him" (I Samuel 17:34-35).

David and Saul

After David was appointed army captain by Saul, his military prowess and growing popularity with the masses soon aroused the king's jealousy. King Saul was undoubtedly a devoted son of his people, a man of generous impulses, fine appearance, and regal in his bearing. But he bore within himself the seeds of his own destruction. He was the victim of his own tempestuous, jealous, and tyrannical nature. He could not tolerate opposition and so he was gradually forced into hostility toward those about him. He had broken relations with Samuel, and now he became insanely jealous of David when the people applauded this youth, who was "ruddy, and withal of beautiful eyes, and goodly to look upon" (I Samuel 16:12). As it happened, David was indeed richly endowed with many and diverse qualities—a handsome appearance, an ingratiating and charming manner, a capacity for making and holding loyal friends, and inexhaustible energy.

Ultimately, after King Saul had made two attempts to kill David, the latter had to flee for his life. Saul, kept informed by spies as to David's whereabouts, pursued him from place to place. Living the life of an outlaw, David fled to the little town of Nob where Ahimelech, the priest, hid him. When the king's soldiers followed David, he fled to the Judean fortress of Adullam. David's parents and brothers looked to him for protection against Saul, and many penniless adventurers, rebels, and outcasts joined his growing band of loyal followers.

Saul's most ruthless and heinous act was the murder of the priests of Nob because they had given temporary asylum to David. Abiathar, son of Ahimelech and the only priest to escape, and also a prophet named Gad, joined David's forces. In order to maintain himself and his followers, David was forced to extort tribute from the peasants and small landholders of southern Palestine.

Much is made of David's magnanimity of spirit toward Saul; though the latter was trying to kill David, the younger man refrained on two occasions from taking the life of his attacker. Once Saul entered a cave where David and his men were sitting; David stood beside the king so closely that he was able to cut off a piece of Saul's garment. After Saul had gone a short distance away, David called out to him: ". . . See the skirt of thy robe in my hand; for in that I cut off the skirt of thy robe, and killed thee not, know thou and see that there is neither evil nor transgression in my hand . . ." (I Samuel 24:12). On another occasion, when Saul had fallen asleep in camp surrounded by his soldiers, David and his companions managed to enter behind their lines and found Saul sleeping on the ground, his spear and a vessel of water at his head. David quietly took the spear and cruse of water, left the camp, and having arrived at a safe distance, reproved Abner for his carelessness in guarding his king. King Saul awakened and recognized David's voice. David said: "Behold the king's spear! let then one of the young men come over and fetch it" (I Samuel 26:22).

But Saul was inflexible and continued his pursuit of David.

In time, David's followers crossed over the boundaries between Palestine and the Philistines to Gath, the nearest of the five Philistine city-states, and hired themselves out as mercenary troops to its ruler. King Achish gave David the town of Ziklag as a kind of fief; it was David's first step toward power.[4] For over a year Ziklag served him as a base for plundering expeditions against the nomadic tribes to the south. When the final struggle came between King Saul and the Philistines in the Battle of Gilboa, David was spared the ignominious choice of deserting King Achish or of fighting against his own kinfolk; the rulers of the other four Philistine towns refused his services, not trusting a former follower of Saul.

The Road to Kingship

Before he had fled from Saul, David undoubtedly had planned a kind of Judean kingdom.[5] He therefore avoided any action that would turn his own tribal kinsmen against him. David was too shrewd to alienate potential adherents by acts of brigandage. Instead, he maintained close communication with the people of Judah, and even sent gifts to them from time to time.

King Saul and his sons, among them Jonathan, were slain at the Battle of Gilboa, a disastrous defeat for the Israelites. Saul's successor Ishbaal (Ish-bosheth) fled to Mahanaim in Jordan. On the brink of complete disintegration, Israel was saved only by the decisive action of David and his followers. David secretly encouraged the Judeans to proclaim a separate kingdom. After political maneuverings, including gifts sent to the elders of Judah, and by reason of lack of opposition on the part of the Philistines, who wrongly regarded David as their friend, David came to Hebron where he was anointed king of Judah in about the year 1005 B.C.E. During a reign of seven and a half years, he developed what must have been his long-range plan to become king of Israel. With all the tribes united behind him, he could then face the common enemy, the Philistines. To advance his scheme, he wisely and shrewdly ingratiated himself with the elders of Israel by showing proper deference to the memory of Saul. He had the fallen king's body brought back from Jabesh-gilead for honorable burial together with that of Jonathan, David's beloved friend.

Abner, Saul's commander-in-chief, after the defeat at Gilboa, had retired to Mahanaim and proclaimed Ishbael, the surviving son of King Saul, to be king. On hearing the news, David sent troops to investigate under the leadership of his nephews, Joab, Abishai, and Asahel (II Samuel 2:12-23). They clashed at Gibeon,[6] where Abner slew Asahel. Later, when Ishbael reprimanded Abner for some misconduct, Abner in resentment secretly sent word to David that he was ready to use his influence to have the crown of Israel offered to him. Before he would negotiate with Abner, David insisted on and succeeded in having Michal restored to him as his wife, for after David's flight Saul had given her in marriage to a certain Palti b. Laish. David must have believed that this marriage into the house of Saul would make him more acceptable to Israel.

When Abner appeared before David, Joab, brother of the slain Asahel, assassinated him, thus taking vengeance for his brother's death and eliminating a potential rival. Ishbael also met a violent end at the hands of Rechab and Baana, who had borne Saul's house a special grudge.

The way was now clear for David to ascend the throne of Israel.[7] The elders felt free to change the dynasty of Saul for that of David because the Northern Kingdom had never held to the principle of hereditary kingship as did the Southern Kingdom. And so it came to pass that David, having ruled Ziklag and then Judah, acquired his third and most important title—king of Israel.

World of David

Whatever other significance King David holds for the Jewish people, he remains above all the creator of Israel the nation.[8] To understand his genius as the founder of Israel as well as the ruthlessness, conniving, and the occasional chicanery he was forced to adopt to achieve his goal, we must envisage the world in which David lived and the desperate chaos within Israel after the defeat and death of King Saul.[9] That world—western Asia about 1000 B.C.E.—was a stormy one of fundamental and revolutionary changes. The Babylonian Empire in the north-east, ever eager to find an outlet on the Mediterranean Sea, had been in decline, with inner weaknesses and turmoil that pre-vented it from adventuring abroad. The Hurrian state and the Hittites no longer threatened from the north. The Egyptian Empire to the southwest of Palestine had fallen into the hands of weak Pharaohs, turning the attention of Egypt away from warlike interests abroad to matters of closer concern at home. The Arameans (Syrians), though in the ascendancy, were still weak. Phoenicia, to the northwest, was friendly because of close economic and political ties with Israel. Hence, when David rose to power about 1000 B.C.E., he was confronted by the challenge of beating back and overcoming the attacks of the lesser nations which surrounded his country—Moab, Edom, Ammon, Aram—and thus enlarging the frontiers of Israel.

Conquest of Philistines

Before King David could seize the opportunity presented him, he had to face the powerful Philistines, as Saul had had to do. A century and a half earlier, a number of Aegean peoples had been driven from the shores of the Mediterranean and from the island of Crete. They took to the sea, and were first heard of in the days of the Judges, when they flooded into Canaan and in time gave their name to Palestine.

These "Sea Peoples"—as the Egyptians called them—deep-ened their inroads into the hinterland from the Palestinian coast. They had established five city-states, each headed by its "tyrant" king or chieftain; in one of these, Gath, David had found refuge from Saul. Having superior military and political organization, they constituted a continuous threat to Israel, attacking one tribe, then another. Sometimes the tribes of Israel joined forces to repel the invaders, occasionally winning suc-cesses, occasionally suffering defeats. As the Philistines multi-plied, they became more and more the major threat to Jewish survival because, unlike other foes, they were well organized and well armed.

The Philistines possessed a revolutionary power—the secret of smelting a new metal, iron—which they guarded closely.[10]

This enabled them to hold a small nation like Israel at their mercy.

> Now there was no smith found throughout all the land of Israel; for the Philistines said: 'Lest the Hebrews make them swords or spears'; but all the Israelites went down to the Philistines, to sharpen every man his plowshare, and his coulter, and his axe, and his mattock . . . So it came to pass in the day of battle, that there was neither sword nor spear found in the hand of any of the people that were with Saul and Jonathan (I Samuel 13:19-22).

The earliest agricultural implements found in Palestine by archeologists were discovered in Saul's fortress at Gibeah, and were made of bronze and wood. To King David undoubtedly goes the credit for shifting his agricultural and war economy to iron, the hardier, more modern metal, and for initiating the Age of Iron in ancient Israel. The shift from the use of bronze, a comparatively soft metal, to iron brought important economic and political changes. Plows as well as axe heads, sickles, and chariots could now be made of iron, and the productivity of the farmers could be increased. So important was the introduction of the use of iron into the economic and military life of Israel that centuries later the first Book of Chronicles (22:3, 14-16), speaking about the reign of King David, takes trouble to record that he prepared "iron in abundance for the nails for the doors of the gates, and for the couplings."

Undoubtedly, the earlier disastrous defeats of the Israelites under King Saul resulted from the inequality in arms related to the Philistine's use of iron. To this might be added the poor strategy of King Saul—his direct, frontal attacks on the Philistines—which made military disaster inevitable.

David met the Philistine challenge bravely by resorting to guerrilla tactics; he inflicted two crushing defeats upon them in the battles of Baalperazim and Gibeon. He finally freed Israel and Judah from Philistine domination for all time. After these battles the Philistines are hardly mentioned again. Philistia probably was made tributary to David and had to hand over the pick of its standing army to him.

Organizing the Kingdom

With what political instruments did King David face the powerfully organized group of city-states of the Philistines? In this as in all his actions, David acted swiftly with the determination, prudence, and brilliance that marked his whole life. He built upon whatever foundations had been laid by Saul. Whereas Saul had helped forward the movement of unity in the Tribal Confederacy, he had not been able to weld the tribes into complete union. The rabbis with startling intuition ascribed Saul's failure to his "too great mildness," which they call "a drawback in a ruler." [11] What Saul had lacked—a dash of iron in his make-up—King David possessed in full measure.

In the first place, there had been no central authority among the tribes of Israel. Each tribe maintained complete autonomy. The Book of Judges ends on the note: "In those days there was no king in Israel; every man did that which was right in his own eyes" (Judges 21:25).

The Tribal Confederacy, as a modern biblical scholar calls it, had been loosely organized under King Saul. The presence of the powerful Philistines had compelled the tribes to unite from time to time for self-protection; but the moment the pressure was removed, each tribe took to pursuing its own individual welfare.

Besides the inevitable jealousies and rivalries among the individual tribes, there was a more fundamental and serious division that was destined later to tear Israel apart—the geographical separation of the tribes, the lack of adequate communication, and their conflicting backgrounds and interests. Ultimately, the people were to be divided into northern and southern tribes, but in the time of King Saul and King David, the immediate weakness of the Israelites lay in their lack of centralized control and unity.

A growing awareness of the Israelites' peril had begun to make itself felt even in the days of the later Judges, and the drive for greater unity had expressed itself sporadically under various strong leaders. Ultimately, even so powerful a spiritual leader as the priestly seer Samuel had to yield to the people's demand for a king, and, having selected Saul, had to present him for ratification by the people.

Fear of the kingly power was natural in the ancient world, for the kings were dictators and masters of the people. In the mind of Samuel, fealty to an earthly king whose word would become the law violated all reverence and obedience due the heavenly king, the God of Israel, who alone was Israel's true sovereign. It was, therefore, with profound misgivings— which he voiced openly—that the old seer had reluctantly acceded to the people's demand. Indeed, Samuel had clearly warned: "And ye shall cry out in that day because of your king whom ye shall have chosen for you; and the Lord will not answer you in that day" (I Samuel 8:18).

Jerusalem Made Capital City

Once David came to power, in an act of sheer political genius, he moved to create a political and religious capital that would be beyond and above the influence of tribal jealousies— a center that would symbolize a united Israel. He captured Jerusalem—a Canaanite city-state in the heart of the hill-country between Israel and Judah—from the Jebusites. In time it became known as "the city of David" (II Samuel 5:9; I Chronicles 11:5-7). Down to its destruction in 586 B.C.E., Jerusalem retained its religious and political supremacy, being bound to Judah only by personal ties through the king.

After David had made himself undisputed ruler of Israel and Judah, he inevitably followed the course of kings in other lands. Unwilling to depend upon a people's army made up of volunteer contingents that the tribes chose to send to meet emergencies involving their own interests, as in Saul's time, David established a small professional army that was loyal not to local leaders, but to him as king, and to him only. He was fortunate in finding in Joab ben Zeruiah, his nephew, a military leader who faithfully served him to the end of his days as head of the army.[12] In addition, the king surrounded himself with a personal bodyguard of foreign mercenaries, including Cherethites, Pelethites (coming from Crete and elsewhere), and Hittites; among them were Uriah the Hittite and Ittai of Gath (II Samuel 8:18; 15:18).[13]

David launched offensive campaigns of conquest and aggrandizement. The greater part of his reign was spent in foreign wars, and many nations became dependent upon him. In truth, the heavy levies on the people for troops in Israel and Judah laid the ground for later restlessness and discontent that became acute and ultimately almost destroyed the kingdom.

The king also recognized the need for fortified sites throughout the land. Recent discoveries by archeologists indicate that "the casemated walls of Dabir and Beth-Shemesh were built by David as part of a line of defense against the Philistines." [14]

Archeologists have further disclosed the great part that the Negev played in the destiny of the ancient kingdom of Israel and Judah. The Negev was heavily populated in those days, with busy towns and interconnecting roads on which trade and commerce travelled back and forth between Arab lands to the southeast and in North Africa. King David was the first to recognize the importance of the Negev; and how much of his and King Solomon's foreign policy was determined by their determination to hold the Negev with its outlet at the Gulf of Aqaba. One might add that the modern State of Israel is also acutely aware of the importance of Negev and has done much to revive, replant, and reconstruct this desert area. [15]

Administration of Government and Law

Another step toward greater unity and personal control of the government was taken by King David when he reorganized the administration of the government. [16] According to certain biblical scholars, David adopted the Egyptian system of governmental organization, either directly or by way of Phoenician adaptation. He created new administrative officials such as scribes, recorders, ministers, stewards, and secretaries. With the need to raise new taxes to support the army, the growing body of bureaucrats, and his many building projects, David had to increase the number of supervising officials, and to discover ways of obtaining sufficient funds.

To set up and maintain a court worthy of the new kingdom, David increased the body of attendants who were legally "servants of the king" or royal officials and dependents. They are referred to by such names as the king's "friend" (II Samuel 15:37), or "counselor" (II Samuel 16:23; I Chronicles 27:32-33); he also had house guests or retainers. Many of his former comrades-in-arms, upon whose loyalty he could depend, filled these and similar posts.

Another advance made by King David lay in the administration of law, which had previously been vested in the tribal "elders" who sat at the gate, or in the judges of the Tribal Confederacy.The function of judging was now taken over by the king himself; but of course he delegated this responsibility to judges whom he appointed (II Samuel 14:4-17; 15:1-6). Mention is also made of other royal officials (II Samuel 8:15-18).

The Ark Brought to Jerusalem

Having established his court at Jerusalem and having centralized the governmental agencies there, thus making sure that unified control over the people would rest in his hands, King David was now ready to stabilize the religious life of his people. Heretofore, the unity of the Israelites had been weakened by the lack of a religious center which could provide sustaining spiritual power to bring together the intensely individualistic tribes of Israel. Shiloh, once the central sanctuary of the Tribal Confederacy, had held the sacred Ark of the covenant, tended in the early days of Samuel by Eli, the high priest, his sons, and then by Samuel himself. In the wars between the Philistines and the Israelites, at the battle of Ebenezer, the elders, seeing the battle going against the Israelites, had summoned the Ark to be brought from Shiloh. But the Israelites had been defeated and the Ark had been captured by the Philistines and taken into captivity (I Samuel 4:1-11). Though from that time on there was no more reference to Shiloh, we now know from archeological excavations that Shiloh was destroyed by the Philistines, most likely during or immediately following the battle of Ebenezer.[17]

The loss of the Ark and Shiloh had been a shattering blow to the very foundations of the Tribal Confederacy. According to tradition, no matter where the Ark was taken by the Philistines —Ashdod, Gath, Ekron, Beth-Shemesh—trouble came to them. Finally, it had found lodgement in Kiriath-jearim, from where it was brought to Jerusalem with great pomp and ceremony; the king himself danced before the Ark.

By establishing the Ark in his city David sought to ensure that the God of Israel would make His home there (II Samuel 6). The city of David now became "Zion, city of God," for God's presence once again dwelled in the midst of Israel.

David followed this step by appointing new heads of the priesthood. One was Abiathar, a descendant of Eli, who alone had escaped the slaughter of the priests of Nob and who had befriended David during the days of his outlawry. Zadok was also appointed as head priest. Both were of distinguished ancestry, and both were loyal to the king. In this way David strengthened his crown with the religious halo of the past.

Tradition attributes to King David improvements in the holding of divine worship, for we read about how he conceived and arranged "the courses of the priests and the Levites and all the work of the service of the house of the Lord" (I Chronicles 28:11-19). According to tradition (I Chronicles 25), David organized the temple musicians into guilds.[18]

King David wanted to go one step further and build a magnificent temple patterned after the royal temples of other nations as the religious symbol of his kingdom, but Nathan the prophet, voicing the more conservative opinion of the Tribal Confederacy, dissuaded him from doing this. David, inherently a religious man, yielded to Nathan, as he had done on other crucial occasions. However, David was said to have purchased later the threshing-floor of Araunah the Jebusite, where he erected an altar to God to stay the plague that had swept over the people, and where the Temple of Solomon was later supposed to have been built (II Samuel 24:18-25).

Taking of the Census

King David initiated and pursued other policies calculated to lessen the independence of the Tribal Confederacy, and which brought murmurs of complaint from the populace. Among these were the census of all Israel and the beginning of the system of forced labor.[19] For various reasons, the Israelites had always resented the taking of a census. Contrary to the advice of his counselors, however, King David instituted such a process under the leadership of Joab. What his purposes were can only be guessed. He may have desired to weaken the tribal set-up of the nation by shifting the tribal boundary lines. Or he may have wanted to establish a wider basis of taxation, since his military efforts, his building program, and his defense fortifications required large sums of money.

The census possibly had another objective, namely, the institution of the corvée system or the drafting of labor. Perhaps it was this that the people so bitterly resented, a resentment that was to explode later, after the death of King Solomon, who had enlarged the system, and during the reign of his arrogant son Rehoboam. The man David placed in charge of the draft was Adoniram, a sinister figure who became the symbol of rebellion. The use of such a man reveals the despotic feature of much of King David's rule (II Samuel 24; II Samuel 20:24; and I Kings 12:18).

These unpopular policies that lost King David much favor in the eyes of the people can be understood only in terms of national need.[20] He had to face hostile powers on all Israel's boundaries. He had initiated a vast building program, including the erection of palaces for governmental officials, because he sought recognition for Israel as a strong and powerful nation. David's victories over the Philistines, together with his conquest of Edom, Moab, Ammon, and Aram brought vast sums of tribute into the royal treasury. But more was needed; and labor had to be obtained. The nation was on the march. Samuel had warned the people of the meaning of kingship; his predictions proved altogether true (I Samuel 8:10-22).

Cities of Refuge

A final policy that King David instituted reveals his astuteness as an event-maker in Jewish history. He reestablished the Levitical cities throughout the tribes and also the ancient "cities of refuge." The religious leaders of the tribes, among whom the Levites were very influential, were often the centers of rebellion against the king. King David, therefore, held it to be better for the unification of Israel to have them scattered over the country so that their power and influence could be weakened. On the positive side, their dispersal over the land would assure their bringing the message of the God of Israel to the people (Joshua 21; I Chronicles 6:54 ff).[21]

By reinstituting the "cities of refuge," David sought to destroy once and for all the disruptive effect of the ancient and time-honored practice of the "blood feuds" or internecine conflicts among individuals, families, and sometimes tribes. Blood revenge codes resulted in vendettas that time and again had wrecked communities in the tribal history of Israel, and King David believed that no stable government could coexist with such an institution.[22]

The Closing Years

King David was himself the victim of acts growing out of blood feuds, as when Joab, Saul's general, killed Abner at a critical moment of negotiation with King David because in an earlier conflict Abner had slain Asahel, Joab's brother. Even more poignant was the sorrow of King David when his son Absalom, enraged at the brutality of Amnon toward his half-sister Tamar, brutally murdered Amnon and had to flee. Later, when Absalom returned and led a revolt against his father, Joab in defending David killed Absalom. Because of this, a bitter blood feud disrupted the long friendship and devoted loyalty that existed between the king and his able commander-in-chief; even on his deathbed David demanded of Solomon that he exact the death penalty of Joab (I Kings 2:1-6).

David's personal life was by no means free of blemish. The incident which most deeply mars his character and which brought down upon him the wrath of the prophet Nathan was his passion for Bathsheba and the death he contrived for her husband Uriah. The episode between Tamar and Amnon, described above, and later Absalom's attempt to seize King David's throne robbed the aging king of peace and happiness. The revolt of Absalom, the son whom he loved most dearly, was actually recognized to be in the nature of a popular movement, as was the later revolt of Sheba b. Bichri, a Benjaminite (from which tribe Saul had come and whose members nursed grievances against David as his successor).

As the years closed about him, David made no public commitment as to who should succeed him. His eldest living son, Adonijah, sought to be king. But Bathsheba, supported by Nathan the prophet, Zadok the priest, and the military under

Benaiah and Shimai, succeeded in getting David to proclaim Solomon, her son, as king.

King David died about 973 B.C.E., having reigned seven years in Hebron and thirty-three years over the united kingdom.

Emergence of the Ideal David

"In one sense, David was a victim of his own greatness, of an indomitable will that urged him to scale the tempting heights of power," a modern scholar writes of King David. "Yet, in spite of his drive for success and national glory, he was never lacking in the magnanimity and winsomeness that endeared him to friend and enemy alike. But in a deeper sense David was involved in the conflict with the God he sought to serve, the God with whose will he had to reckon in the practical affairs of daily life." [23]

As the human David and his troubled times receded into the past, his shortcomings and his sins were largely overlooked; his virtues loomed large and were embellished. He had been faithful to God and his people. He had led Israel from a loose confederacy of tribes to a united nation. He had set up courts of law to bring justice to his people. He was remembered as one who guarded the rights of the poor and oppressed.

Later generations, in the midst of their struggles and sorrows, looked back upon the reign of King David and regarded it as Israel's "Golden Age." The prophets undoubtedly had it in mind when they urged the restoration of a united Israel. And they held it as a confident faith that among the descendants of David they would find their true leader. Thus in Isaiah and other biblical writings we find the ever-changing image of David growing into idealization:

And there shall come forth a shoot out of the stock of Jesse,
And a twig shall grow forth out of his roots.
And the spirit of the Lord shall rest upon him,
The spirit of wisdom and understanding,
The spirit of counsel and might,
The spirit of knowledge and of the fear of the Lord. . . .

And it shall come to pass in that day,
That the root of Jesse, that standeth for an ensign of the peoples,

Unto him shall the nations seek;
And his resting-place shall be glorious.
                    (Isaiah 11:1-2, 10)

In post-biblical times, too, after the fall of the Temple in 70 C.E., as the people's need for help and their yearning for salvation grew more intense, the image of King David became more and more idealized. The rabbis, masters of the Midrash, poets and creators of tales and fables, embroidered upon his name and memory the qualities of piety and the values of learning and wisdom they needed to sustain them through bitter suffering and martyrdom.

Rabbinical writings are full of references to King David. Some sages sought to eliminate the human weaknesses David exhibited so that he would be acceptable to the spiritually sensitive in later years. Others found in David the ideal scholar, who studied Torah until dawn, and who held high the ideal of learning. Some tried to fill the gaps in David's beginnings and life. Still others sought a more reasonable explanation of what seemed to them the strange and miraculous in his achievements.

Out of the desperate hunger to survive and keep alive the memory of King David, the Jewish people created the ideal ruler of the future—"the son of David." And when Christianity appeared, it described its vision of the end-time in the shape of God's kingdom ruled by a Messiah descended from the house of David. It was King David who gave his people and humanity, according to the sages, an eternal blessing. On the Day of Judgment, it is said, God will turn to David with the words:

"Take the cup and say the blessing, thou sweetest singer in Israel, and Israel's king." [24]

FOR FURTHER READING

"David," in *Encyclopedia Judaica,* Volume 5, pp. 1318-1338 (Jerusalem: 1972). Comprehensive survey of David in the Bible, Talmud, Liturgy, Kabalah, Christianity, Islam, modern Hebrew literature, arts and music.

FRIEDMAN, David, Noel, "The Age of David and Solomon," in *The World History of the Jewish People—The Age of the Monarchies: Political History,* 4th ed., pp. 101-125 (Jerusalem: Massada, 1979). A literary and conceptual study of the period of David and Solomon.

MAZAR, Benjamin, "The Era of David and Solomon," ibid., pp. 76-100. A historical and archaeological study of the period of David and Solomon.

SARNA, Nahum, M., "The Biblical Sources for the History of the Monarchy," ibid., pp. 3-19. An analysis of the biblical literature on the monarchy.

ROSTON, M., *Biblical Drama in England* (Evanston, IL: Northwestern University Press, 1968). Survey of the significance of David in the arts.

Jeremiah the Prophet

The four centuries that separate David and Jeremiah, usually referred to as the period of the First Commonwealth, constitute a study in contrasts. On the one hand, those years are characterized by a succession of Jewish kings, few of them outstanding, and the rise and fall of a political state not significantly different from many others in the Middle East; on the other hand, it is during this era that the great Hebrew prophets arose, who constitute what is perhaps the greatest religious movement in the history of mankind. The story of Jeremiah represents the climax of this age of kings and prophets.

The reign of Solomon as the third king of Israel was marked by peace, prosperity, and external splendor. Trade flourished with the entire Mediterranean world; the Temple and magnificent palaces which Solomon built were part of a huge building program which made Jerusalem the religious and political center of Palestine. These structures, however, were made possible only by burdensome taxes and forced labor. The Judeans in the south, as the direct beneficiaries of this program, accepted these hardships. But the northern tribes resented these burdens, and revolted after the death of Solomon. The Hebrews became a house divided: for the following two centuries Jewish history is the story of two rival states who periodically exhausted themselves in internecine warfare.

The history of the Northern Kingdom was characterized by civil wars, insurrections, and continuous instability and unrest. During the two centuries of its existence it was governed by nineteen different kings, about half of whom met violent deaths. During the reign of Ahab and his consort Jezebel (876-853), daughter of the king of Tyre, Baal worship in its grossest forms became widespread in the land. The seizure of power by Jehu and the dynasty he inaugurated, which lasted a century (843-745), stayed some of the foreign influences for a while. Jeroboam II, the last of the dynasty, strengthened his country's commercial position and ushered in a period of luxury, at least for the upper classes. But this was not to last. Subsequent rulers were caught in the struggle for power between Egypt to the south and Assyria to the north, and after a period of semi-anarchy the Assyrian Empire swallowed up the land of Israel and deported its prominent citizens to Assyria (622 B.C.E.). It was those exiles who came to be known as the "lost ten tribes."

Judah to the south could not match its northern neighbor in size, population, territory, or accessibility to the great trade routes. Judah's role in international affairs was negligible and for a time it was subservient to the north. But the Southern Kingdom enjoyed political stability, and it was here that national consciousness and the religious tradition were preserved. The fall of Israel, however, made Judah's position even more vulnerable as a buffer state between Assyria and Egypt, and it remained at best semi-independent for most of the last century and a half of its existence.

What these years lacked in political glory, however, they made up in the great contributions of the literary prophets, who suddenly appeared on the scene in the middle of the eighth century. Long before, the Book of Samuel tells of groups of early ecstatics also known as prophets who went about singing and dancing, and thus stirring up the religious ardor of the people. Later, inspired and courageous men like Nathan, Elijah, and Elisha befriended the victims of injustice and had the courage to rebuke the kings themselves for their wrongdoing. Thus, Nathan appeared before King David to denounce him for his sin with Bathsheba, and Elijah did not fear to confront Ahab in the vineyard which he had taken from Naboth with the words, "thou hast murdered and taken possession."

But it is the appearance of Amos, the shepherd of Tekoa (c. 765 B.C.E.) which marks the new era of classical Hebrew prophecy. Amos lived in a period of economic prosperity, but underneath the surface existed many acute social problems: the exploitation of the poor by the rich, and the perversion of justice in the courts, the market place, and the Temple itself. Seeing this injustice, Amos sternly warned that God would punish the people for their wrong deeds. Amos' great contribution was his emphasis on the universal God of justice who would tolerate moral evil neither in Israel nor among the other nations.

Hosea, a generation later, also predicted the downfall of Israel as an act of judgment. But he looked forward to a final redemption. God was not only a God of justice but equally a God of love, who forgave the Jewish people as a husband forgives an erring wife.

One of the greatest of the prophets was undoubtedly Isaiah, who carried forward the movement begun by Amos and Hosea. Emphasizing the holiness of God and His moral purity, Isaiah too warned against social injustice in all areas of life. He was opposed to foreign alliances either with Egypt or Assyria. "If ye have not faith, verily ye shall not endure." Isaiah's own faith was vindicated when Sennacherib laid siege to Jerusalem during the reign of Hezekiah and the city and temple were saved. By his visions of the Messianic age and of the ideal Messianic ruler, Isaiah fired the imagination of his own and later generations.

After the death of Hezekiah a reaction set in. Manasseh, the new king, became a vassal to Assyria, and Assyrian religious practices became prevalent in Judah. For a period of sixty or seventy years the prophets were persecuted and had to work secretly until the days of King Josiah (c. 640), when they were able to emerge from retirement. The new generation of prophets included Zephaniah, Hulda, Nahum, and Habbakuk. The greatest of these prophets in the last years of the Jewish state was Jeremiah.

3 . Jeremiah the Prophet

[c.645-585 B.C.E.]

SIMON NOVECK

IN THE long line of literary prophets who emerged in ancient Israel from the middle of the eighth century B.C.E. until the fifth, Jeremiah probably has the greatest relevance for our time. His emphasis on the covenant relationship between man and God, his identification of the essence of religion with integrity and sincerity in human relationships, his recognition of the deep-rootedness of sin and yet the ever present possibility for repentance and inner change, the doctrine of Jewish patriotism which he was the first to enunciate, and finally his belief in the eternity of Israel in spite of all the suffering and calamity—all these make his utterances profoundly meaningful for our age.

Beyond its relevance the message of Jeremiah also provides an insight into the nature of the prophetic life. His prophecies, lyrical and emotional in character, reveal his inner conflicts, his doubts and frustrations, the sense of his own unworthiness, and are an illustration of the sustaining power which faith in God can bring. Jeremiah is therefore more accessible and closer to the average person today than some of the other prophets.

Ironically, Jeremiah has come to be known as the "prophet of sorrows and lamentations" or the "weeping prophet," partly because of his constant denunciation and predictions of the doom that would befall his people, in part because the Book of Lamentations was incorrectly ascribed to him, and perhaps too because he led so lonely an existence without the comforts of home or the joys of family life. And yet Jeremiah is actually a prophet of courage and hope. His confidence in the future of his people is shown by his purchasing land and sealing the deed in the midst of the siege. His concept of the religious meaning of the Exile grew out of his faith that eventually Babylon would be overthrown and the Jews would be returned to their land.

Finally, more than any of his predecessors, the life of Jeremiah mirrors the historical events of his time, the story of the last four decades of the First Jewish Commonwealth. His writings constitute the most authentic record of this critical era in Jewish history. There are difficulties in reconstructing the history of the period from Jeremiah's writings since they are not in chronological order, and in many instances it is impossible to determine when a particular prophecy was uttered. However, we still know more about this remarkable man and his period than we do about any other biblical hero except King David. This is due, in part, at least, to his secretary and friend, the young aristocrat, Baruch ben Neriah, who joined him about midway in his prophetic career, to whom he dictated his prophecies, and who shared the last two decades of his life. Jeremiah's prophecies reflect the events in the kingdom of Judah during the period of Josiah and his successors, the religious reform movement and its gradual decline, and the great international rivalries culminating in the rise of the new Babylonian Empire. They also depict the vacillation and intrigues under the last three kings of Judah, which led to the revolt and destruction of the Jewish state, and the final days of Jewish autonomy under Gedaliah. These accounts, as we have seen, have been at least in part confirmed by Babylonian and Assyrian chronicles and the findings of modern archeologists which help fill in some of the background and give us a vivid picture of Jeremiah and his time.

World of Jeremiah

Jeremiah was born to a priestly family in Anathoth, a small village in the Judean hills, about three miles north of Jerusalem. His father Hilkiah may have served as a priest in the Temple and was perhaps a descendant of Abiathar, the survivor of the priests of Nob, who after serving David for many years was banished by Solomon to Anathoth. But of this we cannot be certain.[1]

While we have few specific details about Jeremiah's background and early training, it is clear from his writings—and certain similarities of phrase and outlook—that he must have read the prophecies of Hosea in northern Israel almost a century before. He may also have read in his childhood part of the legal code of Deuteronomy, which, according to some authorities, was available in prophetic and priestly circles long before it was "discovered" in the Temple a few years after Jeremiah had become a prophet.[2]

The times in which Jeremiah grew up were critical for the Jewish faith because of the prevalence of pagan cults. The Assyrian Empire, which had emerged as a world power a century before, had reached its pinnacle toward the middle of the seventh century. Ashurbanipal, the greatest of its kings, had succeeded in capturing Thebes, the Egyptian capital far up the Nile, and in bringing Egypt, Palestine, and the entire Near East under his cruel domination.[3]

The religious practices of the Assyrians were imported into Judah by Manasseh, king of Judah. Worship of Ishtar, the "queen of heaven," soon became a favorite among the people. Together with this went child sacrifices to Molech,* King Manasseh offering his own son as a sacrifice. Witchcraft, necromancy,† worship of Baal, and other Canaanite practices which had been forced underground now became widespread.

Jeremiah as a young boy saw these cults and superstitions all about him. "The children gather wood, and the fathers kindle the fire, and the women knead the dough, to make cakes to the queen of heaven" (7:18).

Jeremiah's Call to Prophecy

Jeremiah began to prophesy at an early age, probably before he was twenty. As he recalled many years later, it was in the

---

* A pagan deity to whom children were sacrificed in the valley of Hinnom outside Jerusalem. See Leviticus 18:21, II Kings 23:10, Jeremiah 32:35.
† Necromancy is the foretelling of the future by communicating with the dead; also used loosely for all forms of divination. See story of Saul and witch of Endor (I Samuel 28).

thirteenth year of Josiah's reign that he felt the call of his destiny:

> And the word of the Lord came unto me, saying:
> Before I formed thee in the belly I knew thee,
> And before thou camest forth out of the womb I sanctified thee;
> I have appointed thee a prophet unto the nations.
>
> (1:4-5)

Like Moses before him, Jeremiah was hesitant to accept the call. "Then said I: 'Ah, Lord God! behold, I cannot speak; for I am a child.'" This reluctance was due to a natural shrinking from so great a task and to his own temperament—timid, sensitive, introspective, and distrustful of his own abilities. But the word of God came to him:

> Say not: I am a child;*
> For to whomsoever I shall send thee thou shalt go,
> And whatsoever I shall command thee thou shalt speak.
>
> (1:6)

Decrying the visionaries who prophesy "a thing of naught, and the deceit of their own heart" (14:14), Jeremiah like all the great prophets before him was not to speak his own words. The message he was to utter was the word of God. Herein lay the function of the prophet—to be a spokesman of God.

> Then the Lord put forth His hand, and touched my mouth;
>   and the Lord said unto me:
> Behold, I have put My words in thy mouth.
>
> (1:9)

God would also give him strength to endure the opposition which he would inevitably arouse. From a timid youth he would be transformed into a "fortified city and an iron pillar and a brazen wall against the whole land, against kings of Judah, the princes, the priests and the people of the land."

Jeremiah's commission had a negative as well as a positive side, each an intricate part of the task he was undertaking, "to

---

* The Hebrew is *naar*, meaning "boy" or "youth," thus stressing the prophet's humility.

root out and to pull down . . . to destroy and to overthrow; to build, and to plant." The mission would be a difficult one— the princes and the people would fight against him. But he had divine assurance that though "they shall fight against thee . . . they shall not prevail against thee" (1:19).

In the Days of Josiah (626-609 B.C.E.)

Jeremiah began his prophetic career in his hometown of Anathoth. Like Hosea, his primary concern during this period was to speak out against the idolatry and apostasy that he saw about him, the breach of faith with God. In the desert period God and Israel had enjoyed a close covenant relationship. But since coming to Canaan the people had forgotten all that God had done for them and lost their sense of gratitude. Even the leaders of the people, including the priests, the rulers, and the prophets, had been faithless.

In simple, forceful parables Jeremiah tried to bring home to the people the truth concerning the evil of their ways. The flowering of the almond tree (in Hebrew, the "wakeful tree") which he saw, signified to him that "God watches (is wakeful) over His word to perform it" (1:11). When he beheld the vision of "a seething pot: and the face thereof is from the north," he warned that "out of the north the evil shall break forth upon all the inhabitants of the land" (1:13-14). As a result of her sins Israel was to be punished: Judah would be attacked by a mighty and ancient nation which will be "cruel and have no mercy"; its people would roar like the sea, and they would "ride upon horses set in array as men for war" [4] (6:23).

While the burden of the prophet's message was denunciation of evil and threat of destruction, for Jeremiah there was always the possibility of repentance. The day of wrath could be averted. Later, however, he was to become so discouraged at the perverseness of the people and their refusal to repent as to cry out:

Can the Ethiopian change his skin,
Or the leopard his spots?
(13:23)

But in his early days, he still had hopes that disaster might be forestalled. About four years after he began to prophesy, a series of events took place which seemed to confirm his hopes.

Jeremiah and the Reform

In the year 621 B.C.E. a movement for religious reform which had probably been long in the making started in Judea. Ashurbanipal, the great Assyrian king, had died in 626, and the Empire had begun to decline. It was therefore now possible for Judea to go its own way, at least religiously. The Bible gives an account of what happened. In the eighteenth year of King Josiah's reign, the "book of the Law" was found in the Temple and read before the king. This was probably the Book of Deuteronomy, undoubtedly known to a few scholars and priests but either unknown or forgotten by the others. When the king heard the words of the book, he rent his clothes, and pledged to renew the covenant with God "to walk after the Lord and to keep His commandments" (II Kings 22). Josiah then proceeded to introduce a series of reforms. He purified the Temple by burning the vessels of Baal, destroyed the "high places"* where the priests had brought offerings, and defiled the *Topeth†* so no man might make his son or daughter pass through the fire to Molech. The king also destroyed the altars made by his grandfather Manasseh, centralized all sacrifices in the Temple, and put away those persons that divined by using ghosts or spirits. Then the people celebrated Passover in a manner which they had not done for a long time.

It was the most thorough religious reform ever tried in ancient Judea. There had been previous attempts in the past, particularly during the reign of Hezekiah, Josiah's great-grandfather, in the days of the prophet Isaiah, which had proved abortive. Undoubtedly, the ideals continuously preached by the succession of prophets had not been without effect. As the de-

---

* "High place" is the translation of the Hebrew word *bamah*, which signifies both "elevation" and "sanctuary." Not all the *bamot*, however, were on hills. They were also found in valleys and elsewhere. The corrupt influences of foreign idolatry rendered the continued existence of *bamot* a danger to the holiness of God and to national survival.

† Topeth is the place where the sons and daughters of Judeans were burned as Molech offerings.

cline of Assyria set in and feelings of nationalism and independence revived among the Jews, the time was ripe for Josiah's reform. The Code of Deuteronomy was now adopted as the permanent guide of the nation.

While these events were taking place, Jeremiah was still a young man of twenty-four, little known outside of his own town. The new covenant made by the king, the removal of the "high places," and the public celebration of Passover must have made an impact on him. He was sympathetic with the ideas underlying the reformation, and felt an obligation to support it by preaching on its behalf.

> And the Lord said unto me: "Proclaim all these words in the cities of Judah, and in the streets of Jerusalem, saying: Hear ye the words of this covenant, and do them." (11:6)

But not all the people were in sympathy with the reforms. The former priests who had officiated at the now destroyed local altars were not reconciled to the new movement, and were irate with Jeremiah because of his efforts in its behalf. They wanted to "cut him off from the land of the living, that his name may be no more remembered" (11:19) because he favored abolition of the local sanctuaries. Jeremiah, sorely troubled, asked the perennial question which Job and later writers were to ask:

> Wherefore doth the way of the wicked prosper?
> Wherefore are all they secure that deal very treacherously?
> (12:1)

It is probably at this time that Jeremiah went to Jerusalem determined to carry out his prophetic activity in the capital city. Here he hoped to find a more congenial environment near the Temple and at the very center of the religious revival. But he soon discovered that it was very difficult to change the habits of a people. At first, he thought that perhaps he had gone to the wrong groups, who did not understand the meaning of the reform, but he soon realized that in Jerusalem, as in Anathoth, sin was deep-rooted and widespread.

> And I said: "Surely these are poor,
> They are foolish, for they know not the way of the Lord,

Nor the ordinance of their God;
I will get me unto the great men,
And will speak unto them . . ."
But these had altogether broken the yoke,
And burst the bands.

(5:4-5)

The reformation did not live up to Jeremiah's expectations. The local altars had been removed, but the heart of the people had not changed. The social and moral evils continued. Realizing how difficult the task ahead of him and sensing the impending doom that was to be visited upon his people, Jeremiah felt that he could not marry or lead a normal life. He regarded himself as forbidden to enter a house of mourning or a house of feasting. By temperament he would have wanted to have a wife and friends, but Jeremiah felt it was his duty to devote himself completely to his mission.

Fall of Assyria

Meanwhile, weakened by intermittent war, the constant need to defend its borders against semi-barbarian marauders, and internal decay, the Assyrian Empire gradually disintegrated. Judah became virtually independent.

In 612 B.C.E. Nineveh, the capital of Assyria, fell, destroyed by the Babylonians as ruthlessly and completely as her kings had once ravaged other cities. The city was burned, and the people were slaughtered or taken as slaves. So little remained that two centuries later, when Greek soldiers marched over the site that had once been Nineveh, they did not suspect that this had once been the site of the ancient capital of a nation that had ruled half the world.[5]

Jeremiah's contemporary, the prophet Nahum, expressed the joy of Israel and the other nations who had suffered from "the bloody city full of lies and robbery." He saw in the fall of Nineveh, for so long the metropolis of the Orient, a moral retribution for the evil it had perpetrated (Nahum 2).

Nahum's prediction that the fall of Nineveh would mark the end of the Assyrian Empire turned out to be correct. Pharaoh Necho, trying to help the remnants of the Assyrian army regain its strength, marched his armies through Judah on the way to the Euphrates. King Josiah, fearful lest Necho would make Judah once again a vassal state, went out against him and was killed at Megiddo in the midst of battle.

Jeremiah, shocked, joined the people in lamenting for Josiah, and composed an elegy for him (II Chronicles 35:25). He had a high regard for Josiah and spoke of him as one who did "justice and righteousness," and who "judged the cause of the poor and needy" (22:15-16).

In the Days of Jehoiakim (608-597 B.C.E.)

After Josiah's death the people, still under the spell of the relative independence they had enjoyed and in defiance of Pharaoh Necho, put on the throne Jehoahaz, son of the slain monarch. But after three months Necho deposed him and made his older brother Jehoiakim king.

Jehoiakim did not follow in the footsteps of his father Josiah in either his economic or religious policies. He was pompous and proud, imposed taxes on the people, and unlawfully employed forced labor in order to build a luxurious palace for himself. For this love of splendor and for his oppressiveness Jeremiah denounced the monarch, contrasting his selfishness with Josiah's sense of justice and piety (22:13-16).

Jehoiakim's reign also represented a return to many of the idolatrous practices of the past. While the centralization of religious worship introduced by the reform still functioned, a religious reaction set in which brought back, with the approval of the king, some of the worst abuses of the pre-reform period —the worship of the "queen of heaven" from the rooftops, and the child sacrifices in the valley of Hinnom. Jeremiah felt compelled to speak out against those who "have built the high places of *Topeth* which is in the valley of Hinnom to burn their sons and daughters in the fire."

The Broken Bottle

To dramatize the consequences of this idolatrous practice, on one occasion Jeremiah took a potter's earthen bottle and went with some of the elders and priests to the valley of Hinnom, the scene of the cult. Breaking the bottle in the presence

of all assembled, he exclaimed: "Even so will I break this people
and this city, as one breaketh a potter's vessel, that cannot be
made whole again" (19:11).

This act of the prophet aroused bitterness among the people,
who mocked him for his predictions, accused him of having
a secret delight in anticipating doom, and rejected his message.
Their hostility increased when, a few days later, he repeated the
same act in the Temple court. It was the struggle all the prophets
had to wage with the priests of their day. Amos was accused
by Amaziah, priest of Beth-el, of conspiring against King Jeroboam (Amos 7:12-13). The priest in charge, Pashhur, struck
Jeremiah and put him in the stocks over night. When Jeremiah
was released the next morning amidst the hatred and contempt
of the people, the prophet was filled with resentment and rage
against Pashhur and began to regret that he had assumed such a
painful burden.

> O Lord, Thou hast enticed me, and I was enticed,
> Thou hast overcome me, and hast prevailed;
> I am become a laughing-stock all the day,
> Every one mocketh me . . .
> . . . the word of the Lord is made
> A reproach unto me, and a derision, all the day.
>   (20:7-8)

Jeremiah was determined not to speak any more; the conflict and controversy were too much to bear. But something
within would not allow him to give up his calling. Throughout
his life Jeremiah felt impelled by a power greater than himself which compelled him to speak.

> And if I say: "I will not make mention of Him,
> Nor speak any more in His name,"
> Then there is in my heart as it were a burning fire
> Shut up in my bones,
> And I weary myself to hold it in,
> But cannot.
>   (20:9)

Though Jeremiah had expected opposition, the intensity of
his enemies unnerved him. Disturbed over the misconstruction
of his motives, and despondent because of the loneliness and

isolation he had to endure, Jeremiah lamented his fate in a remarkable passage reminiscent of Job, which revealed his inner
feelings of doubt and despair:

> Cursed be the day
> Wherein I was born;
> The day wherein my mother bore me,
> Let it not be blessed.
> Cursed be the man who brought tidings
> To my father, saying:
> "A man-child is born unto thee";
> Making him very glad . . .
> Wherefore came I forth out of the womb
> To see labor and sorrow
> That my days should be consumed in shame?
> (20:14-18)

But these regrets were only momentary, and before long
Jeremiah was once again speaking in the Temple. The prophet
was particularly disturbed by the smugness of the leaders, who
felt that, regardless of what acts they performed, the Temple
would remain indestructible.

Sermon in the Temple

In a memorable sermon delivered in the Temple court during one of the festivals when the people had gathered from all
parts of Judah, Jeremiah pointed out the incompatibility of their
actions with the ideals symbolized by the Temple.

> Trust ye not in lying words, saying: "The temple of the Lord, the
> temple of the Lord, the temple of the Lord, are these" . . . Will
> ye steal, murder, and commit adultery, and swear falsely, and offer
> unto Baal, and walk after other gods whom ye have not known,
> and come and stand before Me in this house, whereupon My name
> is called, and say: "We are delivered," that ye may do all these
> abominations? (7:4-10)

If they did not change their ways, Jeremiah warned, God
would "make this house like Shiloh* and this city a curse to
all the nations of the earth" (26:6).

* Shiloh was destroyed by the Philistines during the days of Samuel.

It was a daring and blasphemous speech. Since the days of Isaiah, when the Temple had been miraculously saved during the invasion of Sennacherib, the people had been led to believe that the Temple itself was inviolable. Jeremiah's words, as he must have suspected, bordered on treason.

When the priests and the people heard Jeremiah's words, they took hold of him, shouting: "Thou shalt surely die" (26:8). At this point the princes of Judah came up from the king's house and took their places near the new gate to sit in judgment. The priests repeated their demand that Jeremiah be put to death. Undaunted, the prophet remained firm and insisted on the legitimacy of his cause. As for himself, Jeremiah warned, if they put him to death, "ye will bring innocent blood upon yourselves, and upon this city" (26:15). Jeremiah's heroic words, reminiscent of those of Socrates before the Athenian jury, had an effect on the princes and the people, who joined him in remonstrating with the priests and the prophets: "This man is not worthy of death; for he hath spoken to us in the name of the Lord our God" (26:16).

Some of them then spoke up, citing the precedent of the prophet Micah in the days of Hezekiah a century before, who had also predicted ruin to the Temple and had been spared. Others, however, put forth the more recent example of Uriah, who had prophesied against the city and had fled to Egypt, whence Jehoiakim had had him extradited and then executed.

Through the intercession of Akiham ben Shaphan, one of the most merciful of the princes, Jeremiah was saved from death. But though the principle of freedom of speech had prevailed for the moment, Jeremiah knew that his escape from the vindictive crowd was only temporary.

Burning of the Book

The prophet, therefore, resolved to write down his prophecies in the hope of reaching the people and impressing on them the seriousness of their situation. He was aided in this by his friend and scribe Baruch ben Neriah, a young man of aristocratic background who probably joined him at this time, and who remained with him through the next two trying decades, until the end of his life in Egypt.

Jeremiah collected all the prophecies, warnings, and admonitions which he had delivered during the previous twenty-two years, and dictated them to Baruch, which the latter wrote "upon a roll of a book" (36:4). The following year, in the winter of 603 B.C.E., on a fast day, Jeremiah, restrained from going to the Temple, sent Baruch to read the words "in the ears of the people" (36:13). This made a great impression, and Baruch was summoned by a group of influential princes to read the scroll to them. Having heard the prophet's message, they told Baruch and Jeremiah to hide while they went to report this to the king. "Now the king was sitting in the winterhouse in the ninth month; and the brazier was burning before him. And it came to pass, when Jehudi had read three or four columns, that he cut it with the penknife, and cast it into the fire that was in the brazier" (36:22-23). In vain, the princes entreated the king not to burn the book. He wanted to seize Jeremiah and Baruch, but they could not be found.

Still Jeremiah would not give up his spiritual mission. He heard the divine command: "Take thee again another roll, and write in it all the former words that were in the first roll, which Jehoiakim the king of Judah hath burned" (36:28).

In the process of rewriting the material, "there were added besides unto them many like words" (36:32).

First Exile to Babylonia

Meanwhile, events taking place outside of Judah had a direct bearing on the fate of the country. In the fourth year of Jehoiakim's reign a new power emerged in the Middle East to fill the vacuum left by the decline of Assyria. Nebuchadnezzar, son of Nabopolosar, king of Babylonia, who had destroyed Nineveh, marched against the Egyptians, and defeated them in a decisive battle at Carcemish on the Euphrates. The Egyptians were driven out of Syria, which they had hoped to dominate along with Palestine (II Kings 24:7). Babylonia became the dominant force in the Near East, and Nebuchadnezzar emerged as the undisputed master of Syria and Palestine, occupying the throne for forty-three years. He rebuilt the city of Babylon with its famous hanging-gardens and many great public works, and extended the boundaries of his kingdom until they were virtually identical with those of the old Assyrian Empire.[6]

Heretofore Jeremiah had concerned himself primarily with the religious and social transgressions of his people. But with the rise of the Babylonians he understood that their very survival was dependent on a correct interpretation of the course of political events. Jeremiah recognized the battle of Carcemish as one of the turning points in Jewish history and regarded the new empire as a constructive force. It was to be the "foe from the north" he had spoken of in his youthful prophecies. Nebuchadnezzar was "the instrument of God" to punish the Israelites for their evil-doing. Since they had not repented, they must undergo a period of divine chastisement. By accepting the yoke of Babylonia they were indicating their desire to repent. "Bring your necks under the yoke of the king of Babylon, and serve him and his people, and live. Why will ye die, thou and thy people, by the sword, by the famine, and by the pestilence? . . . And hearken not unto the words of the prophets that speak unto you, saying: Ye shall not serve the king of Babylon, for they prophesy a lie unto you" (27:12-14). The new empire would not last forever, Jeremiah predicted, and after a few generations God would punish the rulers and make their land desolate. But for the foreseeable future Jews should accept a state of dependency.

For a time Jehoiakim, who had been pro-Egyptian, transferred his loyalty to Babylonia. At first Nebuchadnezzar was probably no more severe than Assyria's rule had been during the last years of its decline, and he was satisfied with expressions of loyalty. But when after a few years Jehoiakim faltered in his loyalty and stopped paying tribute, Nebuchadnezzar instigated bands of Chaldeans together with Syrians, Moabites, and Ammonites to invade Judah (II Kings 24:2), and the following year he himself besieged Jerusalem (597 B.C.E.). Jehoiakim died during the siege, possibly in battle, and was succeeded by his eighteen-year old son Jehoiachin. Jeremiah referred to the king as a "despised broken image" and recognized that he would not last long.

After a three-month reign, the king "went out," that is, surrendered to the enemy (II Kings 24:12). The Temple was despoiled and Nebuchadnezzar carried off the king, the queen mother, and members of the court to Babylon as well as "all the men of might, even seven thousand, and the craftsmen and the smiths a thousand, all of them strong and apt for war" (II Kings 24:16). Jehoiachin remained in prison in Babylon for thirty-seven years until he was released by Evil-merodach, Nebuchadnezzar's successor[7] (II Kings 25:27).

In the Days of Zedekiah (597-586 B.C.E.)

After this first deportation to Babylonia, Zedekiah, youngest son of Josiah and uncle of the exiled Jehoiachin, was appointed king over the plundered land and the remaining Jews. Zedekiah found himself in a difficult situation from the very outset of his reign. At heart he was sympathetic with Jeremiah's conciliatory point of view, and probably preferred to accept the suzerainty of the Babylonians, but he was too young and weak to withstand the pressure of the new nobility, many of whom were in favor of revolt. Ezekiel, who was among the exiles of 597, must have known of Zedekiah's weakness; in one of his prophecies in Babylon, he referred to the situation in Judah:

> There is in her (Judah) no strong rod
> To be a sceptre to rule.
>   (Ezekiel 19:14)

Jeremiah was critical of these new nobles, comparing them to a basket of "very bad figs that cannot be eaten" (25:2).

Letter to the Exiles

Using the occasion of a mission sent by Zedekiah to Nebuchadnezzar in Babylon, Jeremiah sent a message to the exiles warning the captives not to hope for an immediate return. In this letter he urged them not to listen to the false prophets and agitators who appeared in Babylonia with such predictions of speedy return, but instead to settle themselves in the land and become good citizens. It was possible to practice their religion outside the Holy Land without the Temple, for God was a universal God whose sway extended to all lands. Thus Jeremiah laid the foundations for the Jewish sense of patriotism and for loyalty to the various countries in which Jews have lived through the centuries.

> Thus saith the Lord of hosts, the God of Israel, unto all the captivity, whom I have caused to be carried away captive from Jerusalem unto Babylon:
>
> Build ye houses, and dwell in them, and plant gardens, and eat the fruit of them; take ye wives, and beget sons and daughters; and take wives for your sons, and give your daughters to husbands, that they may bear sons and daughters; and multiply ye there, and be not diminished. And seek the peace of the city whither I have caused you to be carried away captive, and pray unto the Lord for it; for in the peace thereof shall ye have peace. (29:4-7)

The emotional effect of this letter must have been great, and probably changed the people's attitude to life in exile. The false prophets, whom Jeremiah had attacked in his letter, however, struck back against him by denouncing him to the priesthood and to the people in Jerusalem, urging that he be prosecuted (29:24-29).

The Yoke of Iron

As a dramatic symbol of the importance of submitting to the yoke of the Babylonians, Jeremiah went about wearing a wooden yoke on his neck; he sent similar yokes to the kings of Edom, Moab, Tyre, and other Near Eastern nations who were trying to enlist Judah's aid in a rebellion against Babylonia. In the fourth year of Zedekiah's reign (593 B.C.E.), one of these prophets, Hananiah of Gibeon, spoke to Jeremiah in the Temple in the presence of the priests, predicting that within two years God would bring back all the vessels of the Lord's house that Nebuchadnezzar had carried away, and that Jehoiachin and all those taken captive would return. Jeremiah, taken aback for a moment by his adversary, could only answer "Amen! the Lord perform thy words which thou hast prophesied" (28:6). However, he warned Hananiah that he was going against the precedent of the prophets of old, who had foretold evil and doom, and that he must prove his prediction of peace. His opponent then grabbed the bar off the prophet and broke it in the presence of the people, saying, "Thus saith the Lord: 'Even so will I break the yoke of Nebuchadnezzar king of Babylon from off the neck of all the nations within two full years'" (28:11). Jeremiah's reply was that while Hananiah had broken the bars of wood, God had made in their stead bars of iron (symbol of Babylonia). He accused Hananiah of making the people "trust in a lie" (28:15), and predicted his early death.

The Final Rebellion

Zedekiah was not able to restrain the princes, who were encouraged by the anti-Babylonian policy of Egypt's new king. When the latter organized an expedition into Asia in 588, Judah joined Egypt in revolt against the Babylonians. Soon the Babylonian armies were encamped around Jerusalem and besieged the city for the third time. Nebuchadnezzar was determined not only to bring Judah to task but to dispel any ambitions that Egypt might have.

In this new crisis Zedekiah sent messengers to inquire of Jeremiah what would be the result of the siege. The prophet repeated his view that resistance was hopeless, that the inhabitants of the city would die, and that Zedekiah and the people who remained would be delivered to Nebuchadnezzar. Only those who would fall away to the Babylonians would live.

At this juncture, under the impact of war and invasion, King Zedekiah made an agreement with the people that each one was to release his Jewish slaves. As this act of emancipation was being carried out, the Babylonians, hearing that the Egyptians were advancing against them, lifted the siege and turned to the Judean cities to the south. The owners of the slaves, seeing the seige was over, violated the agreement and brought the slaves back into servitude. Jeremiah denounced this act of treachery, predicting the return of the Babylonians and the destruction of the city.

When the Babylonians withdrew their armies from Jerusalem, Jeremiah went one day to take possession of some property in his home town and was arrested on the charge of deserting to the Babylonians. He was thrown into a dungeon in the house of Jonathan, the king's secretary, where Zedekiah, worried whether or not the Babylonians would return, secretly sent for him to seek his counsel. Jeremiah repeated his warning: "Thou shalt be delivered into the hand of the king of Babylon" (37:17). Then he pleaded with the king not to send him back to the house of Jonathan, the scribe, lest he die there. Zedekiah, who was not unsympathetic with the view of the prophet, commanded that he be returned to the court of the prison and that he should be given daily a piece of bread (chapter 37).

Before long the siege was resumed, and Jeremiah continued from the court of the guard to urge the people to give themselves up to the Babylonians. The princes now demanded that the prophet be put to death, for "he weakeneth the hands of the men of war" (38:4). The weak king, in spite of his kindly feelings toward Jeremiah, turned him over to the princes, who threw him into an unused underground cistern in the court of the guard, from which he was rescued by the intercession of an Ethiopian eunuch, employed in the palace. The prophet was confined as before to the court of the guard where he remained until the city was taken.

Destruction of Jerusalem

Zedekiah did not give in, and twenty months later Jerusalem was taken. In the summer of 586, on the ninth day of *Av*, one of the saddest days for Jews throughout their history, the Temple was burned. Unfortunately, no historian was present to record the details; the authors of the various elegies in the Book of Lamentations wrote their accounts somewhat later, though two accounts are based on memories of the actual events.[8] When the north gate of the city gave in to the pounding of the battering ram, Zedekiah and all the men of war fled during the night southward, but they were overtaken in the plain of Jericho by the Babylonian armies. They brought the king to Riblah, where Nebuchadnezzar "gave judgment upon him" as guilty of treason. His sons were killed before his eyes; then Zedekiah himself was blinded and carried off to Babylon. Some seventy others of the nobility, including the chief priest and his second, were condemned to death. Between thirty and forty thousand additional exiles were carried off to Babylon, including many who had deserted to the Babylonian side.

Only the poorest of the land were left to be "vinedressers and husbandmen" (II Kings 25:12). Many of the towns devastated in that war are still barren mounds. The area that once was Judah has still not fully recovered from the blow.[9]

As the exiles were being taken to Babylon they marched through Ramah, not far from Jerusalem, where Jeremiah heard the voice of Rachel, the ancestress of northern Israel, wailing from her tomb on a nearby hill over the plight of her descendants. Jeremiah's reply reveals him to be a prophet of hope.

> Refrain thy voice from weeping,
> And thine eyes from tears;
> For thy work shall be rewarded,
>   saith the Lord;
> And they shall come back from the
>   land of the enemy.
>
> (31:16)

Even before the final destruction had taken place, Jeremiah was already certain that after a period of time the exiles would return. As a dramatic symbol of his confidence in the future, he bought a tract of land, though many fields lay fallow for the taking. His signing a deed was an act of faith that "fields and vineyards will yet be planted in this land" (chapter 32). When destruction came and the groups of captives began their long trek to Babylon, Jeremiah urged them to set up markers and observe the road carefully so that they could find their way back. He predicted that the exile would only last seventy years,* after which Israel would be redeemed. At that time the land would be rebuilt and "the children will return to their borders." His description of the returning exiles has a contemporary ring to it. They will come from all ends of the earth wherever they live—"the blind and the lame, the woman with child. . . . A great company shall they return hither. They shall come with weeping, and with supplications. . . ."

> I will cause them to walk by rivers of waters,
> In a straight way wherein they shall not stumble.
>
> (31:8-9)

---

* Jeremiah states several times that redemption will come after seventy years, using this round figure to indicate beyond his own generation or lifetime.

Meanwhile, Jeremiah was taken from among the captives by the Babylonian general Nebuzaradan because of the pro-Babylonian counsel he had given Zedekiah and the people. The prophet chose to remain in Palestine, particularly since Gedaliah, son of Ahikam, who shared his views and whose father had once saved him from death, was appointed governor. His secretary and friend Baruch was allowed to stay with him.

Last Days

The new governor established his headquarters at Mizpah and made an effort to bring life back to normal. He urged the survivors to gather wine and summer fruits "and dwell in the cities that ye have taken" (40:10). Gradually, the Jews who had fled to surrounding countries during the siege began to return; for a while it looked as if Gedaliah would be successful in organizing a government for the survivors.

Unfortunately, however, the Ammonites urged on Ishmael, a descendant of the royal house of Judah, to murder Gedaliah. Though the governor was warned that Ishmael was planning to kill him, refusing to believe that Ishmael was capable of such evil, Gedaliah courteously received him in Mizpah. While they sat eating together, Ishmael arose with his ten men and assassinated Gedaliah, carrying away as captives the residue of the people, who were left in Mizpah, including the royal princesses. While the murderers were soon overtaken and the captives redeemed, Ishmael and eight of his men escaped.

At this point, the people, fearing the vengeance of Nebuchadnezzar, asked Jeremiah to inquire of God whether they should flee to Egypt. After ten days, Jeremiah replied, urging them to remain in the land and not to be afraid of the king of Babylon; but they refused to heed his counsel. Taking Jeremiah and Baruch with them, they went down to Egypt, where the people, especially the women, began worshipping heathen idols again. The prophet warned them against these practices, but they replied that as long as they had served the "queen of heaven" it had been well with them, and that they would serve her again. Jeremiah, as he had done so often during the previous forty years, predicted their extermination and announced that

Pharaoh Hophra would suffer defeat at the hands of his enemies. This is the last we hear of Jeremiah; with this warning he disappears from the pages of history.

MESSAGE OF THE PROPHET

The message of Jeremiah represents, in a sense, a summing up and restatement of many of the ideas articulated by Amos, Hosea, and Isaiah during the previous century. Though he did not mention them by name, it is evident that he knew of their work and shared their outlook on life. In particular, as we have seen, there was an affinity between Jeremiah and Hosea, expressed in their denunciation of idolatry and corruption, their use of the metaphor of marriage to describe God's love of Israel, and their faith in the possibility of repentance.

Doctrine of the Covenant

One of the central ideas in Jeremiah's prophecies is his emphasis on the covenant which exists between God and Israel and the mutual character of this bond. The relationship of man to God in ancient Jewish thought was conceived of as a *brit* (covenant) or spiritual agreement, whereby God promised to take care of and protect man, who in turn committed himself to follow God's precepts. Such was the covenant God made with Noah and his sons, requiring them to show regard for all human life, while pledging the preservation of the universe. The rainbow was the sign of this covenant. A similar covenant or agreement was made with Abraham and his descendants, in which Palestine was promised to them while they obligated themselves to do justice and to worship only God. The circumcision ceremony was the sign of this spiritual agreement. The covenant with the patriarchs, as has been pointed out,* was renewed at Sinai, where God chose Israel as His people, and Israel in turn pledged itself to live according to God's

* See pp. 28-30.

precepts. This covenant was to be an everlasting one, with the Sabbath and the book of the law as the signs.

It is this covenant relationship, periodically renewed in the intervening generations, to which Jeremiah constantly refers in his prophecies. He looks back nostalgically to the formative period of Israel's history, the sojourn in the desert, when, according to the prophet, the people had kept the covenant and shown their faithfulness and gratitude.

> I remember for thee the affection
>   of thy youth,
> The love of thine espousals;
> How they wentest after Me
>   in the wilderness,
> In a land that was not sown.
>   (2:2)

But after the Israelites settled in Canaan, the prophet reminds them, corruption had set in. Israel had forgotten the Lord who brought them through the wilderness and had gone after other gods. It was the purpose of Josiah's reform, of which Jeremiah became an enthusiastic supporter, to renew this covenant relationship. But the people did not live up to the agreement and it soon became apparent that the reform was not successful. Jeremiah emphasizes the eternal nature of the bond and its mutual character, denouncing the people for their worship of idols and for the lack of steadfastness in their relationship to God. "For according to the number of thy cities are thy gods, O Judah" (22:28). They had forsaken God, the "fountain of living waters and hewed them out cisterns, broken cisterns that can hold no water" (2:13). The prophet warns them of the punishment that will be visited upon them because of their apostasy.

Jeremiah himself experienced this covenant relationship in very personal terms, calling God his "father" and "friend of my youth" (3:4). The prophet had an intimate and vivid consciousness of the omnipresence of God, who was to him a "refuge in the day of affliction" and "a joy and a rejoicing of the heart."

There were, of course, times, as we have seen, when the prophet began to doubt God's help and whether he could rely on Him.

Wilt Thou indeed be unto me as a deceitful brook,
As waters that fail?
>   (15:18)

But Jeremiah always managed to overcome his doubt. He recognized that the elimination of evil was not simple, for the tendency to sin was deep-rooted in human nature.

The sin of Judah is written with a pen of iron, and
>   with the point of a diamond;
It is graven upon the tablet of their heart.
>   (17:1)

The heart is deceitful above all things,
And it is exceedingly weak—who can know it?
>   (17:9)

But in spite of this human tendency to sin, man is capable of rising above his weaknesses, for the call to repentance is always available. To bring about a whole-hearted repentance, however, requires more than a renewal of the historic covenant between God and the Jewish people. What is needed is not merely another formal agreement or compact, as in the past, but a new covenant, more personal in character, that will affect the hearts of the people. Spiritual regeneration will be achieved not by means of a written code, but through a broadening and deepening of inner religious feeling.

Behold, the days come, saith the Lord,
that I will make a new covenant
with the house of Israel,
and with the house of Judah . . .
I will put My law in their inward
parts, and in their heart will I write it;
And I will be their God, and they shall
be My people;
And they shall teach no more
every man his neighbor,
And every man his brother, saying:
"Know the Lord";
For they shall all know Me,

from the least of them
to the greatest of them,
saith the Lord.
  (31:31-34)

Primacy of Morality

To Jeremiah the sustaining force of the covenant relationship was in the belief in God's justice, righteousness, and truth.
He spoke frequently of the importance of knowing God, by
which he meant not a full intellectual understanding, but a
knowledge of God's ethical character.

. . . let not the wise man glory in his wisdom . . .
Let not the rich man glory in his riches;
But let him that glorieth glory in this,
That he understandeth and knoweth Me,
That I am the Lord who exercises mercy,
Justice, and righteousness in the earth.
  (9:22-23)

Like the other prophets, he was not concerned with proving
God's existence, or with abstruse metaphysical questions. It is a
characteristic of the biblical writings to take God's existence for
granted. Nowhere in the writings of the prophets is there an
attempt to analyze the nature of God or the world in the
Greek philosophical manner. When Jeremiah stressed the importance of a "knowledge of God," he was suggesting the importance of following God's ethical character.

Insistence on justice and truth also required that these be the
criteria for the worship of God. Therefore, no ritual or prayer
in the temple can atone for moral corruption.

Like Amos and Isaiah, he makes clear that the primacy in the
religious life lies in ethical living.

Your burnt-offerings are not acceptable,
Nor your sacrifices pleasing unto Me.
  (6:20)

For I spoke not unto your fathers, nor commanded them in the day
that I brought them out of the land of Egypt, concerning burnt-
offerings or sacrifices; but this thing I commanded them, saying:

"Hearken unto My voice, and I will be your God, and ye shall be My people" (7:22-23).

Based on these and similar passages, many non-Jewish scholars have maintained that Jeremiah repudiated religious ritual, and helped Judaism shift its emphasis from the ritualistic to the ethical aspect of religion. Actually, Jeremiah, like the other prophets, was not opposed to religious ceremonies or to the national cult. At the time of Josiah's reform, the prophet offered no objection to the reinstitution of the Passover celebration. Also, in his vision of Palestine after the restoration, he included priests and Levites whose function was to maintain the temple ritual (31:13). In the view of the prophets, rituals, to be meaningful, must be performed with integrity and sincerity, and not made a substitute for righteous living. Jeremiah warned that unless Judah eliminated the houses "filled with deceit" and kept the house of the Lord from being a "den of robbers," destruction would come upon the nation.

Eternity of Israel

With the rise of the Babylonians to power in the Middle East and the refusal of the Jews to accept their suzerainty, Jeremiah foresaw a period of exile for his people. This would represent not so much punishment as a form of religious discipline and moral education; for out of the crucible of exile would come a purified and refined people. Thus Jeremiah was the first to teach the religious value of the Exile. Amos had referred to the Exile as a "defiled land" (7:17), and Hosea had mentioned it (chapter 9), but it was Jeremiah who first approached the problem posed by the expulsion with a constructive program. While exile was a misfortune which he described as a divorce between God and Israel (3:8), one could worship God not only in the Temple, but also in Babylonia, where God would hear all supplications.*

For a period of time the exiles would have to live outside their homeland, but the prophet had complete faith that regard-

* Ezekiel developed this idea further in the following passage: "Thus saith the Lord God; although I have cast them far off among the nations and although I have scattered them among the countries, yet I will be to them as a little sanctuary in the countries where they shall come" (Ezekiel 11:16).

less of impending events, Israel would not be entirely destroyed: "the whole land shall be desolate; yet will I not make a full end" (4:27). ". . . I will make a full end of all the nations whither I have scattered thee, but I will not make a full end of thee; For I will correct thee in measure, and will not utterly destroy thee" (30:11; also 46:28). More than the other prophets, Jeremiah emphasized the eternity of the people of Israel. Just as the sun will not cease to give light by day, and the moon and stars by night, so it is not possible that Israel should cease to be a nation.[10] From the outset of its history, God has loved the Jewish people and because of this love He will not desert it.

> Yea, I have loved thee with an everlasting love;
> Therefore with affection have I drawn thee.
> Again will I build thee, and thou shalt be built.
> (31:3-4)

In his famous restoration prophecies uttered at the time of destruction, Jeremiah predicts that "the city will be rebuilt on its mound," and visualizes the land as ruled by a descendant of the house of David. It will be a united kingdom to which the children of Ephraim (Northern Israel, which had been exiled to Assyria 136 years previously) as well as Judah will return (31:31). Jeremiah, unlike Ezekiel, does not give full details in his vision of the restored land, but he seems to look forward to a more simplified pastoral life than had existed before the destruction.

> Yet again shall there be in this place . . . and in all the cities thereof, a habitation of shepherds . . . In the cities of the hill-country, in the cities of the Lowland, and in the cities of the South, and in the land of Benjamin, and in the places about Jerusalem, and in the cities of Judah, shall the flocks again pass under the hands of him that counteth them . . . In those days, and at that time, will I cause a shoot of righteousness to grow up unto David; And he shall execute justice and righteousness in the land.[11]
> (33:12-15)

INFLUENCE OF
JEREMIAH

These ideas of Jeremiah as well as the example of his prophetic life have had a permanent influence on the course of Jewish history. Though the people in his lifetime did not heed his words, the prophet was not without influence on his own generation. There undoubtedly was a prophetic party which agreed with his viewpoint and supported him in his struggle. Three men are mentioned in the Book of Jeremiah who were helpful to him in his time of need: Ahikam at the time of the Temple address when the crowd demanded his death, Baruch ben Neriah, who remained faithful through all the vicissitudes of the last half of his prophetic career, and the Ethiopian slave who rescued him from the pit.[12]

The historian Graetz has suggested that it may have been Jeremiah's letter to the exiles that inspired the prophet Ezekiel to step to the front in Babylon and become a prophet.[13] If the exiles retained their faith in God and their sense of unity, it was at least partly due to the teachings of Jeremiah. During the period of the Second Commonwealth the prophet is mentioned in several documents including Chronicles, the Book of Daniel and the second Book of Maccabees. The fact that both Lamentations and the Epistle of Jeremy in the Apocrypha are attributed to him indicates the hold he had on the Jewish mind during this period.

Rabbinic literature contains many legends about his birth, various events during his lifetime, and his death.[14] His resemblance to Moses is pointed out in several such legends. Unwittingly, Jeremiah had an influence on Christianity, particularly through his concept of the new covenant which furnished the title for the New Testament. Christian writers often describe Jeremiah as the Jesus of the Old Testament, one going so far as to say that without Jeremiah there would have been no Christianity.

The echoes of Jeremiah are to be heard in the prayer book in the High Holy Day liturgy, in the daily *Amidah*, the grace after meals, and the marriage ceremony. Some of the phrases in the Book of Jeremiah have become memorable in many languages. Such words as "peace, peace, when there is no peace"

(8:11), "Is there no balm in Gilead" (8:22), "can the Ethiopian change his skin or the leopard his spots?" (13:23) have become part of world literature.

In modern times the pacifistic leanings of Jeremiah inspired Stephan Zweig, the famous Austrian-Jewish writer, to compose a poetic drama based on the message and last years of the prophet's life, and Franz Werfel's novel *Hearken Unto the Voice* is also based on the prophet's life.

The Zionist movement is very much indebted to the message of Jeremiah, particularly to his vision of the restoration. His words have provided hope to dispersed Jews that they would return to their own border. The prophet's emphasis on redemption as bound up with the land has helped inspire the work of the Jewish National Fund. In Tel Aviv a monument erected on the occasion of the fortieth anniversary of the city bears an appropriate passage from Jeremiah:

> Again I will build thee
> And thou shalt be built.
> (31:4)

Jeremiah's influence, however, lies not only in the specific doctrines he taught, but also in his unique personality and the inspiring example of his prophetic life. Ahad Ha'am, the modern Jewish essayist and thinker, describes the Hebrew prophet as distinguished from the rest of mankind by several fundamental qualities. "First, he is a man of truth . . . and he tells the truth as he sees it, without regard to the consequences . . . Secondly, the prophet is an extremist. His ideal fills his whole heart and mind; it is the whole purpose of his life . . . He can accept no excuse, admit no compromise . . . Being a man of truth, he must also be a man of justice . . . His justice is absolute justice, limited neither by social necessity nor by sentiment . . . The only reality for him is his inner vision of what is to be in the latter end of days." [15] These prophetic qualities are reflected in every event in the life of Jeremiah, and in all his utterances. They represent the noblest part of his legacy to the people he loved.

FOR FURTHER READING

BLANK, Sheldon *Jeremiah, Man and Prophet* (Cincinnati: Hebrew Union College Press, 1961).

BRIGHT, John, *Jeremiah*—Anchor Bible (New York: Doubleday, 1965). Comprehensive exegetical-historical study.

HESCHEL, Abraham, J., *The Prophets,* pp. 103–139 (New York: Harper & Row, 1962). A magnificent study of prophetic experience.

"Jeremiah," in *Encyclopedia Judaica,* Volume 9, pp. 1345–1361 (Jerusalem: 1972).

Philo of Alexandria

Five and a half centuries intervene between the Babylonian Exile and the period of Philo. This period marks the transition from the world of the Old Testament to the Hellenistic and Rabbinic ages in Jewish history.

The Babylonian Exile lasted two decades less than the seventy years predicted by Jeremiah. In 536 B.C.E., when Cyrus, king of the Persians, conquered Babylonia and gave the Jews permission to return to their homeland and rebuild the Temple, several thousand took advantage of the opportunity. The returned exiles soon discovered, however, how bare and uninviting the country was. The territory granted them—primarily Jerusalem and its surroundings—was much smaller than the original state. After many hardships they managed to rebuild the Temple (516 B.C.E.) but on a much smaller scale than its predecessor.

Many challenges faced the new settlers as they set out to reestablish their religious life. The walls of Jerusalem were still broken, worship was conducted in a lax fashion, the Sabbath was not observed, and the neighboring peoples looked with contempt on the Jews. Intermarriage was prevalent, and the new community remained in a demoralized state for several generations.

In the middle of the next century, however, new life was brought to the discouraged pioneers. Nehemiah, who had a commission from the Persian king as royal governor, rebuilt the walls, improved the worship, reinstituted the Sabbath, and made Jerusalem the center again. Ezra, who had led five thousand new immigrants from Babylonia, was a kind of second Moses who read the Torah publicly for the people, and made it the constitution of the new commonwealth. At a public ceremony that recalled the giving of the Torah at Sinai the people pledged loyalty and faithfulness to the covenant between themselves and God.

Few details are known about Jewish life during the century preceding the conquest of Palestine by Alexander the Great (334 B.C.E.). His coming brought about momentous changes in the cultural patterns of the ancient world. Wherever he penetrated, Alexander founded Greek cities in which he tried to reproduce Greek institutions. Because he was a pupil of Aristotle as well as a conqueror, he encouraged a fusion of Greek and Oriental cultures.

After Alexander's death Palestine was ruled for over a century (300-198) by the Ptolemies of Egypt. The latter continued the tolerant policies of Alexander, leaving the Jews free to develop their own law and consolidate their way of life. Though there was every opportunity for the Jews to become acquainted with Greek ways, for a time their inner life was not seriously affected. But after Palestine passed to the Seleucid kings of Syria, Antiochus Epiphanes (the tyrant of the *Hanukkah* story), with the help of Jewish Hellenizers in Palestine, tried to impose Greek practices by force. Unfortunately, the Hellenism that was introduced was not the lofty culture of Athens in the classical age but rather an amalgam of Greek practices and Oriental luxury which emphasized polytheism and worldly pleasures. When Antiochus went so far as to establish heathen altars and forbid Jewish religious observances, the Maccabees, a priestly family from Modin, led the Jews in revolt (165 B.C.E.), and freed Judea from Syrian oppression.

After the victory of the Maccabees, Hellenism ceased to exist as an active political program in Judea, and Jewish life was again free to pursue its traditional course. During the years that followed, Palestine achieved independence under the Hasmonean kings for a period of seventy years until 63 B.C.E., when the land came under Roman domination. During that period Hellenistic influences, at least in an external sense, increased, and the Greek language and Greek architecture, games, and gymnasia became prevalent throughout the land. Judaism as a religion and a way of life, however, was able to continue its own organic development.

Meanwhile, a large Jewish community had grown up in the new city of Alexandria, which had become one of the cultural centers of the Hellenistic world and the most important Jewish community outside of Palestine. The Jews of Alexandria had originally been brought from Palestine to Egypt as prisoners by Ptolemy I (323-

283), and were imprisoned in fortresses to protect the country or given to Ptolemy's soldiers as slaves. About a century later they were freed by Ptolemy Philadelphus and allowed to become part of Alexandrian society. In the course of events, Alexandria's Jews began to speak and write in Greek. Greek prevailed in their synagogues and in the official assemblies of their communities, which were modelled on the political institutions of the Greeks. Hellenistic law and Greek education also cast their spell, and at least some of the Alexandrian Jews read Plato and other Greek philosophers.

Since many Jews no longer understood Hebrew, the Bible was translated into Greek (Septuagint) during the third century B.C.E. Because Jews were often derided for what was described as the crudeness and primitiveness of the Bible, allegorical interpretations became current, based on the assumption that the Bible intended something other than what was expressed. Thus, the anthropomorphic expressions, the accounts of miracles, and other literal expressions were given a philosophical meaning. The universal values of the Bible were stressed in order to make Jewish teachings more compatible with Greek thought.

Some carried this allegorical approach to the extreme and disregarded the literal sense of the Bible completely. While there were occasional mixed marriages and converts to paganism among the Jews of Alexandria, the overwhelming majority, though assimilated outwardly, retained a sense of loyalty to their ancestral faith. Gradually, a new type of literature was created, including the *Letter of Aristeas, Third Maccabees,* and *Wisdom of Solomon,* in which Judaism was defended against pagan attacks, and Greek and Jewish ideals were blended into a new synthesis. In the course of time many pagans were attracted to Judaism; by the period of the Romans it is estimated that perhaps one person out of ten in the Empire was a Jew.

Philo was the foremost representative of Hellenistic Judaism whose writings have been preserved. Writing for Jews as well as for non-Jews, he was a philosopher, theologian, allegorical interpreter, and commentator on the Bible. Though less known than most of the other figures in this book, Philo, as Erwin Goodenough points out, is particularly relevant because of his attempt to synthesize

Judaism and the culture of his day. Judaism in Alexandria was not destined to survive, but Philo's work was not lost; eight centuries later the Jews in the Arab-speaking world were again to undertake the task of reconciling Judaism with Greek thought.

4 . *Philo of Alexandria*

[*c.25 B.C.E.-c.50 C.E.*]

ERWIN R. GOODENOUGH

PHILO, the Jew of Alexandria,* to give him his traditional title, deserves a high place in the roster of great Jews, even though he has had little direct influence on the last fifteen hundred years of Jewish life. His writings show that he was victorious in a recurrent struggle of Jewish history, the struggle to live a Jewish life and preserve Jewish values in a Gentile world which has great values of its own. Philo faced the civilization of the Roman Empire at its height, faced it in Alexandria where the Greek tradition of science, art, drama, philosophy, and religion still continued their most vital developments. His deep loyalty to the People of the Book and the observances (as he understood them: the Mishnah was not to be written until he had been dead a century and a half) never faltered. But this could not keep him from reading the Greek classics or from taking their insights to himself, just as a Jew now assimilates modern literature and science. Philo's solution, to reinterpret the Torah until he made it teach Platonism and mystic salvation, may not appeal to modern Jews for themselves, but all must see in him a noble and deeply intelligent Jew.

The World of Alexandria

Of his ancestry and life we know almost nothing. He lived in Alexandria at the beginning of the Christian era, when that city dominated the cultural and philosophical life of the Roman Em-

---

* In the present essay the author has quoted freely from his earlier studies, with the kind permission of the Yale University Press.

pire. Some Romans went to study at Athens, as scholars of the nineteenth century went to Italy from America. The great new movements, however, no longer began in Athens but in Alexandria, where, as in nineteenth-century Germany, a new world was being created. The city had been founded three centuries earlier by Alexander, who had collected settlers from all over the eastern Mediterranean, especially Greeks and Jews, along with his own dominating Macedonians. The greatest library of the ancient world was here assembled, and the greatest science (very great science indeed) developed. Here apparently Platonism changed into Neoplatonism, and the religions of the world were fused and given depth as philosophic ideas were read into the cult practices of the settlers' various rites and myths. A few decades later, Christianity was here more than anywhere to become a religion which had to orient itself to the best teachings of the Greek classical philosophers, and to the current mystical tendencies of contemporary pagan thinkers. The artistic remains of the period have largely perished from the city, but the decorations of Pompeii in Italy seem to a considerable extent to reflect a school, especially of painting, that had flourished best in Alexandria.

Jews, who inhabited Alexandria by the hundreds of thousands, could no more be unaffected by such creativity than could Jews in nineteenth-century Germany or twentieth-century America. Philo lived in Alexandria in that period when it was at the height of its glory. Since he called himself an "old man" in a document describing events of 40 C.E., we assume that he was born about 25 B.C.E.; and since he survived long enough at least to write two long treatises, we suppose that he died perhaps between 45 and 50 C.E.

Family Background

Philo must have come from several generations of wealth. It has recently been argued that not only Philo and his brother Alexander, but also their father, were among the select few of the East at that time who enjoyed Roman citizenship. Philo himself says that life without slaves would be unthinkable, and Alexander had one of the greatest fortunes of the ancient world. Such wealth was rarely acquired in a single generation, at least wealth with the political and social alliances of this family.

Dramatic evidence of the family affluence is the fact that, as the historian Josephus tells us, Alexander gave the silver and gold plates which covered the nine gates of Herod's Temple at Jerusalem, a gift which, even allowing for Josephus' exaggeration in dimensions, must have been of incredible value. In another passage Josephus says that Alexander was "foremost among his contemporaries at Alexandria both for his family and his wealth." In the Roman world great wealth involved great public obligation: hence it is not surprising that Alexandria had an official title, "Alabarch," which meant that he was the person responsible to the Romans for the collection of taxes, though whether for the taxes of all Alexandria or only for those of the Jews does not appear.

We have no reason to think that Philo was an exception in this family of wealth and distinction. He kept intimately in touch with all aspects of the teeming life of Alexandria, in spite of the philosophical and religious concerns reflected in his extensive writings. He was a critical observer of the athletics of the day, and speaks with almost an expert's insight about boxing contests he had seen. He tells of being at chariot races where excitement ran so high that some of the spectators rushed into the course and were killed. He describes the enthusiasm of the crowd at a now lost play of Euripides when some brilliant lines in praise of freedom were recited. When he attended banquets he had to watch himself carefully to "take reason along," as he expresses it; or, as frequently happened, he would become a helpless slave to the pleasures of food and drink. With what satisfaction he recalls the banquets he attended when he had *not* lost control of himself!

Contemplation vs. Action

And yet, in Philo's few personal references, he tells how deeply, on the one hand, he desired to live in contemplation as a scholar and mystic apart from men, and how, on the other hand, he was even more strongly compelled to take the responsible place in society which his wealth and position indicated. Here is one of the most passionate outbursts:

There was once a time when by devoting myself to philosophy and to contemplation of the world and its parts I achieved the enjoyment of that mind which is truly beautiful, desirable, and blessed; for I lived in constant communion with sacred utterances and teachings, in which I greedily and insatiably rejoiced. No base or worldly thoughts occurred to me, nor did I grovel for glory, wealth, or bodily comfort . . . Then, ah, then peeping downwards from the ethereal heights and directing the eye of my intelligence as from a watchtower, I regarded the untold spectacle of all earthly things, and reckoned myself happy at having forcibly escaped the calamities of mortal life.

And yet there lurked near me that most grievous of evils, Envy, with its hatred of all that is fair, which suddenly fell upon me, and did not cease forcibly dragging upon me until it had hurled me down into the vast sea of political cares, where I am still tossed about and unable even so much as to rise to the surface. But though I groan at my fate, I still struggle on, for I have, implanted in my soul from early youth, a desire for education which ever has pity and compassion upon me, and lifts me up and elevates me . . . And if unexpectedly there is temporary quiet and calm in political tumults, I become winged and skim the waves, barely flying, and am blown along by the breezes of understanding, which often persuades me to run away as it were for a holiday . . . from my pitiless masters, who are not only men but also the great variety of practical affairs deluged upon me from all sides like a torrent. Still, even in such a condition, I ought to thank God that while I am inundated I am not sucked down into the depths. Rather, though in despair of any good hope I had considered the eyes of my soul to be incapacitated, now I open them and am flooded with the light of wisdom, so that I am not abandoned for the whole of my life to darkness. And so, behold, I dare not only read the sacred expositions of Moses, but even, with a passion for understanding, I venture to examine each detail, and to disclose and publish what is not known to the multitude.

With this goes another statement:

For many a time have I myself forsaken friends and kinsfolk and country and come into a wilderness, to give my attention to some subject demanding contemplation, and derived no advantage from doing so, but my mind scattered or bitten by passion has gone off to matters of the contrary kind. Sometimes, on the other hand, amid a vast throng I have a collected mind. God has dispersed the crowd that besets the soul and taught me that a favorable and unfavorable condition are not brought about by differences of place, but by God who moves and leads the soul in whatever way He pleases.

Heads Commission to Roman Emperor

In spite of these contemplative tendencies and his extended writings it is clear that Philo was a man of practical sense and interests, although we know only a single incident from his life. In the year 40 C.E. the terrors of a Jewish pogrom raged in Alexandria. The mad emperor Gaius demanded honors as a divinity, and punished with paranoid cruelty everyone who showed any reluctance in giving him such homage. The Alexandrian mob, jealous of the prosperity and political favor the Jews were enjoying, saw their opportunity, and insisted that Jews set up cult statues of the emperor in their synagogues. When the Jews refused, the mob proceeded to plunder and murder at its pleasure; rapine was sanctified by pretended horror at Jewish treason. Jews of the city, herded by the thousands from their homes, in hourly danger of death, had only the hope that the insane emperor himself would exempt them from his demand for worship. In their extremity they selected a commission, certainly from among their most gifted political leaders, to take the perilous journey to Rome in late autumn, there to try to win the respite which only the emperor could give them.

Philo was chosen to head this group, and upon him and his associates fell the almost hopeless task. In Rome, the embassy had to trail the mad emperor month after month, stomaching his jibes, holding their peace, and keeping their dignity in the face of unceasing abuse and insult. It was Philo who presented the case and gave the proper answers to the emperor's banter. He also had to hold his group steady throughout the months when upon any or all of them might fall a flippant sentence of death, and their families and race perish with them. Eventually he accomplished the impossible. He won from Gaius a niggardly toleration of the Jews.

Steeped in Greek and Jewish Traditions

Philo's writings tell us, though not directly, that he had had the best education which money and interest in culture could get for a boy in Alexandria. He wrote in Greek, chiefly in the form of biblical commentaries, a form long known to us from the rabbis who called it Midrash, but now familiar also in the Dead Sea Scrolls. His treatises could have come only from one steeped in the text of the Bible, especially the Books of Moses, for his sentences are studded with biblical quotations or phrases, in a way to remind us in English literature of such authors as John Bunyan. Anyone reading Bunyan would know that he had been brought up on the King James Version, since he always reflects its language, and never seems aware that a Hebrew or Greek text had greater authority than the translation. In the same way Philo was steeped in the standard Greek translation made from the Hebrew two centuries before his day, and he comments upon the nuances of Greek phrases in a way to show that he considered the Greek text verbally inspired and correct. He apparently had a guide to the meaning of the strange Hebrew proper names, but never questioned a line of the Greek translation as compared with the original. Scholars in general agree, accordingly, that Philo's careful training in the Bible was in the Greek text, and see no evidence that he knew more than a scattered bit of Hebrew, if any.

To this was added training in Greek literature and civilization. He quoted the classical poets and dramatists freely, seems to have known Greek history well, and had at least a good working knowledge of the classical philosophers. He used many of the phrases, and some of the conceptions, of the Stoics, but was basically of the idealistic school that had by this time thoroughly combined Platonism with the conceptions of the Pythagoreans.

The two traditions of thought, the Jewish and the Greek, so completely blended in his mind that the favorite dispute as to whether he was more Greek or more Jewish has little meaning. Out of the two strands he had woven himself as a single cloth, warp and woof. He read Plato in terms of Moses, and Moses in terms of Plato, to the point that he was convinced that each had said essentially the same thing. Indeed, he used to say that

Plato had cribbed his ideas from Moses. Philo, an open-minded Jew, no more rejected the best of the Gentile world than the modern American Jew should be expected to reject modern science and Shakespeare. He not only remained loyal to Jewish people and customs, but he made a herculean effort to see meaning in the Jewish traditions in such terms of "meaning" as the deepest and most valuable knowledge of his day had taught him.

What then did Philo retain from his Jewish tradition, and what in the Greek background did he unconsciously identify with his Judaism? And what was the blend that resulted?

Value of the Bible

The Jewish people, at least since the time of Ezra, have been the People of the Book. If Jews had not believed in the unique quality of both their people and the Bible there would have been no surviving Judaism. In Philo's eyes each created and strengthened the other, and he had not the least thought of discarding either. His loyalty to the people involved him in political activities on its behalf, and his immense literary production was dedicated to its defense and advancement. In the Bible (which for Philo, like the rabbis, usually meant the Pentateuch) the Jews had a revelation of God's nature and will that was utterly unique among sacred writings. A Jew was one who accepted this revelation. If Philo got ideas from other sources, as he patently did, he felt uneasy until he could find some way to read them into the Bible. However differently from the rabbis he often interpreted the text, no rabbi ever revered the text more than did Philo.

Philo's Writings

The writings of Philo fall into several divisions, but we have no inkling of their relative order of composition and so cannot trace any "development" in his thinking. Several of his philosophical and ethical writings are preserved, as, for example, a dialogue with his nephew Alexander on whether dumb animals have the power of reason. But these seem little side excursions, the latter apparently written well on in Philo's maturity, in a career oriented in quite other directions. We have fragments of his answers to attacks upon Jews which some hostile Gentile, at some time or other, provoked. Philo also wrote two treatises on the pogrom of the year 40 already mentioned, certainly done in his later life, and apparently written directly for the new Roman rulers after the violence had ended.

The great body of his writings, however, consists of three independent Midrashim on the Pentateuch, where again no trace of development of ideas can be detected in their composition. We know from his own allusions that he wrote the later books in a given series after the earlier ones, but he may well have been writing the three concurrently. The same fully developed way of thinking guides all his writings, though he varied his technique of presentation for each of three audiences.

Treatises for Gentiles

One of these series was designed for friendly Gentiles, to point out to them the supreme value of the Jewish Bible. For this audience he apparently began with a single treatise on the "Life of Moses," which was so well received that he prepared a whole series of treatises for them, a group of writings which we now call the *Exposition of the Law*. In the "Life of Moses" he had first glorified Moses as having fulfilled all Gentile dreams of the ideal king, lawgiver, priest, and prophet. He writes for people who have obviously not read the Bible so that he has to tell each incident as for those who have never heard of it. If the incidents are all biblical, however, the Moses that emerges is the divine saving king for whom Gentiles were eagerly looking; for Moses had so unique a relation to God that he could codify the great law of nature or God, which Gentiles felt had to be brought thus to men if society, or individuals, could ever hope to live aright.

In similar vein, Philo devoted the *Exposition of the Law*, which followed, to demonstrate for Gentiles the unique greatness of the Torah as a revelation of God's will. Its first treatise, on the "Creation of the World," shows how Moses, in writing the Law under God, first oriented it in and with the universe itself by telling in the first chapters about the creation, and hence the relation of the created world to God. It is one of Philo's most difficult books, for it completely transforms the stories into a treatise on the Platonic-Pythagorean theory that the structure of the universe is one of numbers or mathematical relations. Few modern readers will have the slightest idea what Philo was driving at, but those who know this type of ancient scientific thinking will see that he was asserting that Moses had mastered all the best of it, and had based the whole structure of the Torah upon it.

The Torah, as Moses had composed it, then goes on to the stories of the great early Jewish heroes. To Philo, these men and their wives revealed the Law of God in a way secondary only to the structure of the universe. He wrote a separate treatise on each of the lives of Abraham, Isaac, and Jacob. The "Life of Abraham" begins by stating this theory very clearly. The greatest revelation of Torah is to be found in the characters of men who actually embodied the Torah in their lives. Such a grasp of Torah, Philo insists, goes quite beyond literal obedience to precepts, and God and Moses wanted to bring this out by presenting the great early heroes as men who lived lives pleasing to God beyond all later men, but who did so before the code of laws was delivered on Sinai at all. For these men went directly to God, found the true way of God for themselves, and without knowing a single statement of law (except circumcision, which God had taught Abraham) completely embodied the Law in its divine sense in their characters. Unfortunately, the biographies of Isaac and Jacob were not copied by later generations, but Philo makes clear their general purport as he summarizes the whole of the series at the end.

Philo next wrote a book on Joseph. We know from his other treatises that he had a rather low opinion of Joseph for his connivings with Pharaoh and his treatment of his father and brothers when they fled to Egypt. But Philo makes a great show of Joseph for Gentiles as one who exemplified how wonderful a ruler in practical life a Jew with such background would be. I strongly suspect he wrote this book as a *jeu d'esprit*, with his tongue in his cheek.

Since Moses had been treated in the earlier essay, this series does not go over that story again for Gentiles. But we see from his other writings that he considered, indeed revered, Moses as by far the greatest of the heroes who lived by the Law before there were laws. In the "Decalogue" Philo presents the Law in its next stage of revelation, and makes the Ten Commandments into the first presentation of the basic general principles of all the laws of God. Every specific law, he believes, falls under one or another of these ten principles. He then proceeds to analyze the detailed laws in four large treatises, "On the Special Laws." Here he interprets the particular laws one by one to show how they exemplify the principles of the Decalogue. Jewish ritual laws are left quite literally to be obeyed, though they are explained as having their value in the mystical implications of the Sabbath, Jewish food, and festivals. The laws which we would categorize as civil or criminal, however, he interpreted in such a way that they would be quite workable in the Greek and Roman courts of Alexandria. There is strong reason to suspect that Philo here tells how he, as a judge in the courts which Greeks and Romans allowed the Jews to have for themselves, actually interpreted provisions for civil and criminal law in the Jewish code. (Philo seems to me so skilled in contemporary Greek and Roman law that I have suggested, in a special study, that he spent a large part of his life as a judge in the Jewish courts of Alexandria.) In any case, even the specific laws of Jewish life came out as an ideal code in terms of Greek and Roman legal practice.

This series for Gentiles ends with two treatises that consider the general problems of the nature of virtue and the ultimate sanction of Law in reward and punishment. Philo outlines virtue in frankly Greek categories, and insists that the Torah offers the best way to achieve virtue as the Greeks idealized it. In the treatise on "Rewards and Punishments" he summarizes the thesis of the entire series, and says that in following the Torah we look not so much for immortality as for a mystic remaking in the likeness of God; the one punishment is, like that of Cain, banishment from the divine presence and connection.

I have given this much space to the *Exposition* for in it we have Philo's only attempt to present coherently his way of thinking. He has done this for Gentiles, that is, beginners, and while we have no such knowledge of the Greco-Roman way of thinking as had his audience, it will be helpful to bear this series in mind as the general outline of his thought as one goes on to his more recondite treatises.

Treatises for Jews

The most famous of Philo's three series of treatises is the
Allegory of the Law, which addresses itself to an inner group of
Jews, individuals like himself who were so steeped in the Greek
Bible that he could allude to passages from various contexts,
without retelling any of the narratives. For these "initiates" he
wrote like a preacher, assuming that his readers already knew
his way of thinking, but would enjoy and be edified by medita-
tions based on that thinking. It seems to me incredible that the
writings of Philo could have been especially original, in the sense
that he was creating a new thought world or solving new problems. The Judaism into which his readers have already been
"initiated" is that made of his own warp and woof, the Pentateuch so interpreted that it becomes a revelation of the metaphysics of Platonism, Platonism itself already far on the road
toward Neoplatonism.

In this series Philo writes Midrashim much more like that of
the rabbis, whose method is also to comment on one verse by a
patchwork of allusions to other verses. Here, however, the resemblance stops. Philo's *Allegories* are a great body of meditation,
with such countless digressions as meditative writers have always
allowed themselves. Eighteen treatises in twenty-one books
(originally many more) begin with the second story of creation,
that appear in Genesis 2, and end with the story of Ishmael.
In the typical discussion, almost every part of the Pentateuch
is brought in, but as a systematic Midrash the whole covers only
a small part of Genesis. The central interest of the treatises is
not to expound a philosophy, though scraps of philosophical
statements by no means consistent with one another frequently
appear, and have been isolated by those interested in construct-
ing Philo's "system." He had, indeed, no system of philosophy,
but he had a passionate sense that Jews who stopped with legal
observance had caught only the crude beginnings of what Moses
had given men in the Pentateuch. Of course, ordinary men can
go no farther, and God mercifully gave the mass of people a
guide in the specific laws. But Philo here writes for those who,
he hopes, will go on, however inadequately, toward such an
appropriation of divine law as did the great heroes of the Bible.

Third Series of Treatises

For this double Judaism, that of the code and that of the mystic life beyond it, the reader finally gets further detailed orientation in Philo's third great series of treatises, the *Questions and Answers on Genesis and Exodus*, a series which may originally have gone on to Numbers and Deuteronomy. Here he addressed the two main types of Jews—those interested in law, and those interested in the spirit—slowly and in detail as he expounded the Scripture verse by verse. Each little section begins with "What does it mean when it says"—followed by the next sentence of the biblical text. Then in almost every instance he gives two answers to the question, one to expound what he calls the "literal" meaning, the other to give the allegorical implications of the sentence for mystic Jews. It becomes quickly clear that Philo has written here for people who would use the work as a basis for popular sermons, probably, I should guess, so that the preacher would have material for either type of address according to the audience. The work is quite the dullest he ever wrote for consecutive reading, but has great value for filling in details he does not explain in his other writings.

What Judaism Meant to Philo

To try to take the popular reader much further into Philo's mystical metaphysics seems futile. His thought centered in the nature of God, and here also he alternated between Greek and Jewish points of view, without ever attempting to systematize the two. God was still the one God of the Bible, with special relation to the Jews. But He was no longer the tribal God of the Book of Judges, or the mythological figure that could walk and talk with Adam. He was now the remote principle. He contained the world, and was its space, but Himself was not spatial, and the world did not contain Him. Eternal, He included time, but was Himself timeless. All objects and qualities emerged from, manifested His nature, though He Himself was beyond qualities. He was the fixed, unmoved, unchanging being, in whom no emotions, no events occurred. Philo seems sometimes to accept literally the biblical stories of God's dealing with man and the universe, but at other times protests against the impropriety of such stories. "It is quite foolish to think that the world was created in six days, or in general in any measure of time." As for God's "planting and tilling" the Garden of Eden, he says, "let no such myth ever enter our mind."

Jewish tradition made Philo still want a God who was in relation with man and the universe, a God of anger and love, justice and mercy, law and forgiveness, the God of His people and His book. For Philo the Bible supremely revealed the metaphysical as well as the personal God. On some occasions, he finds the personal God of the prophets, Jewish ethics, and law; on other occasions, the abstract God of the budding Neoplatonism.

Philo declared accordingly that in the Bible Jews had a uniquely inspired revelation of God's nature and law, which were not two but one. Pagans (and Jews influenced by pagan thought) considered any verbal code of laws such as the Torah inferior to the true law of the universe; but the best way to recover that law would still be to study the implications of a divinely inspired codification. Such a codification the Jews supremely, indeed uniquely, had in the Books of Moses. Ordinary Jews who followed its literal commands had an ethical guidance superior to that of any other people, a guidance literally formulated by God. But for people of spiritual sensitivity the greater value of the code was that, by allegorizing its words, one could see the supernal law of God itself.

The Torah, then, offered itself as the way to God's utterance, rulership, and light. It is to be doubted that the psalmist had meant all this when he said: "The law is my light"; but this is what such texts meant to Philo, as they have to Jewish mystics ever since.

Perhaps the best single summary of Philo's Judaism is to be found in one of his greatest allegories, that in which he explained the deeper meaning of the cities of refuge in Numbers 35:9-28. These were to function as places where a man who accidentally had killed another could run for protection from the dead man's family, who, in the crude early way of life, were duty bound to establish their honor by killing the manslayer at once without trial. After the refugee reached one of the cities, the passage says, he would be legally tried, and if it was found that he had committed murder by deliberate intent, the family could take him out and kill him. Otherwise he was to remain in the city until the death of the high priest.

Since Philo's own development in law had taken him far beyond any literal value in such a crude procedure, he put new meaning into it. The cities had lain, by the original law, three on the east, across the river Jordan, and three on the west, where most of the Israelites lived. The passage, Philo explained, really indicates the whole system God has provided for man. If one wants to escape sin and its degradation, and live before God, he must flee ordinary human life and, if he is a simple fellow, take refuge in the nearest city, that of the negative commandments of the code. No one is so simple that he cannot, if he will, understand "don't do that." A person with higher spiritual gifts, greater fleetness, will go on to the next city, which represents the code's positive commands. "Love your neighbor," for example, is much harder to fulfill than "don't kill him." The still swifter runner will not stop here, however, but go to the third city, the city where he can live with the God of mercy and forgiveness. In these three cities, Philo has epitomized the life of traditional or "normative" Judaism, for the man at the third city will of course do his best to keep both positive and negative commands; but, like all Jews at *Yom Kippur*, he will know that the true life of the Law is impossible without the God of mercy who gave it, and who forgives the sincere penitent for his human failings.

Quite another world opens to one with such spiritual fleetness that he can cross the river, and find the metaphysical God on the other side. Here are three cities also, the first that of God's cosmic law, the higher law of which we have been speaking; the second that of God's creative energy; and the third the Logos, the supreme manifestation of God's being.

When one thinks of Philo, one must think of a Jew who solved the problem of Judaism in his Greco-Roman world by including in his own life all the cities on both sides of the great divide. Philo summarizes the allegory by saying:

> What need is there of a prohibition for men who are not going to do wrong? Or of positive commands for those whose nature is not erring? Or of mercy for those who have no sin? But our (the human) race has need of those by the fact that it is naturally inclined to both voluntary and involuntary sin.

Philo too lived daily by the negative and positive commands, and his remarks elsewhere on the Day of Atonement show how profound a place the God of mercy had in his life. But the three cities of refuge on the other side challenged him to run to them when he could, and find the deepest values of Judaism in a mystical experience of the true metaphysical nature of deity. All six cities he found in his Bible, and Abraham, Isaac, and Moses showed him the way to the metaphysical cities, quite as really as the code gave him the structure of the three "hither" cities. He had no intention of giving up his careful observance of the laws, for he knew that he was no Abraham or Moses. But he felt that his greatest concern should be not with legal observance, for that took him only a part of the way. Judaism, fully understood, would bring a man increasingly toward the divine way, and in so doing he would come more and more to resemble, even from afar, the true chosen ones of God, the great heroes of the Pentateuch, who had come close to God in their way of living without the benefit of a code at all.

The real Philo was so great a Jew precisely because he so genuinely integrated two worlds. He read Greek or Roman law when necessary into some of the crude legal provisions of early Israel, but he believed that, in doing so, he had only found God's real intent for the people. At the same time, if the metaphysical cities and deity of the "farther" cities began as Greek conceptions, he turned the tables and made them Jewish precisely as he saw the whole presented in the Book. So he Hellenized much of the code, and Judaized the metaphysics, until he could face the Gentile world as a loyal Jew who believed the Jew, among all peoples, had the fullest revelation of reality in any sense of the term.

Philo (and the little group to whom he addressed his most intensive writings) clearly had learned from pagans that the best way of coming to the divine Light-Law was not through a code, not even the code of Moses, but through the true nature of God as revealed in specially endowed persons or "wise men." With a sweep of his hand Philo had dismissed and ignored the mythological heroes and stories of the Greeks; for him the great patriarchs of the Bible represented the "living laws" which all people were seeking. Those early heroes of Judaism, as Philo describes them, had done all that the pagans had dreamed for their "philosopher kings," "wise men," or "divine men." Before Jewish law had been revealed on Sinai at all, Abraham, Isaac, Jacob, and Moses had lived by it, for they were just or righteous, which in both Jewish and Greek thinking meant that they conformed to the law. The patriarchs fulfilled the ideals expressed in terms any pagan would know. Philo was saying what Paul is later reputed to have said to the Athenians: "What you worship in ignorance, I reveal unto you."

In effect, Philo and his group invited all men of the world to find in Judaism the solution of their problems. The archeological remains have convinced me that Jews continued to do this for many years. How long some Jews thus explained their Torah we have no way of deciding, since we have no books at all from the following centuries of Greco-Latin Judaism. All that we have are writings from rabbinical centers and the decorations on synagogues and tombs. In the decade after Philo presumably died, a Jewish group left Judaism altogether, carrying the Torah with them, and proclaiming a "new" and "true" Israel in the followers of Jesus. The Roman world finally came to hear and accept their message, while sooner or later those who remained Jews went back to the Hebrew language and more Hebraic conceptions. They rejected Hellenized Judaism, and we should never have heard of Philo had Christians not preserved his writings.

Philo and the Modern Jew

Philo has thus come into an anomalous situation, and has been studied relatively little by either Jews or Christians. Particularly has he had little standing in Jewish historical writings. Yet I am confident that Philo would indignantly have repudiated Christianity had he ever heard of it. Christians broke from Judaism primarily because most Jews refused to accept three major claims: that in Jesus a new living law had appeared to reveal God's nature in the flesh, to reveal it so fully, indeed, that he completely eclipsed the patriarchs and Moses; that following Jesus meant an annulment of the law of Moses; and that succession to Abraham had nothing to do with lineage—the "true" Israel consisted in those who followed Jesus. Everything I have read in Philo assures me that such a perversion of Jewish tradition would have seemed to him utterly blasphemous. However much his ideas may later have been what he would have considered misused by Christians, he himself remained loyal to the Jewish people and the Book. He should always be recognized as the outstanding leader in one of the most interesting developments of Judaism, one of the truly great Jews of history.

The modern American, Jew or Gentile, will find Philo hard to read and understand. The involutions of his metaphysical thinking and literal absurdity of his biblical interpretations have made one of the best-known contemporary historians of Greco-Roman religion dismiss Philo as a "bore," and teach his pupils to do so. Philo can by no means be so dismissed. Christians also later united the Scriptures (still the Jewish Scriptures) with Greek thinking and did so on the basis of Philo's fusion of the two, a fact which makes him no less great an influence in history.

Jews today will not copy Philo's method, or, usually, adopt his metaphysics. But they may well emulate his breadth of loyalty, intelligence, and courage as they too face problems of being fully Jews in a Gentile civilization that challenges them with its music, art, literature, science, and ideals of society. Philo's solutions will in themselves help very little with the modern problem —that of being Jews in a world of ideas of which Moses, the prophets, or the ancient rabbis never dreamed. We cannot solve new problems with the solutions of old ones. But human nature is a constant, and if the problems of modern Jewry are to be solved, they must be solved by people like Philo who have such inherent greatness that they can find the heights of Judaism in modern science and art, and the heights of science and art still ennobled by their Judaism.

FOR FURTHER READING

BAER, R.C., *Philo's Use of the Categories Male and Female* (Leiden: E.J. Brill, 1970). An intriguing account of Philo's use of gender imagery.

FELDMAN, Louis H., *Studies in Judaica: Scholarship on Philo and Josephus, 1937–1962* (New York: Yeshiva University Press, 1963). An excellent annotated bibliography.

HARRIS, H.A., *Greek Athletes and the Jews* (Cardiff: 1970). Thoroughly documents Philo's love and knowledge of sports.

JUDAEUS, Philo, *Aufstieg und Niedergand der Romischen Welt* (Berlin: Walter de Gruyter, 1984). A whole volume of contemporary Philonic studies.

SANDMEL, Samuel, *Philo of Alexandria: An Introduction* (New York: Oxford University Press, 1979). A very useful introduction for the beginner, especially on the non-philosophic issues.

WINSTON, David, translator and introduction, *Philo of Alexandria: The Contemplative Life, The Giants and Selections* (Ramsey, NJ: Paulist Press, 1981). This excellent anthology emphasizes Philo as exegete, philosopher and mystic.

Akiba

While Philo was creating his synthesis of Judaism and Hellenism, a movement of more lasting importance was taking place in Palestine —the development of *Halakhah* or Jewish law. Its origins go back to the days of Ezra and the *Soferim,** who began to interpret and supplement the Written Law so that it would apply to the new conditions of life during the Second Commonwealth. The method by which this interpretation and amplification took place was known as Midrash,† that is, the exploration and investigation of the content of Scripture to derive its fuller meaning. Often the Written Law needed clarification or did not cover new situations that had developed; at other times, certain ancient laws became outmoded or ethically unacceptable. Such situations made necessary the continuous development of an oral law alongside the written. At first the Oral Law was taught in conjunction with the written text, but the accumulation became so unwieldy that the oral teachings or legal conclusions were detached from the biblical interpretations and taught separately (*halakhot*).

The Pharisees, who succeeded the *Soferim* as interpreters of Scripture, were the outstanding religious teachers during the last two centuries of the Jewish state. In contrast to the priestly group known as the Sadducees, who refused to accept any observance or belief not specifically included in the Law of Moses, the Pharisees supplemented the Torah with a belief in immortality, in resurrection of the dead, and in other religious concepts; they also developed new ceremonials, and applied the priestly laws of purity to the daily

---

* The spiritual leaders of Israel in the centuries between Ezra (450 B.C.E.) and the age of the Maccabees (165 B.C.E.), *Soferim* meant "men of the book," and not, as is usually translated, "scribes." See Louis Ginzberg, *On Jewish Law and Lore*, p. 3.

† This Midrashic method of searching out Scriptures for their deeper meaning is not to be confused with the later Midrashic collections such as the *Mekilta, Sifra, Midrash Rabah*, which were compiled out of the accumulated interpretations and which are popularly referred to as the Midrash.

life of every Jewish family. To the Pharisees the Oral Law was as much an expression of the will of God as the written code.

The outstanding Pharisaic teacher was Hillel the Elder, who came to Palestine from Babylonia about 30 B.C.E. and was elected president of the Sanhedrin. Aside from his saintliness and deep ethical wisdom, Hillel made a contribution to the standardizing of the methods for interpreting Jewish law. He was a liberal to whom legal precedents were not sufficient ground for a decision. To Hillel each generation, with the assistance of logic and reasoning, was entitled to derive new meanings from the Law. Thus, though the Torah provides for a general cancellation of debts every seven years, Hillel created a legal instrument (*prosbul*) whereby creditors could recover their funds in spite of the Sabbatical year.

This courageous approach on the part of Hillel and the Pharisees becomes more remarkable when we recall the character of the times. The last century of the Jewish state was a period of turbulence and civil war, when the Jews suffered from dissension within and harsh oppression from without. In spite of the gladiatorial combats and other Hellenistic practices Herod introduced into Palestine and the executions he visited upon members of his court and his own family, for which the Jews hated him, his reign (41-4 B.C.E.) was in many ways a veritable Augustan age. He strengthened the country's defenses, brought it peace and prosperity, and transformed the face of its cities with a series of magnificent buildings. But after a brief reign by his son Archelaus (4 B.C.E.-6 C.E.), Emperor Augustus annexed Palestine to the Roman Empire and moved the seat of administration from Jerusalem to Caesarea. A succession of procurators or governors was sent to rule the land, one more cruel than the other, who did not understand the religious sensitivities of the people. The country soon seethed with discontent, and outbreaks were frequent until the people revolted against the Romans in 66 C.E. Four years later Palestine was subdued and the Temple destroyed by Titus and the Roman legions.

It is difficult to imagine what would have happened to the spiritual development of the Jew and the authority of Jewish law had not Johanan ben Zakkai, another of the great *Tannaim*, and a disciple of Hillel, come to the fore. Foreseeing the crisis that Judaism would

face with the Temple, the priesthood, and the Sanhedrin destroyed,
Johanan gained permission from Vespasian to establish an academy
at Yavneh, where with the support of his colleagues and disciples
he proclaimed a series of new but necessary enactments (*Takkanot*).
Yavneh was thus established as a new center of legal authority
whence all major decisions were to come. Here, valuable traditions
were collected, particularly those related to the Temple (there was
always the hope that the Temple would be rebuilt). The method of
Midrash was taken up again, and the oral teachings sifted and clarified in an attempt to resolve the differences among scholars.

At Yavneh a new type of personality arose—the rabbi, who was to
exert great influence on the shaping of Jewish tradition. Long before
the destruction of the Temple, teachers of the Law had begun to
occupy a prominent position in national life, but with the fall of
Jerusalem, the scholars became the dominating influence in the life
of the nation. The rabbis were not professional teachers in the sense
that they earned a living by interpreting and teaching the Law. They
were rather artisans, businessmen, workers, and scribes, who devoted their leisure time to scholarship. They were not a clergy or
priesthood but a voluntary profession to which anyone might gain
admittance who could meet the standards. In a sense, they supplemented the work of the prophets, translating their lofty ideals and
visions through concrete legislation into the daily lives of the people.
In the crisis which faced the Jewish nation during the half century
between the fall of the Temple and the outbreak of the Bar Kokhba
rebellion (70 C.E.-132), the rabbinic sages furnished guidance and
comfort to the people. Among the rabbis of this era Akiba ben
Joseph was outstanding.

5 . Akiba

[c.40-137]

LOUIS FINKELSTEIN

R A B B I Akiba ben Joseph dominates the whole scene of Jewish history for eighteen centuries—from the period of the prophets until the rise of the Spanish school of Jewish philosophers in the twelfth century. His originality of thought, his legislative insight, and his colorful personality combined to make him the most revered as well as the most beloved of Talmudic sages. Most of the great scholars of the following generation were Akiba's disciples, and an authority of the third century informs us that the Mishnah, the *Tosefta*, the *Sifra*, and the *Sifre*—those ancient compilations of rabbinic thought which have survived until our own time—all had their origin in his scholarly activity. The method he developed became basic to all later rabbinic reasoning, and everywhere in the massive tomes of the Talmud are traces of his remarkable influence on subsequent systems of Jewish law, ethics, and theology.

In a wider sense, the contour of western thought generally has also been affected by Akiba's philosophy. His ideas molded those of Maimonides, Gersonides,* and Hasdai Crescas.† The influence of these men was felt by a whole series of Latin writers from Thomas Aquinas to Spinoza, who in turn laid the foundations of modern thought. The amalgam of rationalism and mysticism which was basic to the advanced Jewish philosophy of the Middle Ages, the conception of a God who was real but not anthropomorphic, could hardly have taken the form it did with-

* Levi ben Gershom, 14th-century philosopher, mathematician, and astronomer.
† Spanish-Jewish philosopher (c. 1340-1412), author of *Milḥamot Adonai* (The Wars of the Lord).

out the authoritative support of Akiba. Certainly the unequalled freedom and tolerance of later Jewish thought was, in large part, a result of Akiba's victorious assertion of his right to be original. Even the absorbing concern with ethics, which was characteristic of all Jewish thought, and has been perhaps its main contribution to the modern mind, gained in impressiveness from Akiba's teachings.

It is the reconstruction of the social conflicts of his time, however, which makes Akiba's life and thought particularly relevant to us. The issues which confronted him are with us yet, though in somewhat new form. The problems he posed of international peace, universal education, the status of women, the rights of laborers, the removal of superstition from religion, and the advancement of pure scholarship are still unsolved.

The rabbinic sages, always contemptuous of such accidental trivialities as physical characteristics, record only Akiba's exceptional stature and baldness. Surely the strange blend of humor and pathos, rigor and mercy, practical good sense and sentimental mysticism which characterized the man must have found some expression in the cheek, the forehead, and the eye. There must have been something singular and arresting in the contrast between the intellectual preoccupation of the statesman-scholar and the powerful physique of the one-time shepherd. But the Talmud records nothing of this. We are left to recreate Akiba in our imagination out of his pithy maxims, witty answers, ingenious arguments, penetrating decisions, mature theology, pedagogic method, and the memorable events of his life.

Akiba lived during an extraordinary period, intellectually and spiritually productive, marked by new thoughts, widening horizons, daring adventures, heroic martyrs, and memorable teachers. In little more than a century tiny Palestine produced the twin religions of rabbinic Judaism and Christianity.

These contributions to civilization were all the more remarkable in view of the political decline, social disintegration, and economic impoverishment of the times. Before Akiba was thirty years old, the ultranationalists of Judea, maddened by the oppression of the Roman procurators, had persuaded their brethren to undertake a hopeless rebellion which culminated in the capture of Jerusalem and the burning of the Temple (70 C.E.). Half a

century later (115 C.E.) a second rebellion broke out because
the Roman emperors violated their pledge to restore the Temple
and Jerusalem; after another seventeen years came the final
catastrophe of the Bar Kokhba Rebellion and its aftermath of un-
forgettable destruction. The Romans might well have thought
that the destruction of Judea would end the spiritual life of its
people. But the very opposite happened. Judea died, but she died
in childbirth.

Akiba and Paul

In this miracle of destruction turned into creation and death
into life, Rabbi Akiba and Paul the apostle exercised the greatest
influence. Laboring in different fields and with different methods, the two teachers in middle life underwent conversions to
causes which until then they had hated and persecuted. Both
emerged as central figures in their respective faiths; both undertook reformulations of the traditions which they had accepted,
and struggled unremittingly on behalf of their doctrines; both
sought to universalize the teachings of their colleagues and to
impose philosophic breadth and order on their religions; and, in
the end, each crowned his career with a martyr's death.

True, Paul died before the year 70, and Akiba after the year
130; Paul taught the abrogation of the Law, Akiba its perpetua-
tion; Paul gave himself to the Gentiles, Akiba to his own people;
Paul became a Christian, Akiba remained a Jew. These wide
divergences only emphasize their amazing similarities in life and
circumstance.

It is not surprising that the transformation of rabbinic Judaism
was less radical and occurred half a century later than that of
Christianity. While Paul had to contend with traditions which
were only twenty or thirty years old, those which Akiba undertook to recast had the authority of centuries. In the year 50,
Christianity was still entirely fluid; even the founder's sayings
had probably not yet been collected into fixed booklets.

The Oral Law, with which Akiba had to deal, had been
handed down by a chain of teachers which reached back beyond
the beginnings of Pharisaism (second century B.C.E.), and indeed antedated the origins of the Second Commonwealth. To

effect even a moderate change in so ancient a system required
extraordinary genius. Akiba met that requirement and was able
to bring about the rebirth of Jewish law.

Humble Beginnings

Akiba was born in southwestern Palestine, probably in the
vicinity of Ludd (modern Lydda), in the low-lying plain near
the Mediterranean coast. His father Joseph was a poor, landless
peasant, a laborer on the estate of a rich neighbor. He knew and
cared nothing about the literature of his people or the learned
traditions of the scribes. He could probably neither read nor
write. His house had no hewn stone, marble, or wood of any
kind; similar to huts still found among Arab peasants of the
district, it had walls of sunburned brick, without openings for
light or air. Straw mats were the only covering the inhabitants
had over the bare earth. Their food was of the simplest—barley
bread with cabbage, turnip, or garlic, cooked only if a jug of hot
water could be obtained from a rich neighbor or from a central
village supply.

Though Akiba knew hunger, toil, and exposure to the elements, he was outdoors most of the day, and could enjoy the
bright sunlight and country air. Since he lived in the fertile
coastal plain, he could look to the east and see the beauty of the
Judean hills, and steal away to the sea which lay only a few miles
off.

It was impossible for him, however, to acquire any book learning. Twenty years were to elapse before Joshua ben Gamala was
to establish his first system of general rural education for Judea.
In Akiba's day children could learn only from their parents, and
Akiba could get from his father nothing more than the simple
technique of sheep-tending. Condemned to the companionship
of animals and inarticulate peasants, Akiba scorned the scholars.
"When I was an *am ha-aretz*," he reported in later years, "I used
to say, 'Would that I had a scholar in my hands and I should bite
him like an ass.' " Those who knew Akiba in his older, mellow
days, when he had attained profound learning, social charm, and
gentle manners, could scarcely have credited him with such
fierce words.

Marriage and a New Life

From this pit of ignorance, Akiba was fortunately saved by Rachel, who became his wife. Who she was and by what genius she was able to penetrate so graceless an exterior and see the immense potentialities within, we do not know. Whatever her background, she must be recognized as a most remarkable woman. Throughout his life Akiba insisted that he owed everything to her. "Whatever you have achieved, and whatever I have achieved," he said to his disciples when they gathered in hosts to greet him, "belong to her!" Rachel persuaded Akiba to leave his goats and sheep and become a pupil of the scholars whom he envied and loathed. After this decision was made, they were married and entered together on the struggle for his education.

Numerous stories are current about the discouragement which Akiba met and overcame in his first efforts to learn how to read and write. His wife's father, who had opposed the match from the beginning, refused to admit the poor, ignorant shepherd into his home; and Akiba had no house to which he and Rachel might go. His toil barely earned enough for food for the family. Added to these economic troubles were the disappointments over his attempts to learn. Apparently he found his studies so difficult that more than once he was ready to return to his sheep and his ignorance.

In truth, the system of education then in vogue was hardly adapted to the needs of an alert, mature mind. When the pupil had mastered the alphabet and was able to read Hebrew texts, he was introduced not to the fascinating narratives of Genesis, but to the difficult, technical laws of sacrifice in Leviticus. Akiba, unaccustomed to the discipline of book learning, and free to study only after the fatigue of a day's labor, must have found it difficult to keep awake as he struggled to remember which offering was sacrificed in the north and which at the door of the sanctuary; whether the sin-offering of the high priest was a bullock or a ram; whether the presence of yellow hair on a leprous person was a sign of impurity and disease or of purity and healing.

Meanwhile, Rachel had given birth to a child. Akiba may have wondered whether his child too was destined to remain an *am ha-aretz*. Brooding over his own unhappy lot, Akiba came one day, it is said, to a spring, where for the first time he noticed the deep groove which the falling waters had cut into the rock. The spring became for him what the almond tree had been for Jeremiah and the sight of the Temple for Isaiah—the catalytic agent of his conversion. Suddenly his thoughts crystallized, his mind became clear, his purpose assumed definite shape.

Akiba took his child, then a lad of four or five, to a teacher. "My master, instruct us," he said. The middle-aged father and the little boy began to learn the alphabet together. In the effort to help the boy, Akiba found his own learning less tedious and painful. He mastered Leviticus and then the other books which had legalistic significance: Exodus, Numbers, and Deuteronomy. Genesis, which contained only a few laws and was full of stories, was apparently not studied in the regular curriculum. In preparation for advanced rabbinic studies, Akiba also mastered the Prophets and the Hagiographa. He had now far outstripped his little boy, and was ready to apply for admission into the rabbinical academy.

As Akiba approached his fortieth year, in about the year 80, he had not yet entered on his career. But work was waiting for him. The momentous transformation in his private life had coincided with even more fundamental changes in the structure of the body politic. The double process of decay and growth characteristic of the period had already set in.

The Challenge of the Times

As we have seen, while Akiba was still in his infancy, Agrippa's peaceful reign had come to an end, giving way to tumult and rebellion, denunciation and bitter strife. The ancient struggles between the Pharisees and the Sadducees, and among the various Pharisaic factions, had broken out anew, and with redoubled vigor.

This clash of social forces, which was to affect Akiba's public activity so intimately, becomes fully intelligible only in its historical perspective. The fundamental class division in Palestine was that between the semi-nomadic, landless shepherds and the landowning farmers. Neither the shepherds nor the small peasants of the hills could offer effective resistance to the great patrician landowners who dominated Palestinian culture and politics. The common people lacked organization, a program, and class consciousness; it was only in Jerusalem that they achieved partial victory. During the First Commonwealth the defense of the plebeians had been conducted largely by the prophets; in the Second Commonwealth, the prophet was replaced by the scholar, whose forum was his school room.

To emphasize the equality of the two groups within Pharisaism, however, a system of dual leadership was arranged, giving each equal representation. If the first sage (later called the *nasi* or president) was a patrician, the second or associate sage (later called *ab bet din*, or hand of the court) had to be a plebeian, and vice versa. For many generations the two groups worked together, but during the insurrection in 66, which culminated in the destruction of the Second Temple, they became hostile to each other. Rabbi Johanan ben Zakkai was at this time the leader of the plebeians. Vespasian, having warned the Jews, reduced their cities one by one, and was ready, in the summer of 68, to lay siege to Jerusalem, virtually their sole remaining stronghold. This was a difficult moment for Johanan ben Zakkai, who had hitherto abstained from active participation in the rebellion, and had also refused to hold any communication with the Romans. But now a new situation confronted him. Even if the Romans should fail to make a breach in the city's walls, famine and thirst must ultimately compel surrender.

A plan was evolved requiring courage and unbelievable self-control. Johanan feigned illness, then death, and was taken out of the city by his disciples, as if for burial. He then sought out Vespasian in order to establish a new academy in one of the provincial cities already under Roman control. When Vespasian asked, "What shall I give thee?" he was doubtless amazed to hear that the aged scholar had risked his life for no greater boon than permission to establish an academy! The modest request was immediately granted.

Johanan was now ready for a more daring step. He declared the assemblage at Yavneh the true Sanhedrin of all Israel, the authorized successor of the body which had met for centuries in the "Chamber of Hewn Stones" in the Temple. Though the conclave was destined to meet there for only sixty years, while other centers of learning persisted for centuries, the Vineyard of Yavneh holds a permanent, unequaled place in Jewish tradition, for it was there that Judaism was saved in its direst crisis.

In the Vineyard of Yavneh

Shortly after its establishment, Akiba appeared at the Vineyard of Yavneh, seeking higher rabbinic instruction. Though Johanan had passed away and his place was still vacant, the academy had been so firmly established that there was no interruption in its activity, or diminution of its prestige.

It was easy to enter the Vineyard, where the scholars gathered for their deliberations. There were no guards at the gate; the sessions were held in public; the discussions were open. In the center of the whole magnificent group sat the two men who had helped Johanan ben Zakkai found the academy: Eliezer ben Hyrkanos and Joshua ben Hananya. Nothing could have illustrated more dramatically the composite nature of Pharisaism and the Sanhedrin than the juxtaposition of these two leaders, alike in their erudition and piety, but differing from one another in every other way. Eliezer, the foppish, rich landowner, reared as an *am ha-aretz*, had fled from his father's house in order to study Torah, and had finally attained such proficiency that Johanan had compared him to "a well-lined cistern which never loses a drop." Joshua ben Hananya, on the other hand, was ungainly in form and plain of face but possessed of remarkable wit and a melodious voice, a Temple singer who, after Jerusalem was destroyed, had become a needlemaker. In the midst of dire poverty, in a soot-covered hovel, he pursued his studies until he had mastered not only Jewish learning but also the secular sciences of mathematics and astronomy.

In this tumultous and dazzling assembly where so many types with differing gifts, temperaments, and social standing had gathered, Akiba turned first to Eliezer ben Hyrkanos, perhaps because he too had entered on his studies when he was a mature man. Eliezer, however, rejected Akiba, holding that just as God had given the Law to a generation which was fed with manna, so later teachers should accept as pupils only those who had no economic worries to distract them. But Akiba received a warm welcome from the poor Joshua ben Hananya; the latter sent him to Tarfon, Akiba's contemporary, who later became his closest friend. The tradition as he received it from Tarfon did not, however, satisfy Akiba because the former was really a member of the patrician wing of the Pharisees, while his own sympathies were with the plebeian group.

Finding himself in fundamental disagreement on the social issues of the day with Tarfon—in spite of the latter's love of the pupil—and unable to follow the slow-moving, good-humored, half-cynical, easily satisfied Joshua, Akiba turned to the brilliant but comparatively unknown Naḥum of Gimzo. Naḥum's value to Akiba lay in the new method of interpretation which he had developed, by which every word and indeed every letter in Scripture have significance.

Akiba's association with Naḥum continued for twenty-two years. Long after he had become a famous scholar, he would travel back and forth between the village of Gimzo and the city of Yavneh, bringing the sick old man news of the conclave, and taking back to his colleagues ideas born out of those fleeting contacts.

Having mastered the plebeian doctrines of Joshua and Naḥum, Akiba decided to return to Eliezer, who had originally rejected him. This time Eliezer did not refuse to admit him, but neither did he "recognize" him. We do not know how long Akiba remained associated with Eliezer in this way, but it is said that after he had spent thirteen years in study under his various masters, he decided to challenge openly the patrician traditions of the Shammaites, of whom his new master Eliezer was the foremost exponent.

The Great Debate: Akiba vs. Eliezer

One day, in the conclave of Yavneh, Eliezer offered an opinion to which Joshua raised an objection. There was nothing to indicate that the occasion would assume historical importance until Akiba, still comparatively unknown outside the limited circle of his teachers, stood up to oppose Eliezer, who, according to Johanan ben Zakkai, outweighed in learning the entire host of his contemporaries. What followed has become a saga of scholarship, and the arguments, even the invectives, used by the protagonists still echo wherever the Jewish tradition is studied.

Characteristically, the question which precipitated the combat was of purely academic interest at the moment. The law required certain sacrifices to be offered on Sabbaths and holidays, and it had always been agreed that the performance of the labor connected with these duties necessarily superseded the Sabbath and festival prohibitions. The priests further maintained that all ancillary activities, such as sharpening knives and preparing fuel, were also permitted. This the plebeians vigorously denied. The Temple had been in ruins for almost a quarter of a century when Eliezer mentioned the priestly tradition and defended it in the academy. He urged that since slaughtering an animal—a major activity— was permitted, sharpening a knife—a minor activity— must by implication also be permitted. Joshua made a feeble attempt to answer this argument but, in his usual fashion, was about to retire from the field when Akiba stood up to voice his opinion.

"Does not the Bible say," Eliezer shouted, " 'In its due season' (Numbers 28:2)? And does that not mean that sacrifices must be brought at their specified times whether on the Sabbath or on week days?"

"Indeed," Akiba replied, "but show me where it says that knives must be sharpened in the appointed seasons."

This first public argument presumably won Akiba his ordination and full membership in the conclave. The scholar could no longer be called a pupil; he was a master of the Law. By virtue of his new status, he was not only a recognized authority on all ceremonial questions; he could also sit as judge in matters of civil law, which were usually presented before three ordained teachers. He could also act as member of a court to exercise criminal jurisprudence in so far as the Romans permitted the Jewish community to enforce its law.

Both Akiba and Eliezer must have realized that this discussion was only an opening skirmish in a long-drawn-out battle. With unwearying persistence, Akiba returned to the struggle each day, lying in wait for any expression of Shammaitic opinion which he might need to refute.

During the eight or ten years which Akiba spent under the tutelage of Joshua ben Hananya and Nahum of Gimzo, he had become completely transformed: his interests now transcended his provincial origin; he had absorbed the whole plebeian outlook on life. Though his manners and speech were now those of a polished gentleman, his legislation protected plebeian interests. But it was expressed in terms of concrete legal rules and mature, sophisticated urban idealism.

So completely did Akiba win the hearts of both Eliezer and Joshua that when the latter traveled about the country to raise funds for the poor, they frequently invited him to join them. Only one member of the conclave regarded Akiba's rise with ill favor: the patrician scholar Elisha ben Abuyah. While Akiba could afford to ignore Elisha's envy, he could not dismiss as easily the tyranny of Gamaliel, whom the scholars had finally succeeded in making *nasi* or president.

At last, weary of the continual struggle against Gamaliel and the other patricians, Akiba left Yavneh and settled as a village teacher in the small town of Zifron in Galilee. He did not remain there long. The scholars who had taken him for granted while he sat with them in Yavneh suddenly realized all he had meant to them. "The Torah is outside," they declared, referring to his absence from their discussions. Yielding ultimately to their clamor, Gamaliel invited him to return to the conclave.

Though Akiba does not appear to have held any formal office in the academy, he was universally considered a dominant figure, the fourth member of the directing committee. Perhaps it was at this time that he was appointed overseer of the poor, a post for which he was admirably suited by character and which he filled for many years.

About fifteen years had passed since Akiba had come to the academy as a humble shepherd, with little hope. He had risen past colleagues and masters and stood, at last, on a high pinnacle, a dominant figure in Jewish life. At the age of fifty-five, still in the fullness of bodily vigor and mental alertness, he set out on his lifework—the reconstruction of the Law and the establishment of a permanent school.

Visit to Rome

The twenty years which followed the successful revolt against Gamaliel were probably the happiest in Akiba's life. Two sons and two daughters were growing up and showing high promise. His wife Rachel was sharing the fruits of their common sacrifices

—the friendship of their intimate co-workers and the approbation of the general public.

And yet the period began under a cloud. The Roman government, which for fifteen years had pursued a policy of friendship and conciliation, suddenly reversed itself and enacted a series of restrictive regulations against the Jews. In the autumn of the year 95, news reached Palestine of fresh threats against Jews in Rome. No time could be lost; a few days before the *Sukkot* festival, the four leading scholars, Gamaliel, Joshua, Eleazar ben Azariah, and Akiba set sail for the capital of the Empire.

The sages would probably have returned empty-handed had not Domitian died during their stay in Rome. He was succeeded in September, 96, by Nerva, the first of the "five good emperors," who, in his short rule of only sixteen months, managed to bring new hope to Jews, both in Rome and in distant Palestine.

The visit to Rome was a turning point in Akiba's life. Had he died before he undertook this diplomatic task, he would be remembered as the most brilliant member of the illustrious academy at Yavneh. But from that point on, his achievement as a leader competes with and eventually overshadows his reputation as a scholar.

Ordering of the Law

From the time of his return from Rome, in 97, Akiba was held in increasing reverence by both his colleagues and the masses. In the years that followed, while the Jewish community enjoyed unusual prosperity and peace, Akiba devoted himself to the formulation of his juristic principles, the clarification of his theological ideas, and the establishment of his school.

"To what may Akiba be compared?" asked one of his pupils, describing the activities in which the sage engaged at this time. "To a peddler who goes about from farm to farm. Here he obtained wheat, there barley, and in a third place, spelt. When he comes home he arranges them all in their respective bins. So Akiba went about from scholar to scholar, getting all the traditions he could; and then he proceeded to arrange them in an orderly granary." It is probable that the division of the Mishnah into six orders, and even the subdivisions into treatises, goes back to him.

Except for a few treatises describing the ancient Temple and its service, the earlier compilations of Jewish law were not arranged by subject matter at all. They were strings of legal norms put together according to the similarity of their literary formulation but without inner conviction. Akiba realized that while such a method was satisfactory for fragments of the Law, it was altogether inadequate for a complete code, which required logical division and subdivision.

Once he had decided on the method to follow in the arrangement of his material, Akiba even more boldly replaced ancient norms with others which represented his own opinions. Such was the authority he came to enjoy that within a generation the material he had rejected was almost unknown. The trenchant, epigrammatic style which he had developed for his apothegms and decisions proved invaluable to him in his new activity. The effective combination of brevity and precision was a boon to the student who had to memorize the text, and it set a good example for all future codifiers. His Mishnah became so popular in his own lifetime that even those parts which he rejected in his later years continued to be studied. Being oral texts, they could not be issued in new editions; once memorized they could not be withdrawn from circulation, as it were. The original statements were repeated in the academies, with the qualifying remark that Akiba had changed his mind about them, in part.

The later Talmudists rated these achievements so high that they declared Akiba had saved the Torah from oblivion. They ranked his work with the rediscovery of the Law in the days of Josiah. "Had not Shaphan arisen in his time, and Ezra in his time, and Akiba in his time," a homilist of the next century remarked, "would not the Law have been forgotten in Israel?"

For centuries the Mishnah of Akiba was recalled as an outstanding achievement of rabbinic learning. Not only Jewish scholars but Christian Church Fathers referred to it. One of the best-informed authorities of the third century tells us that it became the core of the Mishnah of Meir, which in turn was incorporated into the final redaction of Judah the Patriarch (or Prince)—which still remains the basic codification of rabbinic law.

"The truths which were not revealed to Moses," says a later teacher in his enthusiasm, "were uncovered to Akiba." When he left Palestine on his various journeys, "there remained not his equal in all the land," asserted his younger contemporaries. When he died, "the arms of the Law were broken, and the fountains of wisdom were stopped up."

Akiba's influence in the academy gradually became paramount. The principle, accepted by later Talmudists and codifiers, that Akiba's opinion must be given preference to that of any of his colleagues doubtless originated in the attitude taken toward him in his own lifetime.

Akiba the Teacher

In time Akiba, while still attending the sessions of the conclave, founded a private academy at the little village of Bene Berak, a short distance from Yavneh. The conclave at Yavneh had assembled in a vineyard and Eliezer had given his decisions from a rock; Akiba, however, preferred to lecture in the shade of a broad-leaved fig tree. Students from the most diversified groups flocked to him from all parts of the country.

In his relations with his students, Akiba displayed the same charm and courtesy which had won him the affection of his masters and colleagues. When any one of the young men fell ill, the master was sure to visit him. He did not consider it beneath his dignity on such a visit to arrange his pupil's room, sweep the floor, or perform any other service. "Whosoever neglects the duty of visiting the sick," he taught, "is guilty of shedding blood."

Akiba's power over his disciples arose not merely from his tenderness with them, but mainly from his pedagogic ability. In addition to the codification of the Law, he also arranged the laws and traditions as comments on the biblical verses from which they were derived. Two of his pupils, Judah and Simeon, preferred this method, which they developed even further, while two others, Meir and Jose, made Akiba's codes the foundation of their own compilations.

These works were not put into writing, for it was a cardinal principle of Pharisaism at the time that rabbinic traditions must be preserved orally. They were handed down from generation to generation by a special class of professional memorizers. Only in the fifth century, perhaps even later, when it became obvious that any further attempt to retain the old tradition would result in the disappearance of the whole law, was permission granted to entrust this material to writing. During the three centuries in which the books had remained an oral tradition, they had naturally changed considerably in form. Yet even now the stamp of the opposing schools is still clear, and permits us to reconstruct with reasonable accuracy the methods of teaching and inference current in the days of Akiba and Ishmael, seventeen centuries ago.

Akiba's mode of interpretation of Scripture is a development of that which he derived from his master Naḥum of Gimzo. Superfluous letters, words, and verses were the meat whereon he thrived. By the use of them he was able to read his whole juristic program into Scriptures. But what he called superfluous words would hardly seem such to us. The juxtaposition of the various chapters had a meaning which must be discovered. He rejected the old Hillelite principle of inference by generalization from particulars, and replaced it with a curious and complicated rule of his own invention which he called "Inclusion and Limitation." Neither rhetoric nor grammar offered a bar to his imaginative argument. Indeed, were we to accept at face value the technical reasons he gave for his decisions, we should be forced to the conclusion that, far from being the greatest of the Talmudists, he was simply a brilliant example of extraordinary—but wasted—ingenuity. But the rules which he derived through his curious and intricate logic are so reasonable that when we examine them we are even more impressed with his judgment as a jurist than with his skill as debater. It is obvious that he considered the interpretation of the Written Law merely a form which had to be followed in the derivation of desirable rules from the biblical text.

Akiba was trying to change the complexion of the inherited law. To accomplish this he had to find an authority superior to that of his predecessors and accepted by everyone. Only one instrument could fulfill those requirements—Scripture itself.

The duty of teaching seemed to him paramount. "Though you have given instruction to some disciples in your youth, you must continue to teach in old age," he said. "This is the meaning of Ecclesiastes 11:6, which reads, 'In the morning sow thy seed, and in the evening withhold not thy hand; for thou knowest not which shall prosper, whether this or that, or whether they both shall be alike good.'" Akiba describes the value of a teacher to his pupils in three beautiful similes. "What I received from my teacher amounts to the fragrance given off by the citron, and the light taken from one candle to another, and the water drawn from a brook. The beneficiary enjoys the odor, increases the light, and is refreshed by the water; but the giver has lost nothing!"

Akiba's Juristic Philosophy

Akiba's various utterances regarding ethics, law, religion, theology, and politics form a complete, coherent, and unified system which we may rightly call a philosophy. His various decisions and maxims were applications of general principles which were clear in his own mind, although he did not organize them for posterity in the form of abstract propositions. This was due, first, to the nature of his judicial office, which required decisions in concrete cases rather than philosophic statements of general policy; and, secondly, to the Jewish tradition which, unlike the Hellenic, has never given up its preference for the concrete and individual.

Akiba's fundamental approach to juristic problems may be summarized as follows:

1. Whatever be the inequalities which we find in the world, we must not permit them to intrude on the worship of God. Hence, ceremonial law must be interpreted so as not to exclude the weaker social groups from participation, or to demand too heavy sacrifices from them. This implies that no opportunity may be given to the more fortunate to invent ceremonies or rituals which the poorer cannot imitate. Nor may expensive devices be utilized as evasions of burdensome laws.

In general, Akiba could not brook ostentation, especially in prayer. When he prayed in private, his disciple, Judah ben Ilai, tells us, "one would leave him in one corner and find him in another, to which he had wandered through the multitude of kneelings and prostrations." But when he prayed in public, he "would finish quickly, lest he keep others waiting for him."

2. So far as the civil law is fluid and open to interpretation, it can be used to rectify social inequalities. Hence the rules of law

should favor the oppressed groups: the plebeian, the artisan-merchant, the shepherd, the slave, the women and children.

3. It is especially important that the prerogatives of the priests be limited, and that the gross inequality between them and the Levites be minimized.

4. Akiba's attitude toward women and marriage was influenced by his own experience. When the usual question, "What is true wealth?" was raised among the sages, Tarfon, the great landowner, replied readily, "The possession of a hundred vineyards and a hundred slaves to work them."

Young Meir, Akiba's disciple, said more modestly, "Contentment and satisfaction with one's riches."

But Akiba said, "A wife who is comely in her deeds."

The possibility that the emancipation of women may lead to the disruption of family life should be met by the imposition of severe penalties for infidelity. Suitability in marriage meant not merely mutual compatibility and love; it also implied the absence of any legal or moral hindrance to the union. Hence, he was more severe than any of the other sages with regard to incestuous or forbidden unions, declaring them void, and maintaining that the children born of them were illegitimate.

On the other hand, his defense of the rights of women brought him into continual conflict with the patrician-provincial scholars, who objected to his violent reversal of the tradition of feminine inferiority. He conceded that a married working woman should turn over her wages to her husband, but he ruled that if she earned more than he spent on her maintenance the difference belonged to her.

5. In the attempt to ameliorate the conditions of slaves, care must be taken to protect the status and rights of free labor.

6. Pious merchants must be protected from the handicaps resulting from their observance of the Law.

7. There is no room for superstition in Judaism. In Akiba's opinion, anyone who believed in days of good or bad omen transgressed the biblical law against witchcraft; and those who used magical formulas to cure disease were unfit for immortal life. Tales of miracles which various sects told of their founders he considered pure fiction.

8. The ideals of peace and human equality are fundamental principles of religion. Akiba was determined to grant equality

to all free peoples. When the patricians proposed a rule varying the sum to be assessed for personal injuries according to the social status of the plaintiff, Akiba said, "The poorest man in Israel must be considered as a patrician who has lost his property; for they are all descendants of Abraham, Isaac, and Jacob."

Akiba made no claim that his decisions introduced anything new into Judaism. He regarded himself as the mouthpiece of the Torah, applying its principles to new cases as they arose. "Know before whom ye are standing," he said to the litigants at the opening of each trial. "Not before Akiba ben Joseph, but before the Holy One, blessed be He."

The Tragic Years: Rebellion of Bar Kokhba

The years 110-112 were epochal both in the life of Akiba and in the history of the Jewish people. In his seventieth year the great sage was still at the peak of his strength. His health was perfect, he had retained all the physical and mental vigor of his youth, and his native genius was now supplemented by the skill born of thirteen years of intellectual leadership. If the discovery and development of unsuspected faculties within one's self, the conquest of adverse circumstances, and the achievement of universal applause can give happiness to man, Akiba must certainly have been happy.

The situation of the community was equally happy. Never since the destruction of Jerusalem had Judea been economically more prosperous or politically more tranquil. The aftermath of the war had passed, and the ruined population had once more settled down to normal habits of work and trade; the city of Ludd in the lowland had partly replaced Jerusalem as the metropolis of Judea and had absorbed some of the destitute artisans and merchants. A new generation had grown up, accustomed to the Roman yoke and apparently willing to bear it. In distant Rome, the affairs of the Empire had for a dozen years been in the capable hands of Nerva and Trajan, the first and second of the "five good emperors."

To Akiba and many others it seemed that the Messianic era was at hand. Gradually, however, new oppressions were suffered, and about the year 125 the relations between Jews and Romans took a turn for the worse. It is not known whether the

increasing rigor was due to the suspicion of nationalist activity
on the part of some rabbinic scholars, especially Rabbi Simeon
and Rabbi Ishmael. It is certain, however, that edicts were pro-
mulgated forbidding the practice of circumcision, the pretext
being the Roman law against mutilation of the body, and it is
probable that the recitation of the *Shema* at public services, the
reading of the Book of Esther on *Purim*, and the sounding of
the *shofar* (ram's horn) on New Year's Day were also pro-
hibited as being ceremonies with specifically nationalist implications.

Some of the moderate nationalists were tempted to seek in
exile both safety and the opportunity to observe the Law. But
their consciences would not let them find so easy an escape. To
dwell in Palestine was itself a commandment and, in the minds
of many, one which outweighed all others.

While the scholars, like the people at large, were finding themselves involved in the various factions, the conclave assembled
once more in Ludd to determine on a national policy. Standing
between the extremists on both sides, Akiba insisted that the
practical problem could not be solved until the scholars agreed
on the basic theory of the place of observance in Judaism. The
plebeians had always held that study was more important than
observance; and it was entirely logical for them to maintain that
should observance lead to the destruction of the Torah it would
defeat its own purpose. The patricians had, however, always
opposed this view.

It is highly probable that the severity of the recent enactment
against Jews was related to the Emperor Hadrian's expected return to the East. To the Jews, however, the arrival of the
emperor, in the year 130, seemed a most opportune occasion to
present their petitions and their grievances in person. It must
have been obvious to Hadrian that the Romans had committed
an act of unjustified waste in razing Jerusalem to the ground.
The interests of the Empire demanded the reestablishment of the
great wealth-producing metropolis, which was the center of the
country's commerce, industry, and religion. Hadrian decided to
grant the request of the Jews and to rebuild their city.

The emperor also granted the Jews a temple. But—and in
this he displayed the same blindness that had caused many trage-
dies in Roman history—the temple, like so many others he had

founded, was to be dedicated to the worship of himself, as identified with the Capitoline Jupiter.

The effect of this pronouncement on Akiba, then in his
ninetieth year, was crushing. The last hope for improved relations with Rome had disappeared; the teachings of his whole
lifetime, that a pacific attitude toward the Empire would call
forth reasonable treatment from it, were refuted by the event.
For the first time in his life he began to be uncertain of his views.
Endowed with extraordinary powers of introspection and self-
examination, the old sage must have wondered whether his intellectual powers, which had so long resisted the years, had not
failed him at last.

But the blow which had all but prostrated the old scholar
stimulated the masses of the people to furious action. A decree
of wholesale extermination could hardly have aroused them
more than the news of the emperor's decision to establish his
pagan sanctuary on Mount Moriah. The fanaticism which had
been held in check for decades broke loose.

As the excitement grew, Ishmael and Simeon cast off the
secrecy under which they had heretofore carried on their nationalist activities. The Romans arrested and condemned them to
death, even before the revolution had broken out. Their faith
endured to the last. While they were being led to the execution,
they merely commiserated with each other on the fate which
prevented them from sharing in the glory awaiting their people.
Akiba, speaking over their graves, warned his hearers to expect
no miracles. "Prepare yourselves for suffering," he cried to the
weeping multitude. "If happiness were destined to come in our
time, none deserved better to share in it than Rabbi Simeon and
Rabbi Ishmael. But God, knowing what distress is in store for
us, removed them from our midst, as it is written, 'The righteous
is taken away from the evil to come' " (Isaiah 57:1).

The leadership of the rebellion passed from the intellectual
sages, Ishmael and Simeon, to Simeon bar Kokhba, a soldier and
strategist who at once set out to organize the straggling bands of
patriotic peasants into a regular army. His first few victories
aroused wild enthusiasm among the people, who saw in him not
merely a second Maccabee but the Messiah. The private and
public fortunes of a nation were staked on the personal prowess
and military genius of the unproved leader.

Akiba himself did not long resist the contagion of Messianism. When he saw Roman legions yield to untrained Judean youths, new hope blossomed in his heart. "Yet once, it will be a little while," he quoted from Haggai (2:6), "and I will shake the heavens and the earth, and the sea, and the dry land." He went so far as to encourage the popular delusion concerning the miraculous role to be played by the new leader, and applied to him the verse (Numbers 24:17), "There shall step forth a star out of Jacob." On one occasion he even said outright, "This is the Messianic king."

The story of the denouement is well known: how in a little more than three years the Romans destroyed the last vestige of Jewish resistance, how in their fury they drenched the land with blood, slaughtering hundreds of thousands of people, how they sold tens of thousands into slavery, forbade the few remaining Jews to observe any of their ancestral customs, and took the children forcibly out of their religious schools and put them to manual labor. Hundreds of scholars fled to Babylonia, but many still felt that their duty was to remain in Palestine.

The fact that Akiba was not imprisoned shows that he had not implicated himself actively in the rebellion. Like other Jews, he could observe the Law only in secret; but he was permitted to move about and apparently even to give instruction. Clearly, the Roman generals who were trying to destroy Judaism root and branch did not at this time share the opinion of some modern historians that Akiba himself was the secret instigator of the whole rebellion and that his wide travels, ostensibly for the Sanhedrin and the Law, were really made to foment sedition.

Death of a Martyr

It was not long before the loyalty of Akiba and his colleagues to the principle of study was to be put to the ultimate test. The savagery of the repressions grew from month to month. It was probably in the year 134, just before the capitulation of Betar, that the Romans issued their drastic decree forbidding not only the practice but also the study of Torah. Akiba now knew that he had reached the end of compromise. He had counseled the people to accept the Roman gift of a temple when that had been offered; he had warned them not to be disappointed when the offer was withdrawn; he had asked them to sacrifice the right to observe the Law in order that its study might be perpetuated. But the last stronghold, the innermost shrine, was to be defended at all costs. If the study of Torah was abolished, there was no further purpose of living. And so, at the age of ninety-five, the compromising pacifist once more took up the weapons of non-resistant war. Calmly he gathered his students, gave his decisions, delivered his lectures. He disdained and feared gatherings in secret as unworthy of the dignity of Torah; they were certain to raise the suspicion of political activity. He had always taught in the open, in the shade of a tree; and he would continue to do so. He made only one compromise with necessity. He invited his disciples to dine with him; and they discussed the Law during their meal.

When his old antagonist, Pappias, warned that he was courting death by continuing to teach so publicly, Akiba replied with the parable of the fishes and the fox. The fox, coming to the river's bank, suggested to the fishes that they might find safety from the fishermen by coming on the dry land. But the fishes replied, "If in the water which is our element we are in danger, what will happen to us on the dry land, which is not our element?"

"So, too," continued Akiba, "if there is no safety for us in the Torah which is our home, how can we find safety elsewhere?"

Akiba could not have expected to continue teaching for long. Soon he was seized by the soldiers and carried off to prison. The Romans, still respecting his learning, his reputation, and his distinguished personality, and perhaps also remembering his pacifist and conciliatory teachings, hesitated to put him to death. They kept him in confinement for three years, treating him with consideration, even with courtesy. He was allowed the attendance of his disciple Joshua ha-Garai, who waited on him; and he was permitted to enjoy the visit of Simeon ben Yohai, who had returned from Zidon to be near the master in his affliction. "Continue to instruct me," Simeon begged of him. At first reluctant out of fear that he might endanger his pupil's freedom and even his life, Akiba finally yielded to his importunities. "My son," he said, "more than the calf wants to suck, the cow wants to suckle!"

Although he pursued these audacious activities secretly, Akiba must have known that the Romans would soon learn of them. When this happened, he was transferred to a prison in distant Caesarea, where no one but his servant-pupil Joshua ha-Garai was permitted to attend him.

And still Akiba carried on. The impoverished and leaderless community made unheard-of sacrifices to obtain decisions from Akiba during those days.

Finally Akiba was brought to trial; his judge was to be his former friend Rufus. There was no possible defense against the charges; Akiba had violated the Law by offering instruction to his disciples. He was found guilty and condemned to death. Still attended by his faithful Joshua, he retained his courage and strength of mind until the very end.

The popular story tells that the Romans killed Akiba by tearing his flesh from his living body. As he lay in unspeakable agony, he suddenly noticed the first streaks of dawn breaking over the eastern hills. It was the hour when the law requires each Jew to pronounce the *Shema*. Oblivious to his surroundings, Akiba intoned in a loud, steady voice the forbidden words of his faith, "Hear, O Israel, the Lord our God, the Lord is One. And thou shalt love the Lord thy God with all thy heart, and with all thy soul, and with all thy might."

Rufus, the Roman general, who superintended the execution, cried out: "Are you a wizard or are you utterly insensible to pain?"

"I am neither," replied the martyr, "but all my life I have been waiting for the moment when I might truly fulfill this commandment. I have always loved the Lord with all my might, and with all my heart; now I know that I love him with all my life." And repeating the verse again, he died as he reached the words, "The Lord is One."

FOR FURTHER READING

"Akiva," in *Encyclopedia Judaica,* Volume 2, pp. 487–491 (Jerusalem: 1972).

CASPI, Nadine, *Akiba* (Jerusalem: 1981).

GOLDIN, Judah, Aquiba Ben Joseph," in *Journal of the American Oriental Society,* pp. 38–56, Volume 16, 1976. A study of Akiba's understanding of love of God and love of man.

SANDERS, Edward, "R. Akiba's View of Suffering," in *Jewish Quarterly Review* (Philadelphia: 1972).

CONCLUDING NOTE ON ANCIENT TIMES

After the death of Akiba and the suppression of the Bar Kokhba rebellion, the center of Jewish activity was transferred from Judea (now virtually deserted) to Galilee, where the *Bet Din* was reconstituted and the old life slowly reestablished under the leadership of Rabbi Meir, pupil of Rabbi Akiba and Simon ben Yohai, who was later regarded as the founder of Jewish mysticism. But the dominant personality in the second half of the second century was Judah the Prince (ha-Nasi), the last commanding figure in the Patriarchate.* Many collections and digests of the Law now existed in the various academies, but traditions and interpretations varied greatly from one academy to the other. Because of the ensuing confusion and because conditions in Palestine were not tranquil, Judah undertook to edit and organize the accumulated laws and give them systematic form. Thus there came into being the Mishnah, the first great code in which all the Jewish laws are arranged according to subject matter, divided into six major sections, and subdivided into treatises. Written in a concise and lucid Hebrew, the Mishnah represents a climax of a half millennium of interpretations and supplementation of the Bible by the *Soferim*, Pharisaic teachers, and *Tannaitic* rabbis, and constitutes one of the great contributions of the classical age of Judaism.

Following the death of Judah the Prince, conditions in Palestine began to deteriorate. The heavy taxation and increasing misgovernment of the Romans, the wars between Rome and Persia in which Palestine was often caught in the middle, the recognition of Christianity as the official religion of the Empire, and the beginning of systematic persecution of the Jews all marked steps in the decline. The Patriarchate continued for another two centuries, but the later

* The official heads of Palestinian Jewry from the days of Johanan ben Zakkai until the office's abolition by Theodosius II in 425.

Patriarchs for the most part were not outstanding men. As conditions grew worse, there was danger that all the accumulated traditions and commentaries would be forgotten.

During the fourth century the Palestinian schools began to review the traditions and commentaries (Gemarah) that had accumulated on each treatise of the Mishnah, and subjected them to scholarly examination. Various parts were edited and gradually compiled to form the Palestinian Talmud (containing both the Mishnah of Judah and the Gemarah, which had developed during the ensuing centuries). After the fourth century Jews continued to live in the Holy Land but it was no longer the center of Jewish life. Simultaneously, a great flowering of rabbinic Judaism was taking place in Babylonia, where Jews had been living since the days of Jeremiah. It was just about the time of Judah the Prince that the eastern community showed signs of an intellectual awakening. Two Babylonian scholars, Abba Arika, later called Rav (master), and his colleague Samuel, went up to Palestine to study under Judah. On their return, they were instrumental in intensifying the religious and cultural life of Babylonian Jewry. It was said of Rav that "he found it (Babylonia) an open plain and left it fenced in." Samuel was appointed head of the school in Nehardea, which was destined to become a great center of learning, like the school of Sura, headed by Rav.

In 226, Babylonia came under control of the Sassanian or Neo-Persian Empire, and there began occasional persecution against non-Zoroastrians. About 261 the city of Nehardea, which was the center of Jewish life in Babylonia, was invaded and the academy destroyed. The center was then shifted to Sura, nearer the Persian Gulf, and a new academy established at Pumpeditha. Nonetheless for two centuries Jews enjoyed relative tranquility and were able to fashion their own autonomous life under "Princes of the Exile" or Exilarchs. These were recognized by the government as the official representatives of the Jewish community and, claiming descent from the house of David, conducted themselves with regal dignity. The academies continued unhindered, and a number of outstanding rabbinic teachers called *Amoraim* (expounders) discussed and amplified the treatises of the Mishnah of Judah, two treatises being taken up each year. Students of all ages came in large numbers twice a year during the months preceding Passover and the fall holidays to hear the scholars expound their interpretations. Such *kallahs,* as this institution was called, were a remarkable instrument of popular education whose example has influenced the adult Jewish education movement in America.

The even tenor of life in Babylonia was interrupted in the fifth century by renewed persecutions on the part of the Zoroastrian priests and by the prohibition of many Jewish religious practices. The academies had to struggle for existence and, as had happened in Palestine, the scholars began to fear that the interpretations which had grown up around the Mishnah in Babylon might be lost. They therefore began to devote themselves to the compilation and editing of the material which had accumulated. Rav Ashi, during the fifty-two years that he presided over the Sura academy (375-427), was able to reexamine the entire Mishnah, tractate by tractate, in the light of the supplementary material which he sifted and arranged. At the end of the century Rabina brought the process of redaction (or editing) to a conclusion. Thus there came into being the Babylonian Talmud, usually referred to simply as the Talmud. Very soon it overshadowed the Palestinian Talmud, which through subsequent ages has been studied only by scholars.

The Talmud, written in Aramaic and Hebrew, without structure or style in the modern sense, is made up of *Halakhah*—legal arguments, discussions, comments, and debates of the scholars of the Babylonian academies on the Mishnah—and *Aggadah*, or theology, folklore, wisdom, and narrative tales. It is a vast conglomerate work which the rabbis compare to a veritable sea in which one must submerge oneself in order to appreciate its character.

With the completion of the Talmud the great creative era of ancient times which produced the Torah, the prophetic writings, Hellenistic literature, the Mishnah, and the two Talmuds (not to speak of the Apocrypha and other *Tannaitic* collections besides the Mishnah) came to a close. With the compilation of the Talmud, the basic beliefs and values, customs and ceremonies, and the forms and character of Jewish law were now established. Something of the central character the Bible had for the Jews throughout the seventeen centuries of ancient times the Talmud acquired for them during the thirteen centuries of the Jewish Middle Ages and for most Jews in the modern world. In spite of the great changes that were to take place in Jewish life and the new interpretations and philosophical expositions of Jewish doctrine that were to develop, the shape and substance of Judaism had already been determined.

MEDIEVAL
TIMES

In the history of Western civilization the term Middle Ages is usually used to refer to the period between the sixth and twelfth centuries, when the disintegration of the Roman Empire and the barbarian invasions brought about an eclipse of learning and the loss of the Greek heritage to the Christian world. The medieval period in Jewish history, however, is not synonymous with the Middle Ages in world history. While no agreement exists among historians as to what the term should indicate, medieval Jewish history is generally said to begin with the restrictions on Jewish rights under Constantine the Great in the fourth century, and to extend until the emancipation of the Jew in France at the end of the eighteenth century.[1] In spite of the restrictions which prevailed, Jewish life during this long period, unlike the so-called "Dark Ages," is a record of continuing cultural creativity.

From the middle of the seventh century, Jewish life centered in the Muslim lands, first in Babylonia and then in Spain, where Jews were highly integrated into their environment and enjoyed good relations with their neighbors. While all non-Muslims who were adherents of a revealed religion had to pay a head tax, hostile legislation was passed only occasionally and was only sporadically enforced. The Muslim era marked for the Jew, particularly in Spain, a flowering of Jewish literature which was so rich and diverse in nature as to be described as a "Golden Age." A long series of outstanding figures arose between the tenth and twelfth centuries which, in Babylonia, included Saadia Gaon and, in Spain, Hasdai ibn Shaprut (915-970), court physician and later minister for foreign affairs to Caliph Abd-ar-Rahman as well as patron of Jewish learning, Samuel ibn Nagdela (993-1063), poet, scholar, and statesman, Solomon ibn Gabirol (1021-1056), philosopher and poet, whose poems have enriched our synagogue liturgy, Abraham ibn Ezra (1092-1167), versatile Bible commentator, philosopher, and poet, Judah Halevi, the greatest poet of the entire Middle Ages, and Moses

Maimonides, the most outstanding among all medieval Jewish personalities.

The same era saw the beginnings of Jewish settlements north of the Alps and the Pyrenees in the area of present-day France and Germany. Here Jews lived under a Christian civilization and a feudal society where, though the restrictions were far more severe than in Spain, they lived peacefully with their Christian neighbors. At the beginning of the eleventh century, this area witnessed the development of Jewish scholarship under Rabbenu Gershom and Rashi, a development which was not as varied or colorful as in Muslim lands and was limited primarily to the study of Bible and Talmud, but which nonetheless represented a genuine contribution to Jewish learning.

The Crusades radically altered the position of the Jew in Europe, and ushered in a span of four bloody centuries in which the Church sought to isolate, humiliate and harass the Jew. With the recapture of Spain by the Christians, all of Europe came under the shadow of a single spiritual rule. The "black death," the massacres of 1391, and expulsions from most of the countries of Europe made this a period of trial and tragedy for Jews. Inevitably the literature produced during this period lacked the broad sweep and variety of interest of that of the more tolerant Muslim period. The contribution of Franco-German scholarship was mainly in the field of rabbinic law, mysticism, and pietistic literature.[2]

The expulsion of the Jews from Spain in 1492 led to the rise of new centers of Jewish life in North Africa, Palestine (particularly in Safed), and in Holland. But the outstanding concentration of Jews during the sixteenth and seventeenth centuries was in Poland and Lithuania, which became the cultural center for European Jewry. It was in Eastern Europe that *Hasidism*, with its emotional approach to Judaism, emerged under the leadership of the Baal Shem Tov. Talmudic learning also flourished; at first it was narrow in scope but under the Gaon of Vilna it became broader and more scholarly in approach.

From this period of what may be called the Jewish Middle Ages we have selected three representatives from the Muslim era, one from the Franco-German center, one from Christian Spain and two from East Europe of the eighteenth century. While the Baal Shem

Tov and the Vilna Gaon are sometimes included in the modern period of Jewish history, to us they represent the last distinguished Jewish personalities who lived in closed Jewish communities subject to all the restrictions and disabilities that were characteristic of the Jewish Middle Ages in Christian Europe.

We begin with the three figures who lived in Muslim lands— Saadia, Halevi, and Maimonides—who represent a new type of Jewish personality, the theologian or philosopher. While we do not have the same awe and reverence for them as for the biblical or Talmudic figures, their works have taken a place among the classics of our people, and the anniversaries of their deaths and births have been commemorated in recent decades throughout the Jewish world.*

Though we know them primarily as philosophers, all three were men of wide interests. Saadia was a grammarian, commentator, exegete, and even a poet of sorts; Halevi was, of course, a lyric poet of high excellence; and Maimonides was a master in almost all fields of Jewish knowledge as well as in science and medicine. But it was their philosophical approach to Judaism which permeated all their writings and helped to shape their thought.

How did it come about that the Muslim era produced so many Jewish philosophers? Why is it that Greek philosophy, which in Hellenistic times made so little impact on the sages, should now exert such a great influence on Talmudic and Bible scholars? What was the character of the philosophical movement of which Saadia, Halevi, and Maimonides were such eminent examples?

Medieval Jewish philosophy represents the attempt of the Jew in the Muslim world to meet the intellectual and cultural challenges of his environment. In the days of the Bible and Talmud, Jews lived in a self-contained society both in Palestine and Babylonia. Their cultural activity was largely devoted to the cultivation of Jewish law. While the Books of Job and Ecclesiastes dealt with philosophical questions and the *Aggadic* portions of the Talmud contain some speculations about man and the universe, the views expressed were not arranged in any logical sequence, and can by no means be said to form a systematic Jewish philosophy. In the classical era of Ju-

* The thousandth anniversary of the death of Saadia was commemorated in 1942, the eight hundredth anniversary of the birth of Maimonides in 1935, and the seven hundred and fiftieth anniversary of his death in 1955.

daism (except for the brief interval in Hellenistic Alexandria) there were few intellectual challenges from the outside world, and no attacks on Jewish doctrines for the Jew to withstand. Jews took their concepts and beliefs for granted and felt no need to systematize them in logical fashion or interpret them to the outside world.[3]

With the rise to power of the Muslims, the historical situation changed completely. Within less than a century after the death of Mohammed (632), the Arabs had conquered the Middle East, including Syria, Palestine, and Egypt, and had swept on to take North Africa and almost the entire Spanish peninsula. Soon the peoples in the vast area which stretched from Persia to Spain were using Arabic as the common language of learning and literature, and large cities like Baghdad, Damascus, Cairo, and Cordova became flourishing centers of culture and enlightenment. The Muslims, who before the conquests, had been backward in most fields, now discovered the great classics of Greek science and philosophy, which had been preserved (in Syriac translations) by Christian scholars in Syria. Eagerly the Caliphs arranged for these books to be translated into Arabic; in Baghdad a "House of Wisdom" or scientific academy was set up where a corps of translators were kept busy producing Arabic versions of the Greek classics. By the middle of the ninth century the works of Hippocrates, Ptolemy, Galen, and most of the classic Greek texts in mathematics, astronomy, and medicine had been translated. Gradually the works of Plato, Aristotle, and the Neoplatonists became available, though it was not until the eleventh and twelfth centuries that all the works of Aristotle reached the intellectuals of Muslim countries. As a result, an intellectual awakening took place among the peoples under Arab hegemony and tremendous cultural activity began on every front. By the tenth century a multitude of scientists, historians, and scholars were compiling dictionaries, anthologies, and other summaries of existing knowledge. The Greek classics with their emphasis on reason and independent rational reflection had a tremendous effect on the Muslims, who between the tenth and twelfth centuries produced a number of outstanding philosophical thinkers, among them al Farabi, Avicenna, and Averroes, who concerned themselves with reconciling the teachings of the Koran with Greek thought.[4]

Jews too felt the impact of the Greek spirit and the new emphasis on free rational inquiry. In Baghdad, philosophical circles existed
which "were made up of agnostics, parsees, materialists, atheists, and
Jews" as well as Muslims of all sects.[5] Throughout the Caliphate
there were many meeting places where Jews could join members of
other religious faiths in discussing their respective theological dogmas in an objective, rational manner. In this congenial atmosphere,
where accepted beliefs and practices were questioned, Jews in Baghdad, Cairo, or Cordova began to feel the need, as their forebears had
done in Hellenistic Alexandria, to reconcile their beliefs and practices with the postulates of reason derived from the works of the
Greek thinkers. The impact of Greek philosophy on the Jews in
Muslim lands was therefore more direct and widespread than it had
been in Alexandria. Thus the Muslim philosophers subscribed to a
monotheistic belief in many ways similar to Judaism, while the Jews
in Philo's time had learned Greek philosophy from pagan thinkers
with whom they had less in common. Moreover, the problems which
confronted Arabic religious thinkers and which made it difficult for
them to reconcile the teachings of the Greek philosophers with the
dogmas of Mohammedanism also applied to Jews. Both the Jew
and the Muslim were troubled by questions of creation, divine providence, freedom of will, and descriptions of the deity in human terms
(anthropomorphisms).

For Jews there was also a need to reply to Arab controversialists
who challenged the authenticity of their revelation, ridiculed Jewish
doctrines, or tried to demonstrate the inferiority of the Jewish to
Muslim tradition. Pointing to the elaborate descriptions of God in
human terms found in the *Aggadic* portions of the Talmud, some
Muslims even accused Jews of lacking a purely monotheistic faith.[6]

To these challenges from without must be added the criticisms
which came from the Karaites, a sect within Judaism which emerged
in eighth-century Babylon. According to tradition, the sect was
founded by Anan ben David, an embittered scholar who broke with
rabbinic authority when he was not appointed to the Gaonate.
Actually, Anan was probably the most important of a group of dis-
senters who repudiated the teachings of the Talmud and rebelled
against the authority of the rabbis. The Karaites, like some of the

Muslim polemicists, also reproached rabbinic Judaism for its anthropomorphic expressions about God and prided themselves on the purity of their own conception. Since they attempted to establish a traditionless Judaism based on pure Scripture, and approached the Bible in a rational spirit, they also constituted a threat to historic Jewish beliefs.[7]

The effect of these challenges and criticisms was to create doubts and uncertainties in the minds of many intelligent Jews; the inner conflicts and turmoil which resulted made a reexamination of the basic doctrines of Judaism essential. The rationality of such beliefs as divine providence, freedom of will, immortality and other cherished doctrines had to be demonstrated, and the compatibility of the Bible with reason established. There were instances where Jews rebelled and became skeptics or outright atheists, but for the most part what they wanted was guidance and help in reconciling their ancestral faith with contemporary thought.

The Jewish philosophical movement which emerged in the Judeo-Islamic age represents the effort of medieval Jewish thinkers to cope with the perplexities of their time and to defend the traditional faith of Judaism. They composed their works not so much because of an interest in purely theoretical speculation but as an attempt to justify Judaism for Jews who were wavering in their faith. For the most part, they were not written for the uneducated masses or as missionizing attacks on other creeds, but for the articulate and intellectual Jews who were affected by the rationalism of the age. The theologians and philosophers who arose from the tenth to twelfth centuries, including Saadia, Halevi, and Maimonides, represent another type of Jewish personality—Jewish theologians who stood in the mainstream of Jewish tradition, deeply rooted in Jewish sources, and yet who had absorbed the best in Muslim and Greek thought. Their works are the first attempts to sum up the basic tenets of Judaism and to present them systematically for the Jews of their generation. These men also served as living examples that it is possible for the Jew to draw on the philosophy and science of the day and yet remain true to the tradition of his fathers. Alongside the prophets and Talmudic sages the medieval Jewish philosophers deserve a place among the heroes of Israel.

Saadia Gaon

6 . Saadia Gaon

[882-942]

TRUDE WEISS-ROSMARIN

W H E N Saadia Gaon,* "the father of Jewish philosophy," taught and wrote in Egypt and Babylonia more than a millennium ago, Judaism was faced with challenges not unlike those confronting our own generation. Greek philosophy in Arabic garb seemed more attractive to many young Jews than the culture of their own people. They abandoned themselves to the secular culture of their time in the same manner as do many contemporary Jews who have not had the benefit of a Jewish education. The climate of urban sophistication in Saadia's time, so radically different from the rural pietism of the world of Rabbi Akiba, was very appealing.

As a result, Jews of the tenth century, whose spiritual and physical center of gravity was still in Babylonia, were torn between loyalty to the traditions of their fathers and the lure of religious reforms and new philosophical systems. The religious challenge was represented by the Karaite sect, who accepted a rigidly literal interpretation of the Written Law in the Five Books of the Bible. The philosophical challenge was contained in the ascendancy of Greek philosophy, with Arabic overtones, which aroused doubts in the hearts of many Jews concerning the trustworthiness of the religious teachings of Judaism.

---

* Gaon literally means "eminence," "excellency"; it was the title conferred on presidents of the Babylonian Talmud academies that flourished from about the end of the sixth century to the eleventh century, and later on eminent scholars in Eastern Europe as well—e.g., Vilna Gaon.

Lasting Contributions

In Saadia's time, these twin challenges of Karaism and of rationalistic philosophy wrought such havoc and confusion in the Jewish world that the very survival of traditional Judaism depended upon their defeat or neutralization. Fully conscious of the fact that the Jews of his generation stood at a crucial crossroad, Saadia was virtually the only scholar of his time to take effective steps to safeguard Judaism against the inroads of the Karaites while defending it against the attacks of the philosophers and rationalists. He dedicated his life to strengthening and justifying Judaism in all its aspects and ramifications. This is his immortal achievement and lasting contribution.

Saadia sensed that the best way to prove the validity of Judaism's traditional teachings was by applying the methods of science and philosophy. But the most elementary and basic aids for such a procedure were still lacking. There were no dictionaries, no grammars, no commentaries on the Bible; there was no compendium defining the tenets of Judaism within the framework of a philosophy of life. In short, while earlier Jewish scholars had concentrated on the Law and produced the Talmud, they had not developed the tools necessary for linguistic analysis and philosophic speculation.

Saadia's task, therefore, was to provide some of these indispensable tools. He compiled a Hebrew dictionary and wrote the *Book of Language*, which established the principles of Hebrew grammar. Saadia's lifelong interest in philology was stimulated and nourished by the lively concern with everything pertaining to language, speech, and style of the Muslim majority civilization in which he lived. Grammar and syntax was almost an obsession with early medieval Arab philologists. Saadia's fascination with language must be viewed against the background of the vast production of Arabic linguistic tracts during this period. In due course, he translated the Bible into Arabic and supplied it with a commentary which, besides clarifying philological difficulties, also dwelled on the religious, historical, and philosophical implications of the text. He was a master of Talmudic interpretation, and his decisions in this area were of far-reaching significance. Finally, and most important, he was the first thinker to evolve a systematic philosophy of Judaism. Thus Saadia is primarily known today as a "religious philosopher." This one-sided view of the great Gaon, however, is totally inadequate.

Saadia's works are so numerous that the life spans of several ingenious scholars might have been consumed in compiling them. Yet he died at the relatively young age of sixty. His achievements seem even more remarkable when we remember that the last two decades of his life were largely taken up by his official duties as head of the Talmud academy at Sura, and that his strength and stamina were drained in combatting the enmity he encountered among some of his associates who, overshadowed by his greatness, tried to break his spirit and morale.

Training in Egypt

Saadia, the son of Joseph, was born in 882 in Dilaz, a village of the district of Fayyum in Upper Egypt. Little is known of his youth and education, and except for the name of one of his teachers, the Muslim historian Al-Mas'udi, we have no record of how or where he acquired the background that fitted him for his later tasks.

Yet Saadia did not grow up in an intellectual and spiritual void. From the middle of the seventh century, Hebrew literature and Talmudic scholarship had been well represented among the Jews of Egypt. Hebrew poets specializing in the composition of prayers were active in Saadia's native province of Fayyum. The fame of the first Jewish philosopher-physician of the Middle Ages, Isaac Israeli (c. 852-950), had spread widely through the land. The Bible was diligently studied in accordance with new methods developed by the school of the Massoretes in Tiberias as well as the heretical interpretations of the Karaite sect. Jewish life in the Egypt of Saadia's youth was therefore variegated and influenced by many trends and tendencies, and his writings indicate that he drank to the full from all the sources of knowledge within his reach.

Saadia's works prove eloquently that his religious and secular training were thorough and comprehensive. He mastered the entire range of Jewish literature and absorbed, no less intensively, the philosophical and scientific writings of the Muslim scholars. Saadia did not know Greek and, like most contemporary students of Greek philosophy, he read the Greek classics in the

Arabic vernacular. Likewise, he resorted to Arabic works in acquiring the scientific, astronomical, and geographical knowledge which was part of a higher liberal course of education about the turn of the tenth century, when he was in his teens.

Campaign Against the Karaites

Unlike Rabbi Akiba, who is said to have been completely untutored until he was forty, Saadia was a precocious youth, for he was only twenty when he completed his first work, the Hebrew dictionary and rhyming lexicon, *Agron*. At the same time he began his militant campaign against the Karaites, who enthroned the Bible as the sole authority in Jewish life. Since Anan ben David had founded the sect, the Karaites had gained many adherents. Their success was undoubtedly due to the fact that the biblical Judaism they preached was simpler in theory and practice than Talmudic Judaism which, in addition to the biblical laws, made binding the accumulation of laws and teachings evolved during a thousand years of analysis of every word and letter in the Torah.

Saadia was convinced that biblical Judaism alone would lead to stagnation because it precluded all possibilities of growth by insisting on the unchanging character and literal meaning of biblical law. The Karaites rejected the "fence about the Torah" that had been carefully built and guarded by the teachers of the Mishnah and of the Jerusalem and Babylonian Talmuds. In addition to his firm faith in the divine authority of Talmudic law, Saadia staunchly believed that interpretation and reinterpretation of Scriptures were the only way to retain the vitality of an ancient heritage of religious laws.

Although Karaism was less progressive than rabbinic Judaism, its literature and laws were much easier to master. All a Karaite had to know was the Bible, and all he had to observe was biblical law. His intellectual equipment and religious observance were thus limited, and lacked the richness of the laws, customs, and knowledge that were the legacy of centuries of Jewish scholars. As a result, the Karaite teachers attracted large numbers of Jews who were enticed by the prospect of being released from the "yoke" of Talmudic law.

Saadia was the first to recognize the full implications of

Karaism's threat to rabbinic Judaism. And he was also the first to challenge the theorists and proponents of Karaite doctrines in the arena of intellectual combat. Saadia was a born fighter for the truth as he recognized it, and he possessed the intellectual force, the incisiveness of mind, and the gift of logical argument that made him a formidable opponent.

Saadia embarked upon his career, at the age of twenty-three, as the champion of rabbinic Judaism with his *Refutation of Anan*, aimed at the founder of Karaism. In this as well as his other polemical writings directed against the Karaites, Saadia exposed the faultiness and inadequacy of their reasoning. Unfortunately, except for a few fragments, these writings have not been preserved. They are known from references and quotations contained in Saadia's other works or in the writings of some of his contemporaries. This loss, in a sense, is a tribute to the effectiveness of his campaign against the Karaites. Once his purpose was attained and Karaism was defeated as an influence in Jewish life, these writings became irrelevant and were allowed to disappear, for the Jews of past ages treasured only those books possessing significance for all generations.

As Saadia grew in stature, he was eager to make contact with other Jewish communities. He left his native Egypt in 915 and started on a pilgrimage through the centers of Jewish learning in Syria, Palestine, and Mesopotamia, sojourning for considerable lengths of time in Aleppo and Baghdad. From a letter written by Saadia to three of his pupils in Egypt, we learn that he left behind "a wife and children" as well as numerous disciples and admirers.

Controversy over Calendar

Saadia did not fail to impress the scholars whom he met on his travels with his brilliance and unique gifts of mind. Upon settling in Sura, he soon became a respected personality among the teachers of the famous Babylonian academy. His fame spread throughout the Jewish world, and his opinions were eagerly sought.

On one occasion, he was asked to give his opinion on a controversy concerning the Jewish calendar which had arisen between the Gaonim of Babylonia and Ben Meir, an eminent

Palestinian Talmudist. The controversy revolved about the date on which Passover was to fall in the Jewish year 4681, which corresponded to 921 of the general calendar. Ben Meir declared that Passover should be celebrated two days earlier than calculated by the calendar of the Babylonian scholars, and despite Saadia's remonstrations he clung tenaciously to this view. The Gaonim reacted by dispatching circulars and proclamations to all Jewish communities warning them against accepting Ben Meir's calendar. Nevertheless, most Palestinian and some Babylonian communities followed Ben Meir in celebrating Passover two days earlier.

A schism threatened to divide Jewry if there was no uniformity in the calendar and no acknowledged authority to fix it. No longer would Jewish communities everywhere observe the festivals on the same days. No longer would Jews going up from Babylonia to the Holy Land feel that they had returned "home." Keenly aware of this danger, Saadia put himself at the disposal of the Babylonian Gaonim to destroy Ben Meir's influence and restore unity in Israel. Upon the request of the sages, he wrote (in 922) the *Sefer Ha-Zikkaron* (the *Book of Memory*) in which he refuted Ben Meir so effectively, thanks to his grasp of the mathematical and astronomical details involved, that nothing more was heard of the latter's claims. The Babylonian scholars retained their jurisdiction. This important work is no longer extant, and only a fragment of it has been discovered; but it is thanks to it that Saadia is credited with helping to stabilize the Jewish calendar in its present form.

Gaon of Sura Academy

Saadia's victory over Ben Meir firmly established his reputation; his service in preserving the authority of Babylonian Jewry was rewarded, in 928, with his appointment as Gaon or president of the famed Talmud academy at Sura. In that position he was the official spiritual leader of Babylonian Jewry. Under Persian as well as Muslim sovereignty, the Jews of Babylonia enjoyed a large measure of autonomy. They were regarded as a national minority and had their own civil government. Their highest civil authority was the Exilarch, appointed by the king to rule the Jewish dispersion and be responsible for keeping law and order, raising taxes, and representing them in all official matters. Tracing their lineage to King David, the Exilarchs conducted themselves in a royal manner, maintaining a lavish court, and distributing largesse and favors. Eventually, they attempted to extend their sway over the religious life of the Jews as well. The sages of the Talmud academies, however, were frequently at odds with the "Princes of the Exile," for the Exilarchs often arrogated to themselves religious judicial authority which rightly belonged to the scholars.

In the course of time, the Sura academy, founded by the illustrious scholar Rav, early in the third century, had become the acknowledged spiritual fountainhead of Babylonian Jewry and its presidents the undisputed religious authorities. As a symbol of their position, the heads of the Sura and Pumpeditha academies held the title of Gaon (Excellency); yet, despite their superior scholarship and intellect, they had jurisdiction only in the sphere of religion, while in all other respects the Exilarch ruled supreme. Since Jewish civil law is part of the religious code, it was therefore inevitable that frequent clashes arose between the Exilarchs and the Gaonim.

When Saadia was appointed Gaon of Sura, the first "foreigner" ever to attain that office, it was tacitly understood by the Exilarch David ben Zakkai that the new Gaon would submit to his authority. In 930, two years after Saadia's elevation to the Gaonate, however, a breach occurred between him and David ben Zakkai which ultimately engulfed all of Babylonian Jewry in bitter antagonism and factional strife.

Strife with Exilarch

In a certain law suit, David ben Zakkai had rendered a decision which, if enacted, would have given him one-tenth of the large sum involved in the litigation. In order to make this decision legal, it had to be endorsed by the heads of the academies of Sura and Pumpeditha. When the document was brought to Saadia for his signature, he recognized at once the illegality of the Exilarch's decision and declined to endorse it. In the hope of avoiding a quarrel, he tactfully suggested that his senior colleague, the head of the Pumpeditha academy, be asked to sign first, expecting that he, too, would recognize the spurious char-

acter of the decision. Gaon Cohen Zedek of Pumpeditha, however, gave his signature without hesitation, and the document
was brought once more to Saadia for endorsement.

Instead of signing, Saadia now made his position clear and
pointed out the illegality of the Exilarch's decision. David ben
Zakkai, angered by the daring of the Gaon of Sura, sent his son
and heir Judah to obtain Saadia's signature. But the Gaon
adamantly dismissed the youth with the message: "Tell your
father that it is written in the Torah 'Ye shall not respect persons in judgment.' "

Again and again the Exilarch's son returned to Saadia, at first
pleading and then demanding that he sign. Finally, the young
man threatened to strike Saadia if he did not affix his signature.
In reply, Saadia ordered his servants to throw him out, and the
doors were locked behind him.

Infuriated, David ben Zakkai deposed Saadia, excommunicat-
ing him and appointing a successor as Gaon of Sura. Saadia, in
retaliation, excommunicated the Exilarch and named another
man to take his place. Now there were two Exilarchs and two
Gaonim, each with a considerable following, who warred bitterly against each other. After having appealed in vain to the
Caliph Al-Muktadir to support his position and oust Saadia,
David ben Zakkai and his adherents finally bribed the new and
corrupt Caliph Al-Kahir to pass an edict which deposed Saadia
as Gaon.

In 932, Saadia retired to Baghdad, where he devoted himself
to his studies and writing. During this period he composed his
great philosophical work, the *Book of Beliefs and Doctrines*,
and recorded his stormy experiences as Gaon of Sura in *The
Open Book*. The latter, unfortunately, has been preserved only
in fragmentary form.

Thus six years went by. But the people did not forget Saadia,
and the respect and honor in which he was generally held did
not diminish. On the other hand, David ben Zakkai was criticized and attacked for his conduct in the controversy with
Saadia, and finally agreed to a reconciliation. In a public ceremony, the two leaders were reconciled and maintained from
then on the most cordial and peaceful relations. When within a
period of less than a year (940-941) both David ben Zakkai and
his son and successor Judah died, Saadia took Judah's orphaned

son into his house to prepare him for the high office he was to occupy.

Saadia survived David ben Zakkai by only two years. He died on May 18, 942 (the 26th of *Iyar*, 4702).

Saadia's Philosophy of Judaism

Although not disdaining the more mundane tasks of philological scholarship, Saadia was a keen analytical thinker who was primarily interested in the multifaceted problems of Judaism and its survival. Like Rabbi Johanan ben Zakkai who, some eight centuries earlier, realized that the Temple had served its purpose and should be replaced by the House of Study, Saadia recognized that his time urgently called for a broadening of the scope and definition of Judaism. Saadia was the first thinker, therefore, to present a rationalism-oriented philosophy of Judaism that examined its truths and teachings in the light of reason. This does not mean that philosophical thought and reasoning are absent from the Bible and the Talmud. Such profoundly philosophical books as Ecclesiastes and Job and the hundreds upon hundreds of Talmudic and Midrashic inquiries into the purpose and meaning of the world, man, and the nature of God prove conclusively that what has been termed the Hebrew philosophical genius had been at work long before Saadia's time. Even in those biblical sections where one would least expect philosophical introspection there occur passages which, flash-like, reveal the depth of biblical thought.

Basing his proofs upon the Bible and the Talmud, Saadia defended Judaism and conclusively demonstrated that it was as mature and meaningful as Greek philosophy, which had so great an appeal to the intellectuals of the tenth century. In defending Jewish beliefs, Saadia also considered the difference between Judaism and the religions that stemmed from it—Christianity and Islam.

While some scholars regard Philo as the first great Jewish philosopher, the Alexandrian's writings were more on the order of philosophical allegories in which he sought to impart his concepts of truth and God in symbolic form. Isaac Israeli, Saadia's immediate predecessor in Egypt, has also been singled out for acclaim as a key figure in Jewish philosophy, but on the whole he did not go beyond the statement of isolated philosophical principles. It was left to Saadia to develop the first systematic philosophy of the Jewish religion. As "the father of Jewish philosophy," he pioneered in presenting its beliefs and teachings as a clear, precise, and unified system of thought.

Book of Beliefs and Doctrines

Saadia's *Book of Beliefs and Doctrines* is a milestone in the history of Jewish philosophy and literature. It was written out of his concern over the spiritual plight of many of his contemporaries. "In my time," he wrote, "I saw many believers clinging to wrong beliefs and false reasoning, while many unbelievers, boasting of their heresy and while caught in error, showed contempt for those striving for the truth. I saw men who were submerged in seas of doubt and covered by the waters of confusion, and there was no diver to raise them up from the depths and no swimmer to take hold of their hands and bring them ashore. Since God has given me some knowledge with which I might assist them and has endowed me with some ability that could be employed for their benefit, I felt it was my duty and obligation to help them and guide them toward the truth."

The "wrong beliefs and false reasoning" to which Saadia referred had resulted from the disturbing impact of philosophy upon many intellectuals of his time who found it difficult to reconcile faith with reason. The predicament of Saadia's contemporaries was similar to that of modern Jews who see an apparent contradiction between the beliefs of Judaism and the teachings of science. To the people of the tenth century, as to many Jews of today, an unbridgeable chasm seemed to separate Judaism and reason. They felt that a choice had to be made between the two.

Saadia understood the dilemma of the believing Jew faced by the double challenge of philosophy and science. Asserting that the teachings and commandments of Judaism are not in conflict with reason and logic, but are actually based upon them, he defined faith as "the knowledge which results from the contemplation of the discernible and comprehensible." He insisted that as a source of knowledge the authentic tradition of Judaism is as reliable as reason.

Indeed, Saadia saw no contradiction between knowledge deduced by reason and that taught by tradition as the basis of religious faith. Each, he maintained, has the same purpose—to attain truth. While the intellectual arrives at the truth by philosophical reasoning, the majority of people require Scriptural revelation to know what is true, good, and right. God bestowed the Torah upon mankind so that all men, even those not trained in philosophy, could share in the basic tenets of reason. Saadia hoped that the *Book of Beliefs and Doctrines,* which demonstrates the harmony of faith and reason in Judaism, would "strengthen the faith of the believer and disperse the doubts of the skeptic so that he who believes solely in the strength of tradition will be guided by it to a belief based upon philosophical reasoning and understanding."

After proving, in his Introduction to the *Book of Beliefs and Doctrines,* the principal areas of agreement between Judaism and philosophy, and after clarifying the definitions of faith, reason, and the paths by which knowledge is attained, Saadia proceeded to examine specific beliefs challenged by philosophy. In considering the problem of creation, a burning issue with all medieval Jewish philosophers, Saadia upheld the traditional Jewish belief that God created the universe "out of nothing" (*creatio ex nihilo*), which was rejected by those who adhered to the Aristotelian thesis of the eternity of original matter. Saadia argued that there was a beginning in time. All that exists was once nonexistent; it was created by God, who, after the initial act of creating matter, commanded the form and manner of all that exists.

Saadia was acquainted with all that science and philosophy had to offer in his day. But while scientists and philosophers accepted the fact that knowledge goes no further than what the intellect can discover, Saadia the believer felt certain that there was another type of knowledge which goes beyond the confines set by the intellect: religious knowledge imparted by God's revelation.

From the fact of creation, Saadia went on to prove the logical necessity of the existence of God. Since there is no spontaneous creation in nature, everything that exists has a source and origin. Thus, a creative force, God, must have called the universe into being.

Since biblical times, Jewish teachers had been wrestling with the problem of defining God, only to realize that His true nature and essence cannot be fathomed by the limited intelligence of men. Saadia pioneered in subjecting the God idea to a systematic philosophical inquiry. He was not the first Jewish teacher, however, to express the conviction that all statements about God are, in the final analysis, mere guesswork. God is unknowable and to understand His being requires faculties transcending those of man. Yedaya Bedarasi, the thirteenth-century Hebrew poet, proclaimed, not without despair: "If I could understand Him, I would be He!"

Saadia was keenly aware of this dilemma and understood its inevitability. He knew well that the authors of the Bible could not but describe God as they did: "in the language of man," that is, by ascribing human faculties, actions, and feelings to God. Saadia demanded, however, that we face this dilemma courageously and with intellectual honesty. We must accept the fact that the sacred texts do not mean what their words signify, for "the Torah speaks in the language of men." It resorts to anthropomorphisms, figures of speech and allegory which attempt to describe the indescribable and express the ineffable.

The refutation of God's corporeality as expressed "in the language of man" is the principal aim of the entire *Book of Beliefs and Doctrines* as well as other of Saadia's works. His conception of God was consistently spiritual, cleansed of every vestige of the tendency to view God as possessing attributes and characteristics. He constantly reiterated that God is essentially indefinable, that man's limited intelligence cannot encompass the infinity and actual nature of God. Admitting that this was a source of religious doubt and despair, Saadia concluded that we can never hope to know anything about God beyond the fact that He is one and unique, that He represents the essence of all power, knowledge, and life.

The next step in Saadia's investigation was to ascertain the purpose of creation; he assumed that God did not create blindly and he maintained that that purpose is to bestow happiness upon all the world's creatures, especially upon man, the "crown of creation." Life, Saadia felt, is the gift of God, and it is man's duty to be grateful, to savor and appreciate the remarkable bounty of this gift.

But how is man to live so that he can enjoy the gift of God in gratitude? Saadia explained that a discipline of commandments and prohibitions is necessary for man's self-realization, by means of which he can attain "complete happiness and perfect felicity" in this world. God therefore gave His Torah to mankind —to all of mankind and not only to the Jews—as a trustworthy guide to the good life. While Saadia was emphatic concerning the special place of Israel as the recipient of the Torah, he also stressed that all men are called upon to observe its ethical commandments. It is characteristic of his universalism that he maintained that the Torah was intended for all mankind, and not merely for Jews. Indeed, he states in a much-quoted dictum that "our nation, the children of Israel, is a nation only by virtue of its laws." But this does not change the fact that Jews are bidden to look forward to the days of the Messiah as the time when, in keeping with the promises of the prophets, the earth would be "full of the knowledge of the Lord."

To Saadia, the Torah was revealed reason, and he illustrated with great acumen the rational nature of its contents. He boldly asserted that anything that cannot stand up under the light of reason need not be believed or accepted as historical truth. He deflated the importance of miracles as essential planks of Jewish belief; they merely add strength and confirmation to belief but they cannot establish and substantiate it. As a believing Jew, Saadia was convinced that God can do everything, but he also believed that it is inconceivable and impossible that God will act contrary to reason. The miracles, therefore, which accompanied the Exodus, the Sinaitic revelation, and the prophetic messages have no intrinsic value. The Bible admits that some of these miracles can also be produced by magic. Even the belief in Moses as "the master of the prophets" does not rest on the miracles he performed. "The basis of our belief in Moses and all the other prophets is found in the rightful commandments they imposed on us." Saadia further insisted that all the laws commanded in the Torah are rationally justified, even when our limited human intelligence cannot discern the reasons and motivations of some of the commandments.

Saadia interprets biblical passages in accordance with his rationalistic convictions. He strips revelation and prophecy, the media of the proclamation of the divine commandments and prohibitions, of virtually all vestiges of supernaturalism. This does not detract in any way from the validity of the Torah—on the contrary. The prophets were in all respects like all other men, except that "God conferred a special gift upon them." While distinguishing between revelational and rational commandments, Saadia maintained that reason is the decisive motivation of the Law, even of the revelational commandments which are commanded without the qualification of motives and reasons. Saadia, though a confirmed rationalist, did not make light of the emotional elements of belief. He wanted, however, to teach his fellow-Jews to believe with intelligence and to accept his own religious conviction that "miracles cannot prove what is impossible."

The Torah, Saadia believed, is to be obeyed with understanding. Man, endowed with free will by his creator, is entirely free to obey or disobey its commandments, for there would be no justification for reward and punishment if man's will and decision were not his own. He was the first philosopher to prove systematically that Judaism is uncompromisingly committed to belief in freedom of the human will. The very fact that the Torah speaks of reward and punishment is an indication that man is free to choose between good and evil. In keeping with the Talmudic dictum, "Everything is foreseen, yet freedom is granted," Saadia stated that God's omniscience does not compel man to act either in keeping with or contrary to the commandment; while God knows how man will act in any given situation, this foreknowledge does not determine the action itself.

Well aware of the fact that the righteous often suffer and the wicked prosper, Saadia "justified" God's ways by arguing that goodness is its own reward, even as wickedness is its own penalty, as is stated in the *Ethics of the Fathers:* "The reward of the *mitzvah* is the *mitzvah*, and the punishment of sin is sin." Although God's justice is inscrutable, we know on the strength of Talmudic statements that in this world man is "paid" according to the minority of his actions so that in life eternal he can be "paid" in accordance with the bulk of his deeds. Since even the most righteous are not without sin, he continued, on the strength of Talmudic teachings, even as the most wicked are not without some redeeming merit, the righteous are punished for their few sins in this world so that they may enjoy lasting bliss in the world-to-come. The sinners, on the other hand, are rewarded for their few good deeds in this world so that, in the hereafter, they can be made to bear the full brunt of their transgressions.

Saadia agreed that divine justice makes it imperative that Israel be compensated for its martyrdom in the service of the Torah. Therefore, in the *Book of Beliefs and Doctrines*, he attempted to prove that, although "the righteous of all peoples will share in the world-to-come," the Messianic age preceding that day will be exclusively reserved for the pious among the Jews as a special compensation and reward for all that they had suffered.

From a philosophical point of view, Saadia's concept of the world-to-come is the weakest part of his book. In his beliefs about life after death, he was typical of his time in anticipating an afterworld where concrete rewards and punishments were meted out and where the body was physically resurrected.

Since the aim of Jewish philosophy has always been the improvement of man's ethical conduct—to enable him to know how to do good and to understand why good must be pursued and evil shunned—Saadia concluded his *magnum opus* with a chapter on "What Is the Best Conduct for Man in This World?" This final section points out ways of enjoying life within the bounds of reason and the teachings of the Torah.

What Saadia delineates is a realistic ethics—a blueprint for conduct which takes cognizance also of man's creatureliness, his physical needs and wants. He opposed abstinence, asceticism, and celibacy as unnatural and as hindrances to the practice of genuine piety. He recommended the reasonable and sanctioned enjoyment of food, drink, sex, a comfortable home, and suitable clothing. The body and its needs must be honored, but they should not be wantonly indulged. A sane middle course should be adopted, along the lines recommended by the Jewish sages as well as by Aristotle's "golden mean." Even piety and worship must not be overdone. One should trust in God, but one should also remember that God does not provide miraculously for men's needs. He has appointed ways and means how to earn our livelihood.

To Saadia, as to the sages of the Talmud, this world was but the antechamber of the world-to-come. But this did not lead him to derogate the present world; it led him, however, to view human strivings and endeavors from the viewpoint of eternity.

He held that men are possessed of the love of life and honor because it gives them a foretaste of the rewards of the world-to-come. The essence of Saadia's regimen for the good and happy life is balance, harmony, and moderation.

Saadia's Legacy

In some areas, Saadia remained the son of his age and the heir of its misconceptions and errors. His efforts as lexicographer, philologist, and grammarian were subsequently eclipsed by the works of scholars who built on his foundations. His Arabic version of the Bible, his commentaries, and his polemical writings, being of no interest to Jews in Christian countries, fell into oblivion. Even his Talmudic decisions were permitted to gather dust, so that this aspect of his career is likewise frequently overlooked. But those contributions to Hebrew linguistics and lexicography, Bible translation and interpretation, Talmudic commentary, astronomy and calendation, as well as philosophy, reveal the universality of his mind and interests.

As an analytical thinker Saadia towered above his generation. He advocated views that were revolutionary in his time and which still ring with significance and truth today. And yet, at the same time, he sensed intuitively that the time would come when his own ideas would be in need of the corrective touch of interpretation. In his Introduction to the *Book of Beliefs and Doctrines*, he therefore addressed himself to future scholars in the following manner:

> In the name of God, the Creator of the Universe, I implore the scholar who may read this book to correct any mistake he will find and amend any obscurity of expression. He should not feel restrained because this is not his book, or because I anticipated him in shedding light on subjects which were not clear to him. For the wise care tenderly for wisdom and feel for it as members of the same family are attached to one another.

Saadia was aware that if his ideas were to live on, they would need the tender and understanding attention of those who "say unto wisdom: thou art my sister." Because he introduced reason into the interpretation of Judaism, he stands preeminent as the first in a long line of Jewish scholars to give substance to the conviction that the Torah is *torat hayyim*—the Torah of Life; while regulating life, it is also ready to be molded by life, which is ongoing and dynamic.

Saadia's genius as an interpreter of the Scriptures remains paramount. More than two hundred years after his death, Maimonides wrote: "If not for our master, Saadia Gaon, Torah would have been forgotten in Israel." Whereas Saadia, as the first Jewish philosopher of the Middle Ages, had had to coin his own terminology out of current Arabic philosophical terms, and to experiment with a new style, likewise an adaptation of the Arabic philosophical style then in vogue, which accounted in part for the heavy, labored language in which he wrote, replete with repetitious phrases and hackneyed proverbs, Maimonides had the advantage of being able to build on the foundation which the early Gaon had laid. Thus, Maimonides was able to apply—with new clarity of presentation and ordered structure —the high philosophical standards and insights that Saadia contributed to Judaism as a rational body of beliefs.

The Jews are the "eternal people" because rabbis, scholars, and philosophers—like Saadia—have taught that standing still— refusing to learn from the past or to fit the present for the future—is sinning against the letter and spirit of the Torah. It is Saadia's greatest achievement that he enabled Judaism to hold its place and retain its meaningfulness in a changing world.

FOR FURTHER READING

BARON, Salo, "Faith and Reason," in *A Social and Religious History of the Jews,* pp. 55–137 (Philadelphia: Jewish Publication Society, 1958).

COLLETTE-SIRAT, "Saadia," in *Jewish Thought in Middle Ages,* Chapter 1 (Cambridge: Cambridge University Press, 1985).

EFROS, Israel, "Saadia's General Ethical Theory and Its Relation to Sufism," in *Jewish Quarterly Review*—Seventy-Fifth Anniversary Volume, (Philadelphia: 1967).

FOX, Fox, "On the Rational Commandments in Saadia's Philosophy: A Re-Examination," in *Modern Jewish Ethics* (Columbus, OH: Ohio State University Press, 1975).

KLAPERMAN, L., *The Scholar-Fighter, The Story of Saadia Gaon* (Philadelphia: Jewish Publication Society, 1961). A popular presentation of his life and times.

"Saadia (Ben Joseph) Gaon," in *Encyclopedia Judaica* (Jerusalem: 1972). Scholarly study of manifold achievements.

Judah Halevi

7 . *Judah Halevi*

[*c.1086-1145*]

JACOB S. MINKIN

J U D A H ben Samuel Halevi—or Abul Hasan ibn Alawi, as he was called in Arabic—belonged to that unique period of Jewish history in Spain known as the "Golden Age." He was the greatest Hebrew poet of his time, a man who captured the heart and imagination of the Jewish people. The historian Graetz reflected the affectionate esteem that Jews bear him: "To describe him fully, one would have to borrow from poetry her richest colors and her sweetest song."

There were many strings to Judah Halevi's lyre, and he played upon them with consummate grace and beauty. He was a prodigious creator of songs for the synagogue, and his liturgical pieces are chanted to this day in congregations throughout the world. He wrote of love, wine, friendship, and nature, but it was the fate and future of the Jewish people which was his predominant motif—its pains and sorrows, its grief and suffering. Yet Halevi was not a gloomy poet; he was not a prophet of doom. His muse was capable of bright and lilting tunes, for Halevi loved life. His poetry is a harmony of tears and smiles, of despair and exaltation, of defeat and triumph. Though he lamented the fate of his people, he also envisioned its future with prophetic splendor. In the tradition of David, Halevi too was a "sweet singer" in Israel, the first Jewish national poet.

Student in Lucena

The events in Halevi's career are so shrouded in uncertainty that we can speak authoritatively only of his inner life as revealed in his writings. Not even the year of his birth has been definitely established, each scholar and historian suggesting a different date. It is generally accepted, however, that Halevi was born about 1086 in Toledo, capital of the Christian state of Castile. He was apparently a gifted child, favored by fortune in that he was brought up in an environment of affluence.

Of Judah's early education one can only surmise. The education among Jews living in Arabic Spain was widespread and liberal, not duplicated by Jews anywhere north of the Tagus. The school curriculum was, according to Samuel ibn Abas, a near contemporary, both intensive and extensive, covering Hebrew grammar and poetry, the Bible, Arabic, arithmetic, astronomy, and what was the fashion of the day—verse-making— which must have had a special appeal for young Halevi. These subjects were, of course, crowned by a thorough systematic study of the Talmud.

When, after his elementary education, Toledo had little more to offer, his father sent Judah, about the year 1100, to Lucena to study under the guidance of Isaac Alfasi, a rabbinic luminary famed for his Talmudic compendium. Lucena, a center of Jewish learning and culture, was nicknamed the "Jew town" because of its large Jewish population. Indeed, there is a legend that the city was founded by Jewish settlers. When Alfasi died, the famous academy he established was presided over by his brilliant disciple Joseph ibn Migash, the teacher of Joseph Maimon, and is mentioned in high terms of respect by Moses Maimonides in his commentary to *Avot*. Halevi later eulogized his teacher's demise in an elegy, which became the epitaph on Alfasi's tomb.

> On Sinai's day the mountains bowed before thee,
> Angels of the Lord came forth to greet thee.
> Upon the tablets of thy heart they wrote the Law,
> Upon thy head they placed the crown of glory.
> Even sages cannot learn to stand upright
> Unless they have sought for wisdom from thee.

The youthful student absorbed everything without effort or difficulty. He mastered the Hebrew language until his style became as precise, lucid, and supple as the language of the Bible. He explored the intricacies of the Talmud, and was so proficient in Arabic that he could vie with Muslim scholars in the subtlety of his expression in the language of the Koran. He also devoted himself to the physical sciences, penetrated the depths of metaphysics, and paid his tribute to Greco-Arabic philosophy, then the intellectual fashion, which he later did much to refute. Looking forward to an independent existence, he chose for his profession the "vanity of the medical science," as he called it.

At the Lucena academy, the young scholar-poet relieved the monotony of his studies with some swallow-like flights of song. He sang and lamented both on happy and mournful occasions. He gladdened the hearts of newlyweds and eased the pain of those who grieved over the loss of a loved one. If a distinguished rabbi was appointed to an important post, the ceremony was sure to include an ode by Halevi, and, on more solemn occasions, when Jews were bereaved by the passing of an outstanding scholar, the general feeling of loss found expression in Judah's tragic lyre. Rarely did anything happen in the life of the Jews in Southern Spain without the "silken magic" of Halevi's song.

For whose approval, naturally, would the young eagle of song be more anxious than for that of Moses ibn Ezra, a man of wealth, high position, and a great poet? The elder poet, whose lyre, because of a disappointed love affair, had turned sour and whose verses now lacked their former beauty and freshness, was gracious in acknowledging his young colleague's superior genius:

> How can a boy so young in years
> Bear such a weight of wisdom sage,
> Nor 'mongst the greybeards find his peers
> While still in the very bloom of age?

A close bond of friendship developed between the two men, and lasted until Ibn Ezra's death in 1139.

While yet in his teens, Halevi was surrounded by a brilliant company of friends and admirers who acclaimed his accomplishments and talent. His fame spread throughout Spain—from Toledo to Granada, from Seville to Cordova—and it required all his moral force not to succumb to the heady fragrance of the incense that was burned before him. Mainly through his influence—and that of a younger poet, Abraham ibn Ezra—the Castilian capital began to recover some of its lost prestige as a center of Jewish learning and culture.

Physician in Toledo

Not long after his return to Toledo, Halevi married. We know nothing of his wife beyond the references contained in the adoring poems he addressed to her and the moving lament he wrote when she died. He left us in complete ignorance of her name, family background, and appearance. We do know that she gave birth to a daughter, who did not marry Abraham ibn Ezra, according to the well-known legend, but who bore a son named Judah after his grandfather. While there are few allusions in Halevi's poems to his family life, he was obviously a loving parent, for he left in an ode written in later years on the eve of his departure for the Holy Land a poignant farewell to his daughter and grandson.

While in Toledo, fortune smiled upon Halevi. He occupied a high position as a scholar and poet, and he was greatly esteemed for his medical skill. But in a letter he wrote a friend, he confessed that the practice of his profession did not entirely satisfy him. He had little faith in his medicines, and incessantly prayed to God for deliverance from the profession for which he had little liking. In spite of his care for the sick and the dying, he was troubled in his soul for failing to maintain the ideals of his life. "I occupy myself in the hours which belong neither to the day nor to the night with the vanity of the medical science, although I am unable to heal. The city in which I live is large, the inhabitants are giants, but they are cruel rulers. Wherewith could I conciliate them better than by spending my days by curing their illness . . . I cry to God that He quickly send deliverance to me and give me freedom to enjoy rest, that I may repair to some place of living knowledge, to the fountains of wisdom." Moreover, real healing could come only from God.

My medicines are of Thee, whether good
Or evil, whether strong or weak.
It is Thou who shalt choose, not I.
Of Thy knowledge is the evil and the fair.
Not upon my power of healing I rely;
Only for Thine healing do I watch.

But his desire for financial independence compelled him to apply himself to the calling for which he had prepared. Although he often ridiculed and derided the medical profession, his thorough training in physical sciences, his skill, and, above all, his sympathy for the sick and suffering made him a good doctor with many more patients than he was able to attend.

Still, inwardly, Halevi was restless. A wanderlust possessed him. He was irked by his wearisome, humdrum existence. He who had it in his power to create the most refined and delicate poetry chafed under the prosaic demands of his daily life. Other poets had left their native soil and had come back enriched by what they saw, felt, and experienced, and so Halevi also set forth on his journey. History does not record the turmoil in his mind that made him leave his home and family and become a wanderer, nor do we know the concrete details of his travels, but his steps have been traced to Granada, Seville, Malaga, and Cadiz. Everywhere the Castilian poet was received with delight, for he was an amiable and jovial young man who did not despise the wine houses and was fond of jokes, puns, and riddles. Bright, witty and gay, he was the toast of every party, the center of every circle he visited.

Cordova

From town to town the roving poet wandered, bestowing gifts of verse upon young and old. He sang of the joys of life, the beauties of nature, the blushing maiden's cherry lips. It was in Cordova, the capital of Andalusia—the "bride of Andalusia," as the Arabs fondly called it—that Halevi's fledgling wings grew strong. Cordova, a city that encouraged the arts and prized poetry, was to Spain what Florence was to Italy during the Renaissance some five hundred years later—a city of commerce and learning, of scholars, thinkers, and poets, of magnificent parks and palaces, and vineyards bathed in sunshine. Roman buildings spoke of the early foreign occupation of the city, and Muslim mosques exhibited the exquisite beauty of Moorish architecture. Colleges and learned fraternities made the city a center of education and culture for students from distant Christian and Mohammedan lands. The banner capital of the western Arab empire also boasted of a flourishing Jewish community, with an intensive literary and spiritual activity, and great teachers and writers. It was in Cordova that the foundation of the post-biblical Hebrew revival was laid, where the Jewish spirit was fostered and preserved, and where the national Jewish consciousness was kept alive with loving devotion. Under Hasdai ibn Shaprut, prince and patron of Jewish learning, Talmudic scholarship had thrived and prospered to a point where the academy he founded rivaled the Babylonian schools.

Halevi responded enthusiastically to the sophisticated air of Cordova. In addition to being a seat of learning, the city was filled with an earthiness and an unbridled spirit of passion that admirably suited his poetic temperament. With all the rashness and impetuosity of youth, he wrote hundreds of poems, singing lustily of love, the juice of the grape, the gazelle-like eyes and raven locks of his beloved. His language was bold and forthright, his images steeped in the pleasures of the flesh. Amatory poems charged with fire and passion rippled from his magic lyre:

> Through the veil are seen two serpent-eyes
> A snake coils o'er your cheek—your hair;
> It stings the hearts of many from afar, my fair . . .

> Awake, O my love, from your sleep,
> Your face as it wakes let me view;
> If you dream someone kissing your lips,
> I'll interpret your dreaming for you.

When his older and more serious-minded friends rebuked him for frittering away his time and talent on trivialities, he replied:

> Shall one whose years scarce number twenty-four
> Turn foe to pleasure and drink wine no more?

After some years, however, Halevi, frustrated and disappointed, left Cordova and returned to Toledo, where, for a time, his lyre lay idle. The political atmosphere of his native land had changed, and conditions for Jews had considerably worsened. Alfonso VI, the Christian ruler of Castile, was a judicious monarch, and it had served his interests to be on friendly terms with the Jewish element of his country's mixed population. "The king of two creeds," as Alfonso was called, is said to have been so favorable to Jews that he refused to fight on Saturday for the sake of the Jewish contingent in his forces. But Pope Gregory VII, offended to see such "un-Christian" conduct on the part of a Christian king, had remonstrated with Alfonso, insisting on a sterner attitude toward the Jews. Under this goading by the Church, riots broke out and Jewish homes and shops were plundered. In one of these outbursts, Solomon ibn Farissol, a scholar and leader of the Jews of Castile, was brutally murdered.

Troubadour of God and Israel

These incidents shocked Halevi out of his youthful complacency. When he took up his pen again, he was no longer Abul Hasan, warbler of dainty ditties and erotic songs of love. He was transformed into Judah Halevi, the inimitable singer of Israel, at once the hope and conscience of his people, their seer and patriot-philosopher. In an exquisite transitional poem, he acknowledged the change that had come over him:

> Asleep in the bosom of youth how long wilt thou lie?
> Know that boyhood is like shaken tow,
> Shake thyself from the lure of time—as birds
> Shake themselves from the dewdrops of night.

The man who with his lilting songs and ballads had paid homage to the more frivolous moods of his era now sang of *orah hayyim l'ma'alah*, "the upward way of life." The gay and carefree poet of love became the troubadour of God and Israel.

Halevi sought God in his waking and sleeping:

> Longing, I sought Thy presence;
>   Lord, with my whole heart did I call and pray,
> And going out toward Thee,
>   I found Thee coming to me on the way.

His thirst for God knew no bounds. Without God, he felt, his soul would shrink and wither:

> When I remove from Thee, O God,
> I die whilst I live, but when
> Clinging to Thee I live in death.

Halevi enriched the synagogue liturgy with many sacred melodies. His religious poems, numbering more than three hundred and celebrating every season of the Jewish year, have been incorporated into almost all Sephardic liturgies; even the Karaites included some in their prayer book. His predecessor Solomon ibn Gabirol may rank as the foremost minstrel of the synagogue, for he adorned his maker with a "royal crown" which nearly a thousand years have not tarnished. But while Gabirol sang the song of the Lord with the voice of the philosopher and theologian, Halevi chanted with such emotion and faith that he touched a universal response in the hearts of Jews in every country.

His songs also adorn the religious life of the home no less than that of the synagogue. His Sabbath hymn is one of the most beautiful of his sacred songs.

On Friday doth my cup o'erflow,
What blissful rest the night shall know,
When, in thine arms, my toil and woe
Are all forgot, Sabbath my love!

It was for his patriotic songs, however—the laments over Zion's fallen glory, the visions of Zion's future might—that Judah Halevi is best remembered. He distilled in songs and prayers all that Jews had loved and lost, their severest defeats and most heartening triumphs. He was the steadfast lover of Zion, the mourner over her faded grandeur, the poet and prophet of her restored greatness. He wept over his people's misfortunes, and exulted in its envisioned rebirth.

Singer of Zion

Zion and Jerusalem were like a sacred flame in Halevi's heart, a consuming fever that throbbed inside him. He represented his people's love of home and freedom, and he could boldly proclaim to his fellow Jews: "*Ani kinor l'shiraikh*—I am a harp for thy song." He recalled the loveliness of Zion's youth, the glory and splendor of her prime when the great kings of the earth sought and wooed her. To him Zion was the city of the world, the "life of souls" where the *Shekhinah* dwelled. How sweet, he said, it would be to walk barefoot upon the desolate places where the holiest dwellings once stood:

O city of the world, most chastely fair,
In the far West, behold, I sigh for thee,
O had I eagle wings, I'd fly to thee,
And with my falling tears make moist thine earth.
My heart is in the East, and I am in the uttermost West—
How can I find savor in food? How shall it be sweet to me?
How shall I render my vow and my bonds, while yet
Zion lies beneath the fetters of Edom, and I in Arab chains?
A light thing it would seem to me to leave all the good things of Spain
Seeing how precious in mine eyes it is to behold the dust of the desolate sanctuary.

When he witnessed the despondency of the Jews, their despair of redemption, he soothed their failing spirits:

Bide thou thy time—within thy soul be peace,
Nor ask complainingly when thy pain shall cease;
Speak, rhyme, and sing, for victory is thine,
Nigh thee my tent is pitched, and thou art mine.

Halevi beheld the fate and future of his people clearly and realistically. It was the age of the First Crusade, when Spain was on the very frontier of contending Muslim and Christian forces. The ardent crusading spirit unleashed religious animosities which jeopardized the peace and security of the Jews. How far the poet was himself affected by the changed temper of the time may be judged by his lines:

Men insult me; fools, they know not
That insults borne for Thy sake are in honor.

Little did his Jewish countrymen realize the danger of the erupting volcano on which they were living. In Lucena, Cordova, and Toledo they bought off persecution with heavy gold contributions and continued in the enjoyment of their carefree life. While they drowsed happily in their sumptuous homes, he heard the rolling thunder of the Crusaders' tramping feet, the sound and fury of the Mohammedan destroyers. Bitterly, he cried out:

Have we either in the East or in the West
A place of hope where we may rest?

The Kuzari

Poetry was the instrument of Halevi's genius, his natural mode of expression. In *Kitab Al-Khazari* (better known as *Sefer ha-Kuzari* in Judah ibn Tibbon's Hebrew translation), which Halevi wrote in the latter part of his life, the poet poured out his ideas and feelings with eloquence and force, making it a major contribution to Jewish philosophical literature. Few works of any era have had a greater impact than the *Kuzari* in shaping the intellectual and spiritual currents of present-day Jewish life. It is to this day one of the most widely-read books of medieval Jewish philosophy. Whereas Maimonides wrote the *Guide for the Perplexed* so that few should understand it, and expressly warned Joseph ibn Aknin, his disciple, not to disclose its contents to men without philosophical training, the *Kuzari* was designed to be read by all classes of readers.

The philosophy of Zionism and Jewish nationalism, as we know them, were foreshadowed in its pages. Halevi is first among Jewish medieval poets to dwell upon the tragic consequences of the *galut* (exile) and to conceive of Israel's redemption as a realizable practical ideal. Though written in Arabic so as to be accessible to a wide public, the *Kuzari* is uniquely and characteristically Hebraic, in the sense in which the Book of Job, on which the *Kuzari* is modeled, is Hebraic—in the intense religious feeling underlying its arguments, and its love for Israel and the Holy Land. Halevi was adept in the rationalistic Arabic philosophy of his time, but traditional Judaism—the Judaism of the Bible and Talmud—was his main source and influence.

The *Kuzari*, based on a dramatic and romantic episode in Jewish history, describes the conversion to Judaism in the year 740 of the Khazars, a warlike Tartar people located on the western bank of the Caspian Sea, between the Don and Volga rivers. The language of the Khazars was Greek, and their religion was originally a blend of pagan and Christian beliefs. In his youth, Halevi must have heard the strange story of the Khazars, and their marvelous adventures and ultimate defeat by the Duke of Kiev in 969. It is also possible that he knew of the correspondence that had passed between Hasdai ibn Shaprut, the scholar-diplomat of Cordova who was the leader of Spanish Jews, and Joseph, the last of the reigning monarchs of the Khazars.

The full title of the *Kuzari, Book of Argument and Demonstration in Aid of the Despised Faith,* reveals Halevi's polemic intent as a defender of Judaism. At the time of its composition, Judaism had to fight on at least three fronts: Greek philosophy, Arabic rationalism, and the Karaites, whose aversion to traditional Judaism had won for them a considerable following. In addition, Halevi complained of the religious laxity of his coreligionists, some of whom (in Christian Spain) observed their Sabbath on Sunday, and others (in the Muslim part of the country) on Friday.

In structure, the *Kuzari* is a dramatic dialogue in which a philosopher, a Christian, a Mohammedan, and a Jew appear as dramatis personae, and the Khazar king as interlocutor. The book begins with the story of Bulan, king of the Khazars, a wise and upright monarch who ruled his people with justice and equity and performed the proper obeisance to the gods. Bulan has become disturbed because twice in dreams he has heard a heavenly admonition: "Thy intentions are good, but not thy performance." The king, concluding that he must have acted in a manner displeasing to the gods, summons a philosopher to advise him how to worship. Instead of offering instruction in the correct practices of religion, the philosopher says that the fundamental rule is purity of heart; everything else is non-essential. But the king is dissatisfied with the philosopher and dismisses him.

Bulan then invites representatives of the two major religions in his country, Christianity and Mohammedanism, to appear before him and argue the merits of their respective creeds. When the Christian and Muslim theologians both refer to Judaism, explaining that many tenets of their faiths are based upon the teachings of the Torah, the king's curiosity is aroused and he sends for a Jewish scholar (Haver) to question him about his religion.

The preliminaries are no sooner over than the Haver, Halevi's spokesman, launches into a discussion with his royal master on the philosophy of Judaism, its liturgy, history, and views on

God and His attributes, on prophecy, the Messiah, the laws and ceremonies of Judaism, the Hebrew language and the Holy Land, expounding his outlook in such a way as to provide a skillfully implied critique of the Christian and Mohammedan religions. These topics, of course, reflect in large measure Halevi's position on the thought and faith of the Jewish people and sum up his philosophy of Judaism.

Halevi's Philosophy of Judaism

Halevi was one of the few medieval Jewish philosophers with a sense of history, and the *Kuzari* is as much a philosophy of Jewish history as it is a philosophy of the Jewish religion. Indeed, the *Kuzari* is not a metaphysical or speculative work but an interpretation of God's manifestation in Jewish history. When the Haver explains the position of Judaism to King Bulan, he takes his stand on the revelation of God in history. He not only demolishes the claims of the three disputants—the philosopher, the Christian, and the Muslim—but establishes the standard by which true religion is to be judged. While Maimonides, at a later date, sought for religious truth in philosophic speculation and logical reasoning, Halevi found it in personal experience and the continuous, uninterrupted tradition.

The fundamental difference between Judaism, Christianity, and philosophy, the Haver maintains, is not a difference of creed or doctrine. Judaism, he protests, is neither a philosophy nor a theology, but a factual or visual religion, an historic manifestation of God which the multitude of six hundred thousand people who had been released from Egyptian bondage saw, felt, and personally experienced at Mt. Sinai. It is, furthermore, a religion which did not come into existence slowly, step by step, but appeared in the world by sudden revelation. The Jews were not persuaded to believe in the existence of God by theological or philosophic argumentation, but experienced His being by direct personal contact: God spoke to Moses; He redeemed the people from Egypt, He revealed Himself on Sinai and gave them the Ten Commandments; He brought them to the land of Canaan, and made them a kingdom of priests and prophets.

Halevi was almost alone among medieval Jewish philosophers in his antagonism to Aristotelian philosophy and Greek culture in general, an antagonism he expressed pithily in his famous epigram:

And let not the wisdom of the Greeks beguile thee,
Which hath no fruit, but only flowers.

It was his contention that the Jews had a more direct and accurate knowledge of God than the philosophers, who had no verified tradition to support them and were thus like blind men groping their way in the dark. Unlike Saadia Gaon, he did not hold that the belief in creation "out of nothing" (*creatio ex nihilo*) is fundamental to the conception of God. "The question of eternity and creation," the Haver says to Bulan, "is obscure, the arguments are evenly balanced. The theory of creation derives greater weight from the prophetic tradition of Adam, Noah, and Moses, which is more deserving of credence than mere speculation. If, after all, a believer in the Law finds himself compelled to admit an eternal matter and the existence of many worlds prior to this one, this would not impair his belief that this world was created at a certain epoch, and that Adam and Noah were the first human beings."

The Haver enters into a lengthy discussion of those words and phrases in the Torah and the prophets which seem to ascribe human qualities to God. Maimonides later completely rejected such anthropomorphisms, declaring them to be mere metaphors or figures of speech for the comprehension of immature minds. Halevi, while no less opposed to the corporeality of the divinity, held, nevertheless, that there is something in these attributes which fills the human soul with awe of God.

The Haver then discourses with his royal master about Judaism's stand on free will. Man, says the Haver, is morally free to shape his own life and determine his actions, be they good or evil. While God is all-knowing and master of the universe, He does not interfere with the moral sovereignty of man or predestine his conduct on earth. For if man were to be checked, hindered, or restrained by some force outside himself, what justice would there be for rewarding the righteous and punishing the wicked? Halevi's doctrine of free will was the position adopted by Maimonides and most other medieval Jewish philosophers.

A discussion on immortality and reward and punishment after death follows next. "It does not agree with common sense," the Haver says, "that when a man perishes, body and soul should disappear with him." Immortality is the prerogative of all men who live a pure and righteous life, and not only the reward of those who acquire wisdom, as Aristotle and later Maimonides insisted. If immortality of the soul, the Haver observes, is conditioned by the intellectual nature of the soul, how much intellectual knowledge must one have to be immortal? If any amount is sufficient, then every rational soul must be immortal. Although other religions place greater emphasis on a system of reward and punishment and stress immortality more than does the Bible, there are ample allusions in the prophets to the immortality of the soul and to reward and punishment after death to justify a Jewish belief in them.

On the ethics of Judaism, Halevi felt that man is not meant to live by and for himself, but is a segment of the life and society of which he is a part. As the Haver points out, the relation of the individual to society is as the relation of a single limb to the whole body. Therefore, "it is the duty of the individual to bear hardships, or even death, for the sake of the welfare of the commonwealth." Prayer, besides being a religious discharge of the duty man owes to God, also has its social or community implication.

> A person who prays for himself is like one who retires alone to his house, refusing to assist his fellow-citizens in the repair of their walls. . . . One of the conditions of prayer, craving to be heard, is that its object be profitable to the world. . . . Another is that an individual rarely accomplishes his prayer without slips or errors. It has been laid down, therefore, that the individual recite his prayers with the community, and, if possible, in a community of not less than ten persons, so that one makes up for the forgetfulness or error of others.

Halevi also believed that the Jews are the elect of God, standing in a closer relationship to Him than any other nation as the messengers of religious and moral truth to the world. In his exuberance, he even proclaimed that Israel is the intermediary between God and the nations of the world.

As Halevi's *alter ego*, the Haver is inexhaustible in his praise

of and love for the Jews. Were it not for Israel, there would be
no Torah. "We do not deny that the good actions of any man,
to whichever people he may belong, will be rewarded by God.
But the priority belongs to the people who are near God during
their life, and we estimate the rank they occupy near God after
death." When the Haver rhapsodizes Israel, it is of the Jew as a
religious and not as a racial being that he is thinking. It is his conviction that Israel is the instrument of God for the religious education of mankind. Prophecy is the exclusive right of the Jews,
for although the nations of the world have produced wise and
learned men, where are the prophets they can boast of? "Those
who become Jews," says the Haver, "do not take equal rank
with born Israelites, who are specially privileged to attain to
prophecy. . . . They (converts) can only become pious and
learned, but never prophets."

God implanted His divine love among the descendants of
Abraham, Isaac, and Jacob, and this divine influence has never
departed from them. With an oblique reference to Christianity
and Islam, he says, "We are not called the people of Moses, but
the people of God, as it is said: 'The people of the Lord' "
(Ezekiel 34:20).

To the Haver the suffering of the Jews is not inconsistent
with their role as the chosen people. Indeed, he presents it as evidence of their superiority, for only a superior people devoted
to God would refuse to utter the one word of denial of its faith
that would wipe out its suffering and make it the friend and equal
of its oppressors. When the king contrasts the triumphant out-
come of the early trials and tribulations of the Christians and
Mohammedans with the apparently useless travail of the Jews
through the centuries, the Haver retorts that "poverty and misery, despised in the eyes of man, are of higher merit in the eyes
of God than inflated pride and greatness."

When the Khazar monarch alludes to the degraded condition
of Jews and their low status in the world, the Haver rejoins:
"Do not believe that I, though agreeing with thee, admit that we
are dead. We still hold connection with that divine influence
through the laws of which He has placed us as a link between
us and Him. . . . We are not like the dead, but rather like a sick
and attenuated person who has been given up by the physicians,
but yet hopes for a miracle or an extraordinary recovery." The

Haver then evokes a picture for Bulan of the lifeless bones which, at the word of the prophet Ezekiel, were revived, became clothed with flesh and skin, and again stood erect. He also employs his famous simile of the seed of grain placed in the earth which, to all appearances, decays and rots away, but which, in the course of time, buds and blossoms and provides food for the starving.

Finally, in Halevi's exposition of Jewish history, Palestine becomes the crown and apex of his philosophy. With magnificent imagery, he describes his feeling for the Holy Land, singing of her past glory and her future position in the Jewish revival.

O beautiful of sight,
And sweet of voice;
In you I sight
A beauty choice,
In which there mingle
The rising of the light
And coming of the night.

As the Jews are the heart of the nations, so is Palestine the spiritual home and center of the world. It is the abode of life, the gate to heaven. Whosoever prophesied did so either in Palestine or concerning her. Christians and Mohammedans yearn for her, fight for her, turn their faces in prayer toward her. Without the Holy Land, the Jews are not a body, but scattered limbs and fragments from which all life has fled. When King Bulan asks why of all countries on earth Palestine was endowed with such spiritual perfection, the Haver replies: "Thou, surely, wilt have no difficulty in perceiving that one country may have higher qualities than another. There are places in which particular species of plants, metals or animals are found, and where the inhabitants are distinguished by their form and character and not in other countries."

A considerable part of the *Kuzari* is devoted to a defense of traditional Judaism and a frontal attack on the Karaites. In spite of Saadia Gaon's devastating criticism, they were still a power to be reckoned with in most Muslim countries. The Haver, therefore, sets out to challenge them, criticizing what he calls the perverse doctrine of those who reject the rabbinic interpretation of the Bible without which, he contends, its meaning is incomprehensible. "The view of the rabbis," he says, "was based on the tradition of the prophets, the opinion of the others on speculation. There is harmony and unanimity among the sages while there is perpetual strife and discord among the Karaites."

In discussing the enduring values of rabbinic Judaism, the Haver draws an engaging picture of the creators of that tradition, who, by their piety, learning, and character, approach the prophets. He declares: "Only he can be hostile to them who neither knows nor has studied their work." Poetically he describes the daily life of the pious Jew, follower of the established rabbinic creed. He dwells on his submission to God, his patience under suffering, his devotion to the Torah, and the loving care and attention he bestows upon the most trivial precepts of his daily religious life. He lives as if the divine presence were with him continually and angels walked at his side. Such a man, convinced of the justice of his creator, finds protection in sorrow, and solace in the oncoming shadows of life. "The happy life is only in the fulfillment of the precepts of the Torah."

The great dialogue between Bulan and the Haver unfolds until the king finds himself completely convinced and accepts the Jewish religion both for himself and his people. After this, his mission accomplished, the Haver resolves to fulfill his heart's desire and settle in Jerusalem. The king is loath to see him go, pointing out that Palestine is in the hands of the Crusaders, who kill all Jews. What safety would there be for his life? But the Haver will not be deterred. His soul, he says, is already in Zion —only its empty shell remains in his body. Then the king asks: "What can be sought in Palestine, since the *Shekhinah* has long since departed from her? . . . With a pure heart and desire, one can approach God in any place." To this the Haver replies: "The visible *Shekhinah* has indeed departed . . . but the invisible *Shekhinah* is with every born Israelite of virtuous life, pure heart, and upright mind . . . Heart and soul are only perfectly pure and immaculate in the place which is believed to be especially selected by God."

Pilgrimage to the Holy Land

In the last years of his life, like the Haver, Halevi himself set forth on the long and dangerous voyage to the Holy Land.

Hardly anything is known of the poet's closing adventure, not even whether he ever reached his goal. He traveled part of the way by ship, a journey he described in his nature poem "A Storm at Sea." We know, too, that new poems full of love for Zion matured in his mind on the way to the Holy Land, and that he visited Alexandria, Damietta, Cairo, Tyre, and Damascus. Everywhere he was received with great honor, and attempts were made to detain him. The poet immortalized his benefactors in enchanting lines, but their entreaties to remain fell on deaf ears. Zion obsessed him, and he would not be swayed from his goal. A holy compulsion drove him on to his "highest moment."

Did he realize that "highest moment"? After Damascus, the poet's steps fade away in mystery. There are almost as many theories about Halevi's last days and death as there are stanzas in his famous Zion ode. While some scholars maintain that he never reached Palestine but died either in Damascus or Cairo, other authorities feel as strongly that he reached Zion. A third view is advanced by the literary historian Israel Zinberg that, after a fruitless journey, Halevi returned to Spain, where he died, presumably in the year 1145.

But even if he had reached Jerusalem, what he would have found in the Holy City was something vastly different from the glory and splendor he had seen in his imagination. The city of David was in possession of the Crusaders, who were hostile to Jewish pilgrims.

> To see thy glory long mine eyes had yearned;
> But when at last I sought thy Holy Place,
> As though I were a thing unclean and base,
> Back from thy threshold was I rudely spurned.

Legend makes the song and singer come to an end before the gates of Jerusalem. According to popular belief, the poet was stabbed to death by an Arab at the Temple mount while he was singing his immortal "Ode to Zion."

> Zion! wilt thou not ask if peace be with thy captives
> That seek thy peace—that are the remnants of thy flocks?
> From west and east, from north and south—the greeting
> "Peace" from far and near, take thou from every side.

Chanted by Jews throughout the world on the Ninth of *Av*, the day of fasting and mourning for the destruction of the Temple, the "Ode to Zion" is treasured as the greatest psalm since the songs of David. According to Israel Efros, a distinguished American Hebrew poet, "it is not really one man's song. If the hearts of the Jews of all times could be formed into one great throbbing heart and made to turn toward the East, the song that it would sing would be, 'Zion! wilt thou not ask?' "

Judah Halevi's voice was attuned to everything his people felt and hoped. He was the prophet of his generation, a guide and influence for centuries to come. "The pearl diver and lord of most rare jewels and brilliant song," Moses ibn Ezra called his contemporary. And nearly seven hundred years later, Heinrich Heine, whose aspirations were as wayward and conflicting as Halevi's were single-minded, wrote:

Pure and true and blemish free
Was his singing, like his soul
Which, when his Creator made it,
So delighted Him that He
Kissed the lovely soul, and sweet
Echoes of that kiss e'er after
Lived in all the poet's songs,
Hallowed by this grace complete.

FOR FURTHER READING

BAER, Yitzhak, *A History of the Jews in Christian Spain*, pp. 59–77 (Philadelphia: Jewish Publication Society, 1961).

BARON, Salo, *A Social and Religious History of the Jews—Index to Volumes I–VIII*, pp. 57–58 (New York: Columbia University Press, 1960).

"Judah Halevi," in *Encyclopedia Judaica, Volume 10, pp. 355–366 (Jersualem: 1972)*.

ZINBERG, Israel, *A History of Jewish Literature*, Volume II (Cleveland: Case Western University Press, 1972).

Moses Maimonides

8 . *Moses Maimonides*

[1135-1204]

SALO W. BARON

IN Moses ben Maimon (fondly known as Rambam) medieval Jewry produced its greatest jurist, philosopher, and scientist. Already in his lifetime he enjoyed wide recognition throughout the Jewish world extending from Yemen to France, and when he died a grateful posterity coupled his name with the first Moses: "From Moses to Moses, there was none like Moses." Although opposing voices were not altogether lacking and a short time after his death some Jewish zealots persuaded the Christian Inquisition to burn his philosophic work in a public bonfire, his achievement has remained memorable among both Orthodox and progressive forces in Judaism. His code of laws is still among the most authoritative guides for Jewish ritualistic observance, while his attempt at reconciling the Jewish faith with the postulates of science has illumined the road for many of his "perplexed" contemporaries and successors. His personality and thought have also left an imprint on the larger Christian and Muslim worlds.

Early Years in Cordova

The son of a distinguished Spanish family which included several outstanding judges among his immediate forebears, Moses ben Maimon was born in Cordova on March 30, 1135 (*Nisan* 14, 4895), a crucial period for his people and the world at large. This was the era of the great Crusades, during which the young though still backward Christian nations had assumed the offensive against the richer, more civilized, but decaying world of Islam.

In this divided world, Jews maintained a precarious existence as a sort of "neutralist" group. While in actual warfare they were supposed to side with their respective rulers, they neither were expected nor did they wish to participate in the ideological struggle between the two dominant civilizations. Devoid of military power and dependent on the good will and "toleration" of their Christian and Muslim masters, Jews often suffered severely from their position between the two hostile worlds. At the same time they unwittingly served as the bridge between them. In science, philosophy, and economics, they were able to perform an important mediating role between the awakening West and Islam. Spain, in particular, at the border between expanding Christendom and retreating Islam felt with particular poignancy the great challenge of these world conflicts. Individual Spanish Jewish thinkers and poets had already offered many an answer to that great challenge in Judaism's "Golden Age" of the preceding two centuries. In the twelfth century, as the situation came to a climax, the works of Moses Maimonides provided the most authoritative Jewish response.

The city of Cordova, in which young Moses spent his childhood and adolescence, was a shadow of its former self. Once a great capital, it had in its glory embraced a population of several hundred thousands and prided itself on its famed academies of learning and a royal library of some four hundred thousand manuscripts. In the subsequent period of anarchy and internecine strife among the "petty princes," the city had suffered severely. Most noticeable was the decline in mutual understanding among the various racial and religious groups. Voices of intolerance, certain of which demanded that Muslims not consult a Jewish or Christian physician or lend scientific books to "unbelievers," now developed into a powerful chorus under the impact of the "crusading" spirit on both sides. The Almoravid regime of Spain had already injected a large measure of persecution of non-Muslims. Now, in a direct counter-reaction to the Christian Crusaders, the new Muslim Almohade sect, which believed in the absolute unity and incorporeality of God, felt obliged to suppress both Christianity with its trinitarian dogmas, and Judaism. Sweeping rapidly through North Africa and Muslim Spain, the Almohades completely outlawed all non-Muslim faiths, a policy theretofore unprecedented in the history of Islam.

Maimonides was thirteen when the Almohades conquered Cordova, closing all its churches and synagogues, and demanding the conversion of Christians and Jews to Islam. Since there was no effective inquisitorial body to investigate the private lives of individual citizens and to institute trials against those suspected of secretly adhering to their ancestral faiths, the Almohade authorities had to be satisfied with lip service on the part of their new converts. Maimon and his children may well have successfully dodged any such formal declaration and merely exercised great caution in performing certain indispensable Jewish rituals at home. Outwardly, nevertheless, every subject of the Almohade Empire was considered a professing Muslim, and for this reason Maimonides had to face in later years the accusation of being a relapsed convert, a mortal offense in Islamic law.

Emigration to Morocco

As time went on and Almohade intransigence hardened, the number of secret adherents to the older faiths must have greatly diminished. Continuous clashes between the Muslim and Christian kingdoms ultimately led to the reconquest of nearly the entire Iberian Peninsula by the Christian Crusaders. In the meantime, however, the situation of the "secret" Jews became ever more precarious, many suffering outright martyrdom. In 1158 and 1159 Maimon and his family decided to emigrate to more hospitable regions. Curiously, the Maimonidean family did not seek shelter in Christian Spain or the Provence. Although the people in those regions had made great strides in their economic and cultural pursuits, they must still have appeared backward to citizens of Muslim Andalusia. Jewish refugees found it easier to adjust to conditions in North Africa where, because of the lack of an immediate Christian menace, the surveillance of recent "converts" was less thorough.

Some "secret" Jews, nonetheless, were disturbed by the concessions they had to make to their outward profession of Islam, even in Morocco. To pacify their consciences, the elder Maimon circulated in 1159 an *Epistle of Consolation*, in which he tried to strengthen the heart of his perplexed coreligionists—an epistle which undoubtedly served as a model for the somewhat similar *Epistle of Conversion* later published by his famous son. Both authors urged their fellow sufferers to stand firm on their faith, and to look forward to an opportunity to emigrate to a more tolerant country.

Undoubtedly themselves planning to depart before long, Maimon and his children spent several years in Morocco, from about 1159 to 1165. In the city of Fez they found an intellectually vigorous and alert community which in the preceding two centuries had produced an array of distinguished Jewish thinkers, philologists, and jurists, including Isaac Alfasi, whom Maimonides acknowledged as the greatest of his teachers. Here young Maimonides received further training in both Jewish and general subjects, and in medicine. He also continued with his literary activities, on which he may have embarked as early as the age of sixteen. While still in Spain he had composed a brief manual on logic, analyzing some seventy basic philosophic terms and classifying the sciences, as well as a tract on "Intercalation," which reviewed the main principles of Jewish calendar computation. At the age of twenty-three he began his *Commentary on the Mishnah*, which, when completed ten years later, became a classic in its field. These works were written originally in Arabic, although they became far more influential in their later Hebrew translations.

We are not told what particular event persuaded the Maimonides family, in 1165, to turn their backs on the Almohade Empire. Possibly a new outburst of intolerance in Morocco resulting in the execution of one of Maimonides' teachers forced their departure. In any event, after a stormy voyage, the surviving of which Maimonides thereafter commemorated annually in two family fast days, they reached the Holy Land. They remained there a year or less, probably because most of the country was then part of the Latin Kingdom of Jerusalem, which, at least in its early years, was even more fanatical than the Almohades. Maimon and his family turned to Egypt which, even under the then declining Fatimid domination, was still one of the great economic and cultural centers of the Near East.

Egypt: Physician and Communal Leader

Moses and his family adjusted themselves in a remarkably quick manner to the new Egyptian environment. His younger brother David became a successful merchant, engaging in risky but lucrative trade with India. On one journey to the rich subcontinent, however, David was shipwrecked and lost at sea, along with most of the family's fortune (1174). In a letter dated 1182 Maimonides wrote: "When the bad news arrived, I became ill and depressed for a whole year; I thought I was lost. Eight years have passed; I am still mourning and cannot find consolation. I brought him up; he was my brother and my pupil." Under the impact of that loss and the ensuing financial responsibilities which he had to assume toward his brother's family, Moses began to practice medicine. Quite early he achieved a considerable reputation among his fellow physicians at Fustat, Cairo, who, when requested by a Christian prince of the Latin Kingdom to send him an expert physician, selected Maimonides; he, however, declined the invitation. He soon entered the services of the vizier and counselor of Saladin, Egypt's new and colorful ruler. Maimonides' success was so great that his medical services were sought by many princes and dignitaries of state and mosque. In an often-quoted letter to his French Hebrew translator, Samuel ibn Tibbon, Maimonides described his busy career:

> I live in Fustat while the king resides in Cairo at a distance of two permissible journeys on Sabbath (about three miles). My duties at the royal court are very exacting; I must see the king every day. But if he feels unwell, or if one of his children or concubines falls ill, I must spend most of the day at the royal palace in Cairo. Similarly, if one or another official is sick, I must attend to his medication . . . In any case, I do not return home before noon, quite hungry (and exhausted). But I find my waiting rooms filled with people, Jews and Gentiles, distinguished and common, judges and surveyors, friends and enemies, a mixed multitude awaiting my return.

In spite of his professional responsibilities, Maimonides found time to concern himself with the problems of the community in which he lived. Almost immediately after he arrived in Egypt he assumed a position of leadership in the Jewish community. The general respect for learning and personal integrity overcame whatever resentments may have been nurtured among local Jews by the interference of this "foreigner" in their domestic affairs, which had been quite unsatisfactory for some time. All of Egyptian Jewry was controlled by a single official bearing the distinguished title of *nagid* (prince), and some of the *negidim* used their authority and court connections for personal gain and aggrandizement. The regime of the *nagid* Zuta, shortly before and after Maimonides' settlement in Egypt, proved particularly obnoxious and had embroiled the community in endless controversies.

Maimonides evidently entered the ranks with reluctance. Deeply involved as he was in his studies, he resented any loss of time occasioned by communal strife. He also believed that "all the house of Israel are in duty bound to be united in one indivisible whole, and there should be among them no conflict whatsoever." At the same time, he held to the principle of the obligation of each individual to prevent wrongdoing whenever possible. "He who can protest and does not do so is himself guilty of the transgression for which he had failed to reprimand the transgressor." The growing authority of the great jurist doubtless helped depose the abusive Zuta, but he apparently refused to become *nagid* himself.

Nevertheless, Maimonides was soon recognized by all Egyptian Jewry as its outstanding leader. As early as 1176 he and nine associates issued a sharp ordinance aimed at reducing the Karaite influence on Rabbinite Jews. Although past its intellectual heyday, the Karaite sect generally enjoyed a high social and intellectual standing in Egypt, and their members sometimes intermarried with prominent Rabbinites. A series of other ordinances likewise bears Maimonides' signature and the imprint of his personality.

Maimonides' influence was also soon felt beyond the confines of Egypt. Ancient Yemenite Jewry, in particular, had long maintained intimate relations with the major Jewish centers of learning in both Babylonia and Egypt-Palestine. These relationships had been strengthened by the political and religious influence exercised upon Yemen by Egypt's Fatimid ruler. Maimonides' reputation spread from Egypt to this South-Arabian community, and in 1172, or some seven years after his arrival in the East, he was asked by Yemenite leaders to resolve certain theological difficulties connected with Jewish Messianic beliefs and practices. These difficulties assumed new significance with the appearance in Yemen of a Messianic pretender who found a wide following among his oppressed coreligionists. In his *Epistle to Yemen*, Maimonides delved deeply into both the doctrinal and historical aspects of the problem. Apart from citing numerous Messianic movements up to this time (some unrecorded elsewhere), he presented the traditional Messianic teachings which he sharply differentiated from the related Christian and Muslim doctrines.

The apologetic parts of the *Epistle* enjoyed wide popularity both in their Arabic original and in three independent Hebrew translations. So grateful were the Yemenite communities that they inserted Maimonides' name, while he was still alive, alongside that of the reigning Exilarch in their daily recitations of the *Kaddish*. The historical section of the *Epistle*, however, as well as its outspoken polemics against Christianity, was considered either uninteresting or too dangerous for Jews to be disseminated in the Hebrew version. The Arabic manuscript lay dormant until its publication in recent years.

Jurist and Legal Philosopher

Maimonides was both a jurist and a legal philosopher. His ordinances and responses enabled him, like the other Jewish *Halakhists*, to extend the law, civil as well as ritualistic, by applying it to ever new cases. Reinterpretation of older laws by way of commentaries and recodification had also been a time-honored device to adjust the law to novel conditions in each particular environment. But beyond his concerns with legal practices, Maimonides always searched also for the deeper reasons behind them and, in his systematic mind, formulated categories into which their disparate elements might logically fit.

Not that Maimonides felt the need to defend Jewish "legalism" as a matter of principle. Living in a Muslim environment, which was as little antinomian (opposed to law) as Judaism, he did not have to argue for the necessity of legal orderliness in societal and individual behavior. It sufficed for him to consider mainly the spiritual versus the physical elements in Jewish law and its impact on both body and soul. As he wrote in his *Guide:*

The general object of the law is twofold: the well-being of the soul, and the well-being of the body. The well-being of the soul is promoted by correct opinions communicated to the people according to their capacity. Some of these opinions are therefore imparted in a plain form, others allegorically; because certain opinions are in their plain form too strong for the capacity of the common people. The well-being of the body is established by a proper management of the relations in which we live one to another. This we can attain in two ways: first by removing all violence from our midst; that is to say, that we do not do every one as he pleases, desires, and is able to do; but every one of us does that which contributes towards the common welfare. Secondly, by teaching every one of us such good morals as must produce a good social state. Of these two objects, the one, the well-being of the soul, or the communication of correct opinions, comes undoubtedly first in rank, but the other, the well-being of the body, the government of the state, and the establishment of the best possible relations among men, is anterior in nature and in time.

Maimonides profoundly believed in the rationality of all laws. If his great predecessor Saadia Gaon had tried to draw a line of demarcation between rational laws which the human mind can explain, and irrational laws which must be followed merely because of the divine command, Maimonides rejected this distinction as almost bordering on blasphemy. To him the idea that God might have enacted laws without any good and valid reasons appeared abhorrent, although he admitted that human reason may not always be capable of comprehending their import. But whether one knew the reason or not, Maimonides agreed with all other Jewish jurists that one had to adhere to the commands of tradition undeviatingly. He even recognized unreasoned obedience as a highly meritorious act before the Lord.

Commentary on the Mishnah

A few years after he arrived in Egypt Maimonides completed his *Commentary on the Mishnah*, which he had begun at the age of twenty-three. Seeing in the Mishnah—as well as in the other *Tannaitic* sources—the chief repository of Oral Law, Maimonides early concentrated on deducing from it the principal Jewish legal teachings and spreading their knowledge among the masses. Overtly, his *Commentary* pursued only pedagogic aims. "What induced me to compose this work," he wrote, "was the recognition that the Talmud explains the Mishnah in a way no one could guess through mere reasoning." To understand it, moreover, it was not enough to study the Talmudic comments on a particular Mishnah, but one also had to remember many other rabbinic discussions scattered through the vast "sea of the Talmud." To help students understand, he embodied in his *Commentary* a summary of those far-flung debates in the ancient academies, and pointed out what he considered to be prevailing law. He also wrote commentaries on several tractates of the Babylonian Talmud, and, as one of few medieval rabbis, also studied intensively the Palestinian Talmud. The former are unfortunately lost, while his summary of the Palestinian compendium entitled the *Hilkhot Yerushalmi* appeared a few years ago.

Maimonides stressed the underlying principles alongside the specific provisions contained in the Mishnah. Unlike Roman law and its continental offshoots, but more similar to Anglo-Saxon, Muslim, and other legal systems, biblical-Talmudical jurisprudence was largely "case law." Inductive processes were necessary to reach an understanding of general principles, which Maimonides' logical mind tried to emphasize. At times he felt impelled to expatiate on them in lengthy introductions to individual Mishnaic tractates or even chapters. For example, the introduction to the *Sayings of the Fathers* was divided into eight sections. It soon began to circulate as an independent treatise called *Eight Chapters*, and became an outstanding classic of Jewish ethical literature.

Maimonides' ethics, too, has an intellectual slant. He believed that man's "only design in eating, drinking, cohabiting, sleeping, waking, moving about and resting should be the preservation of bodily health, while, in turn, the reason for the latter is that the soul and its agencies may be in sound and perfect condition, so that he may readily acquire wisdom and gain moral and intellectual virtues, all to the end that he may reach the highest goal of his endeavors." His introduction to the last chapter of "Sanhedrin," in which Mishnah and Talmud dealt at great length with the problems of resurrection and the Messianic era, enabled Maimonides to elucidate the fundamental doctrines of Judaism as a whole. Here he formulated his famous thirteen principles, which stated the beliefs in (1) God's existence, (2) unity, (3) incorporeality, (4) eternity, (5) exclusive claim to worship, (6) prophecy, (7) Moses' uniqueness among the prophets, (8) the Law of Moses as in its entirety given by God, (9) its eternal immutability, (10) God's omniscience, (11) reward and punishment, (12) coming of the Messiah, and (13) resurrection of the dead. Preceded in each case by the declaration "I believe (*Ani Maamin*)," these principles were embodied in the daily ritual of Ashkenazic Jewry. A broader reformulation has been recited monthly in Sephardic congregations for many generations.

The Book of Commandments

Despite his comprehensive treatment, Maimonides must have recognized the inadequacy of his *Commentary* for the practical guidance of judges and students. Gone was the time when the entire Jewish intelligentsia concentrated exclusively on the study of rabbinic letters. While concern with the law remained the major preoccupation of a substantial segment of Jewry, the wider horizons of the renaissance of Islam had attracted many to the study of philosophy, philology, poetry, and the sciences. At the same time the new articulateness of Jewish literature and its diffusion from Persia to the Atlantic Ocean taxed the erudition of even the most learned *Halakhists*. Recodification of Jewish law in well-organized and clearly written handbooks had, therefore, become imperative.

Following established precedent, Maimonides in his Arabic *Book of Commandments* summarized the entire body of Jewish law under the headings of the traditional 613 commandments. From ancient times it has been assumed that the Torah had presented the Jewish people with a set of 248 commandments, similar in number to the limbs of a human body, and with 365 prohibitions resembling the days of the solar year. But nowhere did the Talmud offer any detailed enumeration; it was left to the medieval rabbis to fill in that gap on the basis of their individual traditions and reasonings. Deviating from all his predecessors, Maimonides attempted a new classification beginning with such general principles as the belief in the existence and unity of God and finally descending to individual laws and rituals. Each positive commandment as well as prohibition embraced many specific provisions. Together they covered the broad areas of Jewish law, both ritual and civil. Although some scholars disagreed with one or another individual decision, immediately after publication of the *Book of Commandments*, Maimonides soon claimed with great satisfaction that "many copies of that book have reached Babylonia, the extreme west and the cites of Edom (Christendom)." He only regretted that he had written it in Arabic and hoped that some day he would have the opportunity of translating it into Hebrew.

Here, as elsewhere in his juridical works, Maimonides insisted that all commandments were equal in rank. He refused to follow the gradation of commandments made by Abraham ibn Daud into those relating to faith, morals, social life, and those pertaining to ceremonies. He believed that the very assumption of such a differentiation in biblical laws had been King Manesseh's main transgression because it had led him to take certain commandments more lightly than others. The sage of Fustat would certainly have viewed with dismay those persons of our time who rather arbitrarily consider certain laws as more or less obsolete, while they rigidly adhere to others.

The Mishneh Torah

Still dissatisfied, Maimonides decided to reformulate all of Jewish law in a new systematic code. In intensive labor extending over more than a decade (1166-1176) and with many revisions thereafter, Maimonides restated the entire law of the Talmud. Using the Mishnah as a model, but going beyond it, he omitted all discussion pro and con or the citation of controversial points of view, but merely stated in his own lucid way

the general principles as well as the specific laws. He gave considerable thought even to the succession of chapters and sub-
chapters; for he so strongly believed that such orderliness had
already guided Judah the Patriarch in his redaction of the
Mishnah that he sometimes deduced points of law from
Mishnaic sequences. Legitimately, therefore, Maimonides' commentators and other students of *Halakhah* paid special attention to the implications of the sequences in the Maimonidean
code as well. He was proud of the simplicity of his Hebrew
style and staunchly resisted appeals by friends to translate it
into Arabic. Disregarding the traditional division of the material into six orders and sixty-three tractates, he reorganized
it into fourteen logically integrated sections. Concerned with
presenting the totality of Jewish law, the codifier drew no
distinction between regulations still valid in his time and others
which had become totally obsolete. He treated the laws governing the ancient Temple and its sacrificial ritual with the same
care and detail as he did, for instance, those affecting marital relations, holiday observance, or the consumption of ritual food.
Most remarkably, he devoted the first section of his work to a
discussion of the "fundamentals of the Torah," that is, to the
credal and ethical elements of Judaism, which had hitherto been
left to homilists and preachers rather than to jurists.

This unprecedented method aroused misgivings among those
students of the law accustomed to the traditional arrangement,
and even greater objection was raised to Maimonides' failure to
supply his sources. Although any keen *Halakhist* could detect
behind each formulation the author's familiarity with Talmudic
sources and his careful weighing of the often contradictory
evidence, Maimonides' authoritative declarations sounded pre-
sumptuous and arbitrary. At times, indeed, in spite of its clarity,
many a Maimonidean statement lent itself to misinterpretation
and misapplication by less informed judges and communal
leaders. Only the citation of the older sources themselves, many
leading jurists believed, would enable such legal practitioners
to comprehend the arguments underlying each decision and
to arrive at a more reliable judgment. Maimonides himself,
constantly engaged in revisions of his *Code*, was aware of that
shortcoming and at one time contemplated supplying brief references to the sources. He never accomplished this task; how-

ever, and it was left for the later host of commentators to do.*

Most shocking to traditionalists, however, was Maimonides' self-assurance and his opening declaration that he was trying to summarize the entire body of Oral Law so that "none will be required to study any further book concerning the laws of Israel . . . The present treatise," he promised, "will assemble the whole Oral Law, together with the ordinances, customs, and enactments which had been issued from the days of Moses to the completion of the Talmud, as they have been interpreted by the authorities in all writing composed after the Talmud. For this reason I have called this treatise *Mishneh Torah* (the Second Torah), for one need but read the written Torah first, and then study this book, to learn the entire Oral Law without being required to peruse any intervening tract."

This declaration evoked in the minds of many readers the specter of total neglect of Talmudic studies. For example, the distinguished and self-assertive *Halakhist*, Abraham ben David, of Posquières, reacted immediately with a series of sharp strictures to the *Code* (which he seems to have received in installments). Abraham's *Hassagot* (Objections) have since accompanied most editions of the *Code* itself. By thus stimulating the independent thinking of readers, they helped prevent blind reliance on the *Code* and the ensuing "petrification" of Jewish law, fear of which had long served as an argument against any attempt at codification. In fact, as Maimonides himself boasted to the scholars of Lunel, the distribution of copies of his *Code* in Yemen and vicinity had, from the outset, restored interest in Talmudic learning in communities as far east as India. Ultimately, a fifteenth-century North-African scholar could claim that without the *Code* "we would be unable to fully comprehend the Talmud."

Religious Philosopher

Maimonides became the greatest Jewish religious philosopher not so much out of an inner drive to speculate on the riddles of existence as in response to an urgent social need. Not that he

* No less than 220 commentaries were enumerated in a bibliography compiled some sixty-five years ago by the famous Viennese preacher Adolph Jellinek; many more have appeared since.

lacked intellectual curiosity; in fact, all his life he was deeply concerned with theoretical problems and voraciously read Arabic literature in most fields of learning. His personal contact with Muslim scholars, the influence of a philosophically-minded Jewish intelligentsia in Spain, Morocco, and Egypt, and the teachings of rabbinic scholars like his own father Maimon all combined to arouse his profound interest in philosophical speculation. Had not an outstanding leader of *Halakhic* Judaism, Saadia Gaon, and some of his successors pointed the way toward the reconciliation of *Halakhah* with philosophic studies?

None of these men indulged in speculations in a vacuum. As intellectual spokesmen of their people they were confronted with the powerful challenges of the majority culture, and often had to react to direct attacks on Judaism by Muslim thinkers. Even more important loomed the need to justify the traditional teachings before the growing Jewish intelligentsia itself. True, the outright agnostic trends noticeable in eastern Islam in the ninth and tenth centuries had given way to a more fundamentalist reaction, and in the western Muslim countries the impact of the Almohade reaction had almost obliterated all radical tendencies. Nevertheless, there were still many Jews of Maimonides' generation who were uncertain and perplexed about the seemingly irrational character of many Jewish teachings. To some of them, numerous statements in the Bible appeared controverted by scientifically demonstrable facts and sound speculation. Without abandoning their faith, they searched for guidance in reconciling the verities of their own religion with the philosophical and scientific teachings of the Greek schools now available in Arabic translations, and their further elaborations in Arabic commentaries and independent tracts.

Guide for the Perplexed

It was to such "perplexed" Jews rather than to outright agnostics or atheists (whose number in the medieval Jewish community must always have been small) that Maimonides addressed his *Guide for the Perplexed.* This philosophic masterpiece grew out of a series of essays in Arabic in which he answered some incisive questions put to him by a former pupil, Joseph ibn Aknin. In this work he sought "to enlighten a religious man who has been trained to believe in the truth of our holy Law, who conscientiously fulfills his moral and religious duties, and at the same time had been successful in his philosophical studies." He was addressing himself to persons attracted by reason who found it "difficult to accept as correct the teaching based on the literal interpretation of the Law."

Speaking to that intellectual minority, Maimonides had to be very circumspect so as not to offend the sensitivities of extreme traditionalists. The major question was how to reconcile the apparently naive and often legendary statements in the traditional sources with the dictates of reason, in whose supremacy Maimonides staunchly believed. Without entering into discussions of the complex philosophical problems concerning the reliability of human reason such as had been heatedly debated in Saadia's generation, Maimonides insisted that whenever reason was absolutely certain of its findings, the contradictory statements in the Bible must be explained in an allegorical way, that is, by searching out their hidden rather than literal meaning.

For this purpose Maimonides devoted most of the first section of his *Guide* to a lengthy semantic discussion. He tried to show that the Bible often used homonyms, or words which had one meaning when applied to man and another when used in connection with God. Even the simple formulation that "God is One" did not have the same connotation as that of "oneness" employed in human affairs. Whereas the latter really means that something consists of one rather than of two or three entities, all of which are equally possible, in the case of God double or triple existence is logically unthinkable; hence, God's oneness really means that He is one of a unique kind. This was the core of Maimonides' famous doctrine of "negative attributes," which held that anything attributed to God was intrinsically different from a similar attribute to man, and that we really know what God is not rather than what He is. Whether one asserts that God exists, has power, or knowledge (the three attributes originally used by the Syriac Christians to rationalize the trinitarian dogma), or whether one adds any number of other attributes, they all have a meaning peculiar to God's unique essence.

None of these doctrines was deeply controversial. The overwhelming majority of Christians, Muslims, as well as Jews agreed on the oneness of God and His differentiation from human beings. Nevertheless, like most medieval philosophers, Maimonides went through the motions of proving again the existence of God in Aristotelian terms. He mainly used the argument that a world in motion, caused by previous motions, logically leads back to a prime unmoved Mover, just as the usual chain of causality must somewhere end in a postulated First Cause.

Only one aspect of Godhead led to sharp controversies. The unsophisticated reader of the Bible saw in God a personality of a superhuman kind but one endowed with many corporeal features. God's actions and sentiments were expressed by the biblical writers in purely human terms (God seeing or saying something, His being angry, and the like). The rabbis, too, often stated that the "Bible speaks in the language of man," by which they meant that many of its statements need not be taken literally. Nonetheless, these biblical anthropomorphisms and the even more elaborate descriptions of human qualities in God found in the rabbinic *Aggadah* and mystical literatures became ready targets for Christian and Muslim critics. Some Muslims actually accused Jews on this score of lacking a purely mono- theistic belief. They also claimed that the ancient rabbis must have altered statements in the Bible which could not have been given by God to Moses in that materialistic form.

Like other Jewish philosophers, Maimonides strained his ingenuity in explaining these passages; he declared most of them were homonyms having an entirely different meaning when applied to God. In any case, he felt that since human reason repudiated ascribing human qualities to God, Jewish readers were perfectly free to interpret away the most clear- cut biblical anthropomorphisms. He even counted rejection of the corporeality of God among his thirteen articles of faith. "Therefore bear in mind," he wrote, "that by the belief in corporeality or anything connected with corporeality, you would provoke God to jealousy and wrath, kindle His fire and anger, become His foe, His enemy and adversary in a higher degree than by the worship of idols." Such a rejection angered many of the traditionalists of the time, especially in Europe where the Bible still was largely read with its un- sophisticated *Aggadic* elaborations. Thus Abraham ben David of Posquières noted that "greater and better men than he have followed that trend of thought."

The sage of Fustat was not prepared to accept, however, the somewhat related philosophic teachings concerning the eternity of the world which ran counter to the accepted religious doctrine that it had been created by God out of nothing. He felt that in this respect the Aristotelian demonstrations could be countered by equally valid counter-arguments and that, hence, there was no "sufficient reason for rejecting the literal meaning of a biblical text and explaining it figuratively." More generally he accepted almost all Aristotelian teachings concerning the physical aspects of the earth and its inhabitants, but he declined to follow the Stagirite thinker in matters affecting the superlunary world.

In discussing the relation between God and the universe, or man, Maimonides saw no need of arguing for the prevailing geocentric view of the world. Having accepted the creation of the world in time, he also had little difficulty in persuading himself that the same creator had inspired the biblical writers to compile this authentic record of the divine revelation to man. True philosophically-minded readers required an explanation of the nature of prophecy and miracles, and particularly of the manner in which the incorporeal God had communicated His will to man. Maimonides argued that the same omnipotent creator who had fixed the laws of nature could also alter them at will. Such a breach in the course of nature was not really their reversal but a temporary adaptation to new needs set in advance by an omniscient providence. God also willed it that certain individuals be endowed with special prophetic gifts enabling them to perceive His wishes and to communicate to their fellow men truths unattainable to human reason unaided by revelation.

In Maimonides' analysis of prophecy, which had given him the original impetus to compose the *Guide*, because it was the main line of demarcation between believer and nonbeliever and even between members of different denominations, his rationalism conceded the existence of an imaginative quality in certain extraordinarily gifted individuals which was infinitely superior to human reason. In his methodical fashion Maimonides graded the prophecies recorded in Scripture in eleven degrees.

Above all prophets towered the unmatched personality of Moses, who, in Maimonides' opinion, was as superior to the other prophets as the latter were to ordinary men. Only the poverty of human language accounted for the inability to give the great lawgiver a different and unique designation. Next to psychic endowment, piety, and virtue were qualities indispensable for a genuine prophet, distinguishing him from a false prophet.

Clearly, such doctrines easily lent themselves to an emphasis upon the uniqueness and exclusive truth of the Jewish religion. Mohammed's prophetic endowment was sharply rejected as was Jesus' Messianic mission. True revelation was limited to the law of Moses, given to him on Sinai in the presence of a whole people. Later Israelitic prophets amplified the Pentateuchal teachings by special messages, but, unlike the founders of Christianity or Islam, did not alter them in any fundamental way. The fact that the Jewish people was the sole recipient of that revelation made it the "chosen people," which it has remained in spite of all suffering and persecutions, and which it would unalterably remain until the advent of the genuine Davidic Messiah.

It is because of the Jew's membership in the "chosen people" that he is obliged to observe the 613 commandments in all their ramifications. Next to the first two commandments of knowing that there is a God and believing that He is one, Maimonides placed as the third and fourth commandments the duties of loving and fearing Him. To explain love of God, he wrote: "It means that we ought carefully observe and meditate on His commandments, words, and works, until we grasp Him and enjoy such recognition with the profoundest of pleasure . . . This commandment also includes our obligation to urge all men to the service of God, and the belief in Him."

Although not averse to propagandizing the Jewish faith among Gentiles, Maimonides knew that under both Islam and Christianity such conversion was a capital offense. In Muslim lands even the conversion of Christians to Judaism was sternly outlawed. But in answering the appeal by a particular convert, Maimonides went out of his way to stress the law that after conversion a proselyte enjoyed essentially the same rights as a full-fledged Jew. Maimonides' primary concern in enjoining man's duty to love God was to make each and every Jew not only observe all commandments for himself and his family, but also to induce him to share in the responsibility for his fellow Jews and the community at large.

In general, man's ethical behavior must transcend the requirements of formal law. The moral aspects of Judaism deeply permeated all Maimonidean philosophy and colored his psychology. In his *Eight Chapters* particularly, Maimonides tried to combine the teachings of the fathers with those of Aristotle's *Nicomachean Ethics*. Like most Jewish teachers, but more explicitly, the Fustat sage stressed the doctrine of the "golden mean" as the major rule of human behavior. In his famous "Code of Benevolence" he placed assistance toward self-support of impoverished persons high above outright charity. Maimonides allowed himself occasional outbursts against existing communal practices which he abhorred. Following the old Talmudic preference for the study of Torah without expectation of reward, he sharply censured the widespread commercialization of learning and the professionalization of teaching and the judiciary. "Every Jew," he taught, "is in duty bound to study the Torah, be he poor or rich, healthy or ill, young or old and decrepit; even a pauper living on charity or begging from door to door and obliged to provide for a wife and children is bound to set aside time during the day and night for the study of Torah." Maimonides also condemned sharply the mania for titles which, in emulation of an Arab fashion, had spread in the Jewish community since the tenth century. He saw in them a violation of the old rabbinic ideal of humility which, together with inward piety, law observance, and intellectual aspiration, formed the backbone of Jewish ethics.

Medical Writings

The last dozen years of Maimonides' life were largely devoted to his intensive medical practice. Yet he found enough time to write a number of important responsa and epistles on legal and theological subjects. Some of these letters tried to explain to questioners moot points in his earlier works which he kept on revising to the end of his life. To this period also belong various important tracts which established his reputation as one of the outstanding Jewish medical authors during the Middle Ages.

As a student of sciences Maimonides was primarily concerned with those scientific data which had a direct bearing on his legal and ethical teachings. An assiduous reader of contemporary mathematical and astronomic literature, he effectively utilized the findings in the elaboration of certain rabbinic teachings. He was most interested in expanding his views on medical subjects. Most of his monographs—on hemorrhoids, sexual intercourse, asthma, poisons, fits (of melancholia), and even his semimedical and semiethical tractate on the *Regulation of Health*—were written at the request of various dignitaries, which explains their frequently casual tone and numerous repetitions. Only two major medical tracts seem to have been written on his own initiative.

One of these was a large compendium on drugs, discovered about two decades ago in a unique Istanbul manuscript transcribed by one of the leading medieval Arab pharmacologists a generation after Maimonides. Apparently one of Maimonides' earliest medical works, it may have been written for his own benefit to help identify drugs used in his new Egyptian environment with similar preparations made in Morocco and Spain, which frequently bore different Arabic designations. Moreover, even the study of Hippocrates and Galen require a more precise knowledge of the medical compounds, for many of their prescriptions could not be filled in Egypt because of the absence of certain plants or their extremely high price. In the ensuing quest for substitutes a clearer understanding of drugs of similar qualities, or their linguistic "synonyms," became an urgent necessity.

Maimonides spent many years in formulating aphorisms of a medical-ethical nature, which came to be known under the name of *Pirke Moshe* (*Chapters of Moses*). While frequently quoting Hippocrates and Galen, he also dared to deviate from and at times even opposed the teachings of those ancient masters. In this and other works he tried to instill in his readers the conviction that a physically and mentally healthy way of life was the best means of preventing and curing disease. He was an ardent believer in "mental therapy" and often devoted considerable space in his medical treatises to advising patients to apply psychological cure. In his *Regulation of Health*, written at the request of a sultan who complained of mental depression and forebodings of death, Maimonides describes his approach: "The soul may become accustomed to resist passion by considering the ethical books, the literature and the rules of the religious law, and the sermons and the wise sayings of the sages, until the soul is strengthened and sees the right as right, and the idle as idle. In this way the passions diminish, the bad thoughts disappear, the unsociableness is removed, and the soul is gladdened in spite of all the conditions which may happen to man." Equanimity and calm acceptance of adversity were the keynotes of Maimonides' ethical-medical teachings.

After Maimonides' death, a Muslim student of medicine, with the typical exaggeration of the panegyrists of that age, wrote a poem extolling the mental therapy used by the Fustat sage above Galen's exclusive concern with bodily ills.

Contrast Maimmi's with famed Galen's art:
Health to the body Galen can impart,
But the wise Hebrew, with a two-fold skill
Relieves both mind and body from all ills;
Shows how base ignorance can hurt the soul,
While wisdom, counteracting, makes it whole.
Even the moon, obedient to his cure,
From periodic taint would be secure;
No spots the brightness of her disc would stain,
Nor would rebirth entail her death again.

Though some Muslim physicians denounced him as a relapsed convert to Islam, the majority placed him among the ranking medical authors of his age.

Following the prevailing fashion, Maimonides relied on book learning rather than experimentation. Though in his medical practice even more than in his mathematical and astronomic calculations the scientist had to make use of his personal observation and experience, Maimonides leaned heavily on earlier authorities. Primarily a student rather than a practitioner, he was annoyed at having to attend to the minor or imaginary ailments of his highly placed patients, which left him little time for the study of medical literature. "For you know," he declared, "how exacting and difficult is this profession for any person of conscience and precision, who refuses to make a statement without knowing how to prove it, or else how to indicate its source, or the kind of analogy leading up to it."

Scientific Works

In his astronomic studies Maimonides was even more dependent on literary sources; calculations of the movements of the moon and the ensuing calendar regulations had long been established in the Jewish tradition, and any deviation therefrom was a sign of heterodoxy. Like most of his Jewish confrères, moreover, Maimonides had little access to the few extant astronomic observatories, which had been erected for Muslims by royal patrons. Hence he could not possibly have reached novel conclusions on the basis of direct astronomic observation. Nevertheless, by using sound deductive methods he was sometimes able to improve upon the findings of certain distinguished Arab predecessors.

On the whole, Maimonides' world outlook was confined to the current views of Ptolemaic astronomy. Although some ancient thinkers and even such near contemporaries as the author of the *Zohar* had suggested an earth rotating around its axis or even around the sun, the overwhelming opinion held the earth to be a stationary globe around which the moon, the seven planets, and the sun all rotated. Erroneous as many of Maimonides' underlying hypotheses undoubtedly were, his practical conclusions were on the whole quite sound. In the field of calendar regulation especially, they still form the basis of the Jewish calendar today.

At times, however, when scientific findings ran counter to traditional teachings, a serious dilemma was created for Maimonides. In such instances, he consistently taught that rational certainty must take precedence over the literal meaning of the traditional sources, and that the latter must be reinterpreted in the light of scientific facts. In his *Commentary on the Mishnah* he had stated bluntly: "Thus have taught all the gaonim whose opinions we know, yet I have come to the conclusion that the opposite is true." Later in summarizing the laws governing the calendar, he declared: "Since all these teachings are demonstrated by clear and incontrovertible proofs one does not doubt them because of their authors, be they Israelitic prophets or Gentile scholars." On the other hand, his own medical learning had undoubtedly taught him that predictions of life expectancy always carried with them an element of doubt. That is why he refused to deviate from the Talmudic classification of *terefot* (maimed animals unable to survive), even where it was controverted by veterinary evidence. He apparently felt that even an animal, whose expected life span appeared very short, might nevertheless live much longer.

Fortunately for Maimonides and other orthodox students of science, scientific findings rarely came into conflict with *Halakhic* regulations. The latter were largely concerned with subject matter from the domain of *Aggadah* which, from the outset, had developed in so uncontrolled a fashion that it carried with it inherent contradictions and was subject to an endless variety of interpretations. Its unauthoritative nature had long been conceded by prominent *Halakhists*, and enabled Maimonides and other scholars to follow established scientific facts more freely and to rely on their own reasoning powers.

Death of the Sage

The incessant travail which characterized Maimonides' life —his medical practice, communal activities, and constant writing and revisions of his books—gradually undermined his health. In a letter to Ibn Tibbon he wrote:

> Patients go in and out until nightfall or sometimes, I assure you, until two hours in the night. I talk to them lying on my back because of weakness. When the night falls I feel so weak, I cannot speak any more.

> Thus no Israelite can have a private discussion with me except on the Sabbath. Then they all come to me after the services and I advise them what to do during the week; afterwards they study a little till noon and depart. Some of them come back and study again until the evening prayers.

In spite of his strict regime, to which he devoted a special monograph and according to which he seems to have lived himself, Maimonides did not complete his seventieth year. He died on December 13, 1204 (*Tevet* 20, 4965), and all Egyptian Jewry observed a three-day period of mourning. According to his wish, Maimonides was buried in Tiberias, where his tomb has ever since attracted pious pilgrims. He left behind one son of his old age, Abraham Maimonides, who, as the official *maggid* (preacher) of Egyptian Jewry as well as a jurist and philosopher in his own right, became an important leader of Near Eastern Jewry in the first half of the thirteenth century.

Impact of His Works

The controversy which Maimonides' works had aroused during his lifetime continued after his death. He had purposely written his *Guide* in a more involved style than he had employed in his juridical works and had repeatedly warned his readers to study his words very carefully lest they understand them "to mean the exact opposite of what I intended to say." It is not surprising that his views were condemned not only by ignorant persons, but also by thoughtful and informed traditionalists. Maimonides' insistence that belief in God's corporeality stamped one as a heretic may have been a necessity in the Muslim world, but those residing in the Christian West felt little of that pressure. After all, Christianity itself had gone much further in its doctrine of Incarnation of God, born, living, and dying as a human being. Some other teachings of Maimonides sounded even more extreme and dangerous to western traditionalists.

The assumption of the supremacy of reason and the need to harmonize the revealed word of God with Aristotelian philosophy aroused sharp opposition. In the Provence, particularly, that area of confluence of Islamic and Christian cultures, the anti-Maimonidean controversy reached its climax. Ultimately, the obscurantist faction invoked the aid of the Christian Inquisition. In 1233 it succeeded in persuading the Inquisitors of Montpellier that the Maimonidean *Guide* contained many heretical teachings, dangerous not only to the Jewish community but also to the orthodoxy of Christians. Before very long, however, an enlightened Pope himself promoted a Latin translation of the *Guide* so that he might study it at its source, and then the leading Christian scholastics, Albertus Magnus and Thomas Aquinas, frequently cited "Moses the Egyptian" with approval and respect. Little did the Jewish anti-Maimonidean informers realize that by inviting the Inquisition to interfere with Jewish literature, they were paving the way for the prolonged trial and burning of the Talmud.

At the same time, Maimonides' work inspired more moderate Jewish scholars the world over to concern themselves with philosophic and scientific studies. An ardent admirer like Yedaiah ha-Penini of Beziers exclaimed with the typical exuberance of youth: "We cannot give up science; it is as the breath of our nostrils. Even if Joshua were to appear and forbid it, we should not obey him. For we have a warranty which outweighs them all, namely, Moses ben Maimon who recommended it, and impressed it upon us. We are ready to set our goods, our children, and our lives at stake for it." With less vocal enthusiasm but equal devotion, many students, including some Muslims and Christians, studied the *Guide* with great care. A thirteenth-century Muslim even wrote a commentary on some of its sections. Several distinguished Jews, including Don Isaac Abravanel, wrote extensive commentaries on the whole work, while all later Jewish philosophers constantly took a position for or against some of its individual teachings. With Spinoza, whose philosophy was greatly indebted to that of Maimonides, the teachings of the Fustat sage entered the arena of modern philosophy and have ever since fructified human thought on basic religious problems.

Even more influential within Jewish life and thought was his great *Code* and other legal writings. Many distinguished *Halakhists*, including Joseph Karo, author of the similarly authoritative compilation, the *Shulkhan Arukh*, wrote lengthy commentaries on it. Some poets, even if not endowed with grace divine, reproduced the regulations of the *Code* in verse form. Still today, students of Talmudic lore often exert their ingenuity in first detecting supposed contradictions in the *Code* and then harmonizing them by the use of advanced Talmudic dialectics. The very *Kabbalists* whose mystic teachings were so completely alien to Maimonides' rationalistic mind tried to claim the master as their own. Shem Tov ben Abraham ibn Gaon, one of Maimonides' outstanding commentators, actually reported to have read in an ancient scroll the following auto-graph entry: "I, Moses ben Maimon, descended into the cham-bers of *Merkabah* (the divine chariot of Ezekiel's vision)." Modern *Ḥasidic* rabbis likewise derived many significant teach-ings from the sage of Fustat. Hence, Saadiah ibn Danan (fif-teenth century) was not guilty of an overstatement when he wrote that "under Ben Maimon's guidance all Israel walked from sunrise to sunset."

The Man and His Legacy

As for the Jewish masses, they took a cue from the poet Yehudah al-Harizi, who had sung:

Thou art an angel divine,
Created in God's image,
Though formed in our shape,
For thy sake did God say,
"Let us make man in our image, after our likeness."

A rich web of tales and legends were spun around the person-ality of the master. He became one of the great heroes of Jewish folklore in both East and West. After the appearance of an alleged portrait of the sage, in an Italian work by a Christian scholar, Ugolinus (1744), reproductions were spread through-out the Jewish communities. In the nineteenth century there were, indeed, few Jewish homes which were not adorned with this alleged likeness of the jurist-philosopher.

What does Maimonides mean to our generation? Answers to this question will depend on the personal *Weltanschauung* of each individual. Certainly much of the sage's world outlook, his picture of the astronomic and geographic world, his ac-ceptance of the four basic physical elements (earth, water, fire, and air), and even many remedies suggested in his medical works have become decidedly obsolete. His metaphysical dis-cussions and his intense preoccupation with the problems of creation versus eternity of the universe, his proofs for the ex-istence and oneness of God, or his doctrine of the negative attributes—all bear the imprint of the scholastic philosophy of his day and carry little immediate conviction to men searching after ultimate religious verities today.

Nevertheless, Maimonides' ingenious attempt to solve major religious problems through the instrumentality of reason, and his penetrating effort to build bridges between the traditional sources and the new facts presented by philosophy and science, have set an inspiring example for the following generations. The fact that religious philosophies advanced by such diverse thinkers as Avicenna, Maimonides, and Thomas Aquinas had so much in common and were accepted with relatively little opposition in that religiously enthusiastic age, when denominationalism was the most divisive force in mankind, has served as a testimony to the basic unity of the human mind.

Maimonides' legal and ethical teachings have suffered far less from the obsolescence of the ages. Perhaps because human progress in law and ethics has been much slower, or non-existent, the teachings of ancient and medieval thinkers, as reformulated in his writings, still have a direct bearing upon human behavior today. Certainly, Orthodox Jews living in accordance with the 613 commandments of Judaism still try to live up to the postulates of the thinker of Fustat, even though they know that *Halakhah* has long since overruled many of his individual decisions.

The extraordinary lucidity and persuasiveness of Maimonides' formulations, his penetrating methods of dealing with complex legal concepts, and his monumental effort to derive from the vast, often contradictory, traditional sources a uniform and self-consistent legal system may still serve as a model for all new juridical compilations. In the field of ethics practically nothing taught by Maimonides has become wholly obsolete. Perhaps our generation prefers to place different emphases on and ascribe different values to certain segments of the Maimonidean doctrine. But just as Maimonides himself attempted few innovations in the realm of ethical behavior, so have his successors until the present day departed relatively little in this area from the memorable structure erected by the masterbuilder. Moreover, like other classics, Maimonides' works have provided different values for different generations. If we, too, restudy them in the same creative way as Maimonides did in reinterpreting the older authorities, we shall indeed find that he may serve as a guide for the perplexed of our generation as well.

FOR FURTHER READING

BLEICH, David, *With Perfect Faith: The Foundations of Jewish Belief* (Hoboken, NJ: Ktav, 1983).

GOODMAN, L.E., *Rambam Readings in the Philosophy of Moses Maimonides* (New York: Schocken, 1977).

HARTMAN, David, *Maimonides: Torah and Philosophic Quest* (Philadelphia: Jewish Publication Society, 1976).

HESCHEL, Abraham, I., *Maimonides: A Biography* (New York: Farrar, Strauss & Giroux, 1982). An existentialist picture of the life of Maimonides.

DRENSTAG, Jacob, I., Editor, *Eschatology in Maimumdean Thought, Messianism Resurrection and the World to Come* (Hoboken, NJ: Ktav, 1983).

JACOBS, Louis, *Principles of the Jewish Faith* (New York: Basic Books, 1964).

TWERSKY, Isadore, *A Maimonides Reader* (New York: Behrman House, 1972).

TWERSKY, Isadore, *Introduction to the Code of Maimonides* (New Haven: Yale University Press, 1980).

Rashi

The flowering of philosophy, poetry, and science among the Jews in Muslim lands found no parallel in the medieval world under Christian domination. The environment in Christian Europe during the ninth and tenth centuries was not conducive to the development of Jewish culture, and no figures arose comparable in stature to Saadia, Halevi, or Maimonides.

In the eleventh century, Talmud study began to flourish in the area that is today France and Germany. A relatively small number of Jews had come to the Rhineland with the Roman armies and lived at peace with the Romans, Gauls, and Franks. But life was not easy, particularly after the advent of Christianity; the clergy tried to restrict contacts between Jews and Christians, and the Merovingians and other ruling houses, after their conversion to Catholicism, were often intolerant. Moreover, in the emerging feudal system which was based on a hierarchy of lords, knights, and serfs, there was no place for the Jew.

During the reign of Charlemagne (768-814), the great builder of the Frankish state, however, Jewish immigration was encouraged. Jews were valued for their international commercial connections and were given protection. Numerous Jewish communities were subsequently established in spite of the restrictions enacted by church councils. Occasionally, Jews were banished for a time, but on the whole they managed to maintain friendly relations with their neighbors in southern and northeastern France and in Metz, Worms, Mayence, and other German communities along the Rhine. In comparison with the indignities and brutalities they were to suffer after the Crusades, life was still quite tranquil.

Little is known about the status of Jewish learning in the Franco-German area before the year 1000, when the rabbinic scholar Gershom ben Judah established a school of Talmudic studies in Mayence. While this academy lacked the breadth and sophistication of Spanish-

Jewish scholarship, it laid the foundations for Ashkenazi Jewry for centuries to come. Gershom issued decrees forbidding the practice of polygamy and insisting on the consent of both parties to a divorce. These decrees were accepted as law by Ashkenazi Jews, and Gershom came to be known as the "Light of the Exile," rivalling in authority the last of the Gaonim* who was trying to keep alive the tradition of Saadia in Babylonia.

The school did not last long after Gershom's death, but before it disappeared it gave instruction to a young student who came from France. This student was later to be known as Rashi, one of the great interpreters and teachers of Judaism.

*Hai Gaon, son of the famous Sherira Gaon (968-998), was the last Gaon of eminence, serving for forty years until his death in 1038.

9 . Rashi
[1040-1105]

SAMUEL M. BLUMENFIELD

R A B B I Shlomo Yitzhaki, better known by his initials Rashi, though no longer read and studied as widely and assiduously as in previous generations, is still accepted as the authoritative commentator on the Bible and Talmud. The great impact which his teachings have had upon Jewry is due to the decisive role he played in maintaining the continuity and authenticity of Judaism at a critical juncture in the history of Jewish culture.

By the eleventh century, Babylonian and other Oriental Jewish communities had passed the zenith of their communal and literary creativity, while European Jewry was still in the throes of social and cultural adjustment to the new emerging patterns of western Christian culture. The world of the Bible had already receded to a seemingly hoary past, while that of the Talmud had become increasingly less intelligible since Aramaic was no longer the language of the majority of Jews, particularly in the West. There was, therefore, serious danger that the Bible would be relegated to the past, and, though revered, might no longer be considered relevant to the needs of a Jewry under totally new and different conditions. As to the rabbinic lore of the Talmud, it might have been lost altogether, owing to the sheer lack of knowledge of its language and the inability of most Jews to understand its involved legal dissertations and discussions.

Rashi's commentaries accomplished the remarkable feat of interpreting the Bible in terms and accents of eleventh-century Franco-German Jewry, and of providing the key to the sealed pages of the Talmud. Rashi's literary labors helped to link European Jewry to the chain of tradition of ancient Palestinian and Babylonian Jewries. Rashi's role in the history of Jewish culture can best be summed up in the words of the fourteenth-century Spanish rabbi, Menahem ben Zerah: "He (Rashi) wrote as if by divine inspiration. . . . Without him the Talmud would have been forgotten in Israel."

In spite of the widespread fame that Rashi attained during his lifetime and the many studies of his works by generations of writers after him, precious little is known about him as a person. Rashi, like other Jewish pietists of his day, did not consider it proper to reveal in his writings personal details about himself. The information that is available has been culled from scattered and indirect references in his own voluminous writings and the works of his disciples.

The Wandering Student

Rashi was born in the year 1040 in Troyes, the capital of Champagne in northern France. He came of a pious family which engaged in the prevailing economic, social, and religious pursuits of the Jewish community of Troyes. Rashi seldom refers to his father, but he does refer to his maternal uncle, Rabbi Shimon Hasaken, as "an expert scholar of the Talmud." Rashi married young and had three daughters, two of whom later married scholars of note and were the parents of renowned interpreters of the Bible and the Talmud, including the famous Rabbenu Jacob Tam. Descendants of Rashi, together with other illustrious disciples, became the founders of a school of commentators known as *Tosafists*. Their name is derived from the Hebrew root "to add," for they "added" to the commentaries and explanations of Rashi.

Until Rashi became famous, Troyes was not distinguished as a center of Jewish learning. Like other scholars of his day who were eager to pursue their education, Rashi traveled to Worms and Mayence, centers of Jewish learning in Germany. In these Talmudic schools Rashi received instruction from disciples of Rabbenu Gershom, known as the "Light of the Exile" because of his pioneering and creative rabbinic leadership in Central Europe in the tenth century. Rashi speaks of his own experience when he says that like "doves that wander from dovecote to dovecote in search of food, so they (students) go from the academy of one scholar to that of another in search of inter-pretations of Torah."

As such a wandering student, Rashi's life was full of hard-ships. "Lacking bread and decent clothes, with a millstone on my neck (burdened by marriage), I served before them (the masters)," he writes. After spending eight years of study in Germany, he returned to his native city of Troyes at the age of twenty-five where he began his lifelong career of teaching and writing. Rashi acquired his learning from the available lit-erature on the Bible and the Talmud in Hebrew and Aramaic, but he also had access to writings in French, German, and possibly Latin. Soon after, he organized a Talmudic school of his own, and hundreds of students flocked to receive the benefits of his vast erudition and distinctive method of inter-pretation.

Influence of French Civilization

While our information about Rashi as a person is sparse, recent studies of Franco-German Jewry of the Middle Ages offer considerable information concerning the social and spirit-ual environment in which Rashi grew up and labored. Troyes was then a center of commerce, the seat of government, and the scene of important church conferences. Like most towns of Franco-Germany in those days, Troyes, whose total popu-lation at that period is estimated at about ten thousand, con-tained only about a hundred Jewish families closely knit by economic and religious ties—indeed, many of Rashi's disciples were his relatives. (To this day Troyes has retained an alley named "Rue de la Synagogue.") Like the other residents of this rural community, the Jews of Troyes were farmers and wine-makers. Grape-growing was a major occupation in which Rashi himself engaged for his livelihood. Some Jews also car-ried on commerce with neighboring communities as well as with those beyond the borders of Franco-Germany.

Contrary to conventional notions about the ghetto character of the Jewish communities in the Middle Ages, French Jews in the eleventh century maintained close relations with their non-Jewish neighbors. They used the French language in their daily speech, bore French names (one of Rashi's daughters, according to some scholars, was named Belle Assez), and shared with non-Jews in social and economic pursuits. Jewish scholars had such names as Leontin and Bon Fils, while pious poets composed prayers in French. Recent studies indicate the existence of both isolated *piyyutim* (religious poems) in the vernacular and entire prayer books in French. There are also indications that Jews used Gentile tunes for the lullabies they sang their children, and on occasions taught synagogue melodies to Christian priests. Jews often presented gifts to their Christian friends on *Purim*, while non-Jews would offer their Jewish neighbors on the eighth day of Passover leavened cakes, eggs, and the like. Rashi himself was the recipient of many such amenities. Indeed, according to L. Rabinowitz, "from the detailed account of the social, economic and religious life of the Jews of Northern France during the twelfth to fourteenth centuries in all its important aspects, there emerges one fact with unmistakable clarity, viz., that apart from the purely religious life, the Jews lived in a state of complete social assimilation with their non-Jewish neighbors." [1]

In such friendly circumstances, it was natural that much of Rashi's life and experience should have been influenced by the French society and civilization in which he was born and lived practically all of his life. He refers to French as *bilshonenu* ("in our language"), and in his interpretation of events in the Bible and Talmud he avails himself of terms used in his time to describe political and technical subjects. Some scholars have even suggested that the clarity of Rashi's writings may be attributed in part to the influence of the French language, which because of its preciseness has long been the language of international discourse and diplomacy.

Relations with Non-Jews

Though close social and economic contacts existed between the Jews and their non-Jewish environment, there was little common ground in the area of religious and cultural ideas and practices. The Jewish community of the eleventh century was heir to a cultural tradition of about two thousand years and an institution of education at least a thousand years old, whereas the Christian community of this period was witnessing only the beginnings of what later led to the growth of scholarship and the founding of universities. Education did not become compulsory or universal until the end of the nineteenth century, and in eleventh-century Europe was almost exclusively limited to the training of religious teachers and ministers in monastic centers of scholarship, ecclesiastical authorities, and certain royal courts.

While Christian scholars like Anselm, the Archbishop of Canterbury and a contemporary of Rashi, made a dichotomy between knowledge and faith, Rashi and other Jewish scholars and teachers saw faith leading to the search for knowledge, and knowledge or Torah as the foundation of faith. Had not the rabbis of the Talmud taught long before that "an empty-headed man cannot be a sin-fearing man nor can an ignorant person be pious" (*Avot* 2:6)?

The difference in educational practice between the Jewish and non-Jewish community was fully noted by Christian spokesmen in Rashi's days. A pupil of Peter Abelard made the following comparison: "If the Christians educate their sons, they do so not for God, but for gain in order that the one brother, if he be a clerk, may help his father and mother and his other brothers. . . . A Jew, however poor, if he had ten sons would put them all to letters, not for gain, as the Christians do, but the understanding of God's law, and not only his sons, but his daughters." [2]

This appreciation of the Jewish devotion to learning on the part of some Christians did not, however, lead to an understanding of Jews or to continuous friendly relations with them. Owing to strong spiritual and communal disciplines from within and the rivalries between the political interests of the church and state from without, Jews of Troyes and neighboring communities until the end of the eleventh century enjoyed rights and privileges accorded to ecclesiastics, noblemen, and the ruling count's vassals. They were free to choose their residences, and rulers could not legally seize the property of Jews who had decided to move to other localities. But in 1096, with the advent of the Crusades and the ensuing era of lawlessness and persecutions, these rights and privileges were curtailed and even abrogated. The Crusades must have brought about so many forced conversions that Rashi deemed it necessary to make allowances for unwilling Jewish converts. He called upon his people to show sympathy and forbearance to those who returned to the fold, saying: "Their defection was made under the menace of the sword, and out of their free will they hastened to return to the God of our fathers in penitence."

The Crusades also renewed disputes with Jews in regard to the merits of Judaism and Christianity, especially on the subject of Jesus. Commenting on the verse, "Lord, in Thy strength the king rejoiceth" (Psalms 21:2), which Christian theologians claimed was a reference to Jesus, Rashi argued that "it is more correct to speak of King David." Alluding to the bitterness of the disputations with Christian theologians, Rashi commented: "They hate me . . . because I do not pursue after their falsehood to follow their errors."

Rashi's rebuttal of Christian ideas is to be found in his reference to claims made by the Christian clergy to property rights over the Holy Land. In his first commentary on the Bible (Genesis 1:1), Rashi argues that the Holy Land does not belong either to Christians or Muslims, quoting from rabbinic writings: "The land belongs to the Lord, He created and gave it to whom He pleased. When He willed, He gave it to them and when He willed, He took it from them and gave it to us." In another connection Rashi expressed his views on the same subject even more forcefully: "The Holy Land does not belong either to the Christians or to the Muslims, but remains the perennial property of the Jewish people down to eternity."

Traditionalist and Realist

Far from being a cloistered scholar, confined to the proverbial "four ells of *Halakhah*" associated with the ghetto tradition of later centuries, Rashi displayed broad interests and warm sympathies in worldly affairs. There is hardly an area of human experience of his day that seemed alien to him. His commentaries and writings reveal familiarity not only with the wine industry in which he engaged but also with such subjects as carving, engraving, falconry, fishing and bee husbandry, glasswork, botany, ship repairs, and military affairs. For example, commenting on "the Lord trieth the righteous" (Psalms 11:5), Rashi says:

"The nature of the Holy One, blessed be He, is to chastise and to try the righteous more than the wicked. Just like the flax-man who knows that the better the quality of his flax, the more he beats it; when the quality is poor he does not beat it, as it would dribble away."

Other illustrations of Rashi's interest in everyday affairs and his use of homely similes follow:

> Interest is like the bite of a snake. At first it is a small wound on one's foot, and suddenly it swells up as the head (Exodus 22:24).

> One does not wait on his master while dressed in the garments he used in the kitchen (Leviticus 6:4).

> Merchants show the bad wares first and afterwards show the better ones (Numbers 13:17).

This wide range of interest undoubtedly contributed to what might be described as Rashi's pragmatic and wholesome views on a number of questions of Jewish law and practice. On the question of wine handled by Gentiles (*Yayin Nesekh*), for example, Rashi took a liberal position. According to the Talmud, a Jew was forbidden to use or to benefit from wine touched by non-Jews. Since wine was frequently used among Gentiles for idolatrous purposes, the rabbis of Talmudic times had felt justified in keeping Jews from any possible contact with Gentiles that would lead to a breach of law against idol-worship.

In France, however, many Jews, including Rashi himself, derived their livelihood from the making of wine in a predominantly non-Jewish community. Because of the many restrictions limiting the economic pursuits of Jews in medieval Europe, they were confronted with the choice of either withdrawing from the wine industry and being reduced to poverty, or disregarding the law and breaking with Jewish tradition. Rashi, like other courageous rabbinic personalities, shunned both these alternatives. By facing realistically the new circumstance of Jewish life in Europe he sought and found a formula which made it possible for the Jews of his time to adhere to another important tradition, "He shall keep my statutes" (Leviticus 18:5). He maintained that the prohibition against wine handled by Gentiles does not apply to Christians on the principle that they are not idolaters. Therefore Jews should be permitted to employ Gentiles in the production and distribution of wine.

Rashi is also quoted by his grandson, the Rashbam,* as interpreting the prohibition against doing business with Gentiles on their holiday to be limited only to certain specific festivals, and as ruling that even on such occasions one need not be overly strict. Among the reasons given for this leniency is that "we are in exile and cannot afford to refrain from dealing with people among whom we live . . . and from whom we derive our sustenance." There is also the implied reason that since Jews disregard these prohibitions and restrictions, there is no sense making matters worse by branding those who violate the laws as transgressors. This is based on the rabbinic principle: "It is better that they (the Jews) err unknowingly than deliberately."

Like his contemporaries, Rashi sought to conform to tradition, but this formal loyalty to rabbinic teachings did not preclude his suggesting changes in the law in order to meet a new and urgent need for survival in a Christian community. Indeed, the *pilpul* method of interpreting the Talmud with its ingenious dialectic perfected by Rashi's disciples was another device for squaring innovations in beliefs and traditions with older views and practices. Rashi's views on the wine problem and his decisions on similar questions reveal his courage and ingenuity in meeting new realities while preserving the spirit of old laws and traditions.

Rashi's Major Contribution

The secret of Rashi's influence is to be sought chiefly in his methods and skills as a commentator and teacher. The Jewish and secular lore contained in his writings influenced Jews in all walks of life, from lowly laborers to men of wealth, from young students to accomplished scholars. Indeed, most printed texts of the Pentateuch and the Talmud were subsequently accompanied as a matter of course by Rashi's commentary, which enriched the imagination and warmed the hearts of generations

* Rabbi Samuel ben Meir, also a distinguished French biblical commentator (1085-1160).

of school children and mature students. In fact, Rashi's commentary was among the first to be printed in 1475, seven years before the printing of the Bible itself.

Because of the type of script used in Rashi's commentaries by the first printer (which was then current among the Jews of Spain) and by many printers in succeeding generations, this script became associated with the name of Rashi, and is known to this day as Rashi script.

To understand the extraordinary interest shown in Rashi, one must appreciate the method he used in teaching the Jewish heritage. The question of how to hand down Jewish ideals and practices was a matter of controversy between the Sadducees and Pharisees several centuries earlier, one of their major points of dissension being whether the Scripture should be understood and transmitted literally or freely according to its spirit. This same controversy later led to disputes between the Karaites and Rabbinites.

Clearly, Rashi's problem was a difficult one. To interpret Jewish lore literally or to explain it only rationally would render the Torah a dogmatic, spiritless code. On the other hand, the method of free interpretation had its dangers, for in departing from the literal and rational approach, one incurred the risk of lapsing into farfetched allegory and mysticism. That Rashi was conscious of these dangers appears from the following comments: "Let the interpreter keep on interpreting, but we are interested in the simple, natural meaning of the text" (Exodus 6:9), or from his denunciation of those "who pervert the sense of the Torah by wrong and misleading exegesis" (Berakot, 126).

Rashi's contribution consists in his blending of both *peshat*, literal exegesis, combined with *derash*, free interpretation and homiletic comment. In his *peshat*, Rashi explains the text and conveys its meaning in terms of logic, grammar, common sense, and experience. This rational and logical treatment helped clarify many obscure passages and ideas, and to this day Rashi remains the most widely used commentator by students of Bible and Talmud.

Not being too far removed from the Talmudic age, Rashi was able to project himself into the world of the Talmud and share in it as though he were a contemporary. He succeeded also in steeping himself in the world of the Bible. Having shared vicariously in the life of biblical and post-biblical Jewry, Rashi was able to interpret the civilization of ancient Israel to his contemporaries in a lucid and vivid style which still remains a model of clear, precise Hebrew writing.

When Rashi was in doubt as to whether his contemporaries would understand a certain Hebrew or Aramaic term, he did not hesitate to translate it into French. Rashi's use of the vernacular is another indication of his eagerness to bring the teachings of Judaism to as many people as possible. He used some three thousand *Loazim* or French words, which have been studied by scholars of Romance languages as an important source of information about the French language of the eleventh century. When he was not certain that words alone would suffice to convey the full meaning of a passage, Rashi used drawings (I Kings 6:31) or cited graphic illustrations from daily life and the experiences of artisans and men of affairs.

When Rashi was not certain of the meaning of a text, he would quote an authority, adding that he was not convinced; or he would confess: "I do not know." At times he pointed out his own errors. Even in old age, when men's minds ordinarily tend to become less flexible, Rashi confided to his grandson that if he had the time, he would rewrite his biblical commentary in the light of more recent findings. Such freedom from dogmatism is all the more significant when considered against the authoritarian spirit of the age.

Rashi as Educator

Rashi's method is noteworthy for its sense of fitness and balance. He neither leaves passages unexplained, nor does he explain more than is necessary. As a skillful teacher he veers carefully between "not enough" and "too much," aiming to "help the student to help himself," to use William Kilpatrick's description of the ideal teacher. Drawing upon the distinction made by the rabbis between the *ḥakam* who relies upon authority, and the *ḥabon*, who from his knowledge of one situation understands another, Rashi advises the learner: "Do your own investigations in order to be able to infer one case from another." In his commentaries, instead of doing the work for the student, Rashi stimulates the learner and thus achieves one of the major goals of education.

While Rashi employed the rational approach, he was fully cognizant of the place of emotions and imagination in education. Though it is unlikely that Rashi was influenced by Plato's theory of character-building through the arts, as a true pedagogue he sensed the power of myth and poetry in elevating the spirit and enriching the imagination of the learner. This explains how a man with as clear and realistic a mind as that of Rashi could so often be at one with the world of imagery and poetic fantasy—the Midrash—the rich treasure of rabbinic lore from which he took so many references. Rashi, however, chooses his selections with discriminating taste and with a sense of harmony. "There are many Midrashim (interpretations)," he remarks a number of times, "but I have chosen the *Aggadah* which interprets Scripture according to its proper meaning in its appropriate place" (Genesis 3:9).

In many instances, Rashi, in order to convey more graphically a rabbinic thought or image, departs from the original text and freely uses his own intimate style. That his versions have proved to be more appealing than the originals can be judged from the fact that the one hundred rabbinic dicta which are most current in the Yiddish language are those quoted from Rashi and in his style.

An example of Rashi's effectiveness in selecting rabbinic material rich in emotional content and human appeal is his often-quoted commentary dealing with Jacob's request to be buried in Canaan and his allusion to the burial of his wife Rachel (Genesis 48:7):

> And although I trouble you to take me into the land of Canaan for burial, and I did not do this for your mother, though I might easily have done so since she died quite close to Bethlehem. . . . I know that in your heart you feel some resentment against me. Know, however, that I buried her there by the command of God, that she might help her children when Nebuzardan will take them into captivity. When they pass along the road, Rachel will come forth from her grave and stand by her tomb weeping and seeking mercy for them as it is said, "A voice is heard in Ramah . . . . the sound of weeping. . . . Rachel weeping for her children." And

the Holy-One-blessed-be-He replies to her, "Thy children will return to their own border."

The tender voice and the moving appeal of Rachel pleading for her perpetually wandering children as expressed by Rashi in these lines have found their echo in the hearts of millions of Jews who studied the Pentateuch with Rashi's commentary, and had much to do with preserving the hope that Zion would one day be rebuilt.

Pedagogic Insights

An important pedagogic principle which has its origin in Talmudic literature and is particularly stressed by Rashi is the idea that the learning process can best be achieved if it starts on the level of the learner and with his interest. Rashi missed no opportunity to urge the teacher to consider the student—his tastes, interests, and capacities. He emphasizes that learning can best be achieved through love and joy rather than through fear and pain: "He who does not care for the words of Torah, even reasonable explanations do not appeal to him; but he who desires them, even those parts which he learns with effort and bitterness become sweet to him." He also stresses the thought that "there is no comparison between one who does things out of love and one who does them out of fear. He who does things for his teacher out of fear leaves him the moment they become burdensome."

Rashi further advises the teacher ". . . . teach only the tractate that (the pupil) requests; for if the teacher will use another tractate, the pupil would not know it, for his heart is bent upon the things he likes." Commenting on the expression, "early rain which falls gently," Rashi plays on the similarity between the words *moreh* (teacher) and *yoreh* (rain), and suggests that it refers to a "person who teaches his students with gentleness." Rashi also maintains that "when a person explains his words well to a student and makes his words sweet, he (the pupil) will increase in learning, and if the teacher approaches the learner in a pleasant way, the pupil will succeed in his studies; otherwise, he will not." He exhorts the student: "Learn out of joy and with good cheer in accordance with your heart's dictation and understanding." These exhortations in behalf of the child as the subject (and not object) of education, which are in complete harmony with modern educational theory, are eloquent testimony to Rashi's pedagogic insight.

Rashi is aware of the value of firmness, reproof, and occasional chastisement. He has, however, a fine sense of discernment among types of students and the effect of punishment on individuals of differing intelligence. He stresses the thought of Scriptures that "the humiliation of rebuke will impress a man of understanding more effectively than a hundred blows dealt a fool" (Proverbs 17:10). He also suggests that it is better to inform the student in advance that he will be punished rather than administer sudden punishment. Rashi goes out of his way to warn against unreasonable and harsh treatment: "You are not to punish him more than is necessary to remove him from your presence, but he should sit there together with others and thus he will become attentive." Rashi also suggests that once punishment has been meted out, an effort should be made at immediate conciliation to end unpleasantness as soon as possible.

This liberal attitude to the pupil was quite unusual in his time, which was largely under the influence of St. Augustine, who taught that "a birch, a strap, a cane" are indispensable to "overcome ignorance." Even in the days of colonial New England, schools viewed children as "limbs of Satan" and therefore sought to inhibit their natural appetites and interests as inclinations toward evil.

Like his contemporaries, Rashi stressed the value of drill and systematic study, but at the same time he placed an unusual emphasis upon explanation, understanding, and reasoning. According to Rashi, it was not enough for the teacher to say, "this is the tradition that I received," but he must explain and give reasons for everything possible. Commenting on Exodus 21:1, Rashi interprets "thou shalt set before thee" to mean that one must "set the material (before the student) and give reasons which will satisfy the learner." Rashi expresses the same thought in a letter to his son-in-law Meir ben Samuel. The rabbis of old arrived at decisions, he says, "not because of tradition or proofs from the Talmud but because of the understanding of their heart."

Rashi himself, in spite of his reverence for his teachers, did not hesitate to express himself vigorously against them when he found their views unacceptable. The person who gathers information without understanding Rashi describes as "a basket full of books," carrying a load without appreciating its contents. Rashi used all possible devices to simplify his subject matter and make it understandable to different types of students. That is why his commentaries on the same subject may differ in form, depending upon the kind of student for whom they were intended.

Rashi, aware of the importance of a well-balanced personality, states that "he who kills himself over the words of Torah is not worthy that his views be received and quoted." He thus disregarded the Talmudic statement (*Berakot*, 63b) that "the words of Torah endure only with him who kills himself over them." Rashi is fully conscious too of the great educational value of habit formation and says, "The education of an infant is essentially to enable him to follow his habits when he grows up" (Proverbs 22:6).

Rashi in his utterances is not lacking in a sense of humor. He supports the advice of some rabbis of the Talmud not to dwell in a city which is led by scholars "because they are intent on their studies rather than on the affairs of the town" (*Pesaḥim*, 11ra). Critical of the negligent appearance of many a scholar, Rashi stresses the need for cleanliness. Likewise, he realizes the difficulties of being a servant of scholars for they usually display ill temper (*Sabbath*, 11a), in spite of all the encomium that tradition showered upon them.

Legacy as Rabbi and Teacher

Rashi is in the main stream of Jewish tradition, in which the rabbi and teacher, rather than the ruler and priest, guide the development of the people. Moses is known as Moshe Rabbenu, "our teacher," and the reconstruction of Jewish religious life after the Babylonian Exile is associated with Ezra, the leading teacher of his day. Following the destruction of the Second Temple, the continuity of Jewish development was ensured by the activity of a third great teacher, Rabbi Johanan ben Zakkai. Rashi too made his contribution as a rabbi and teacher.

In his own day, Rashi brought the rabbinic world into the

very life of his people. As a result, Jewry for many centuries did not know of the distinction that existed in Christendom between the clergy and the laity. Because of his lucid, warm style and his intimate manner of interpretation, Rashi helped bring an ancient heritage to life, not for the scholar alone, but for the Jewish people as a whole. While education was until modern times restricted to the few, and in the days of Rashi to the clergy, Jewish learning, because of Rashi, was so widespread that the average Jew could quote Scripture and adorn his quotations with Rashi's commentaries.

In Rashi's writings, one finds sublime expressions of the value of study and teaching. There is hardly an utterance on education recorded by generations of scholars and pietists who preceded him which is not quoted directly or indirectly by him. Torah was to Rashi more than a means of imparting knowledge, training in skills, or even character-building. It was an integral part of religion itself, an essential element of faith and observance.

Like many a great Jewish personality, Rashi shows a deep appreciation of the historic mission of the teacher in the centuries-old struggle for survival of the Jewish people. Teaching to him was not a chore to be relegated to someone else, as among the ancient Greeks and Romans, where the slave performed the function of teacher. To Rashi, teaching was a divine function and the teacher a kind of spiritual father. By bringing out the potentialities of the learner, the teacher helped recreate the human personality and thus partook of the function of God. God Himself is often referred to in Jewish tradition as scholar and teacher. In the words of Rashi, "Even the master still needs instruction, and the Holy One teaches him" (*Temurah*, 16a).

Rashi's impact on Jewish learning can be judged by the fact that more than two hundred super-commentaries have been written upon his commentaries on the Bible and Talmud. His writings stimulated generations of scholars and opened for them new areas of studies and investigation. Recent studies have shown that the contribution of Rashi and his disciples, known as the *Tosafists*, was more than a successful attempt at explaining or interpreting Bible and Talmud. Just as the rabbis of the Talmud, while apparently seeking only to explain the Bible, in reality initiated a new era in the history of Jewish culture, so Rashi and his followers, through their interpretations of the works of their predecessors, ushered in an even newer era in the growth and development of Judaism, namely, the institution and tradition of the rabbinate. A distinguished Talmudist maintains that Rashi was "the founder of the rabbinate in Western and Central Europe" and "responsible for the institution of the rabbinate." [3]

What is particularly significant about the literary labors of Rashi and his disciples is that they also influenced to a considerable degree Christian theologians and commentators in spite of the latter's ingrained bias against the Talmud and rabbinic teachings. It is well known, for example, that Rashi's commentaries were generously used by Nicholas de Lyra, a Christian scholar who in turn exercised a great influence on Luther. Recent studies indicate that Rashi's influence is also to be perceived in earlier Christian scholars as well.

Beryl Smalley, a Christian student of medieval Bible commentaries, speaks of Philo, Rashi, and Maimonides as major influences on Christian scholars. "We hear of controversy between Christian and Jewish scholars, in the form of polemics and disputation," he goes on to say, "yet a Christian wishing to learn Hebrew which he revered not only as the language of the Scriptures but also as 'the mother of tongues,' and which he expected would be the current speech in heaven, was obliged to take a Jew as his teacher. . . . We also hear of the Jew as a 'carrier' bringing Arabic science to Western Europe. But the exegesis of the North French school of Rashi was no imported article: it was a native product, of Jewish manufacture. So collaboration between biblical scholars may have involved a real contact, in which a specifically Jewish method influenced the Christians." [4]

The esteem in which Rashi was held by Jewish posterity is evidenced by the many legends about him—the tribute of inarticulate masses to their favored master. Some legends relate to his forebears, tracing his descent to a venerable Talmudic sage; others deal with Troyes, his birthplace; the honor of being his first home is also claimed by Worms and Lunel. Still another tale tells how his mother, when pregnant, was caught in a narrow street in the midst of a collision of two carriages; to avoid being crushed she pressed against a wall which miraculously opened to receive her. There is also the legend about a chapel Rashi built in Worms and the bench used by him, which are exhibited to tourists.

Rashi has remained a potent influence into our own period, judging by the eloquent testimonies of recent writers. A Jewish scholar records his memories of the time when he studied Rashi: "Great joy seized me when I used to study something difficult that I finally succeeded in grasping. . . . At times I would jump from my seat, startled by the power of Rashi to clarify the most difficult passage by adding one or two words, and at times just one letter." [5] Another contemporary writer states: "Since my childhood, Rabbi Shlomo Yitzhaki fascinated me by his spirituality, kindliness and humility; by his simplicity and wholesomeness; and by the sweetness of his gentle and lucid words that speak to and penetrate the heart."

In his own time and to this day, Rashi succeeded in opening the vast treasures of Jewish lore to the masses of Jewry, thereby setting a unique example of democracy in education.

FOR FURTHER READING

AGUS, I.A., "Rashi and His School," in *The World History of the Jewish People*, pp. 210-248 (Jerusalem: Massada, 1966). Comprehensive review of Rashi's achievements.

GELLES, Benjamin, *Peshat and Derash in the Exegesis of Rashi* (Leiden: E.J. Brill, 1981).

HAILPERIN, H., *Rashi and the Christian Scholars* (Pittsburgh: University of Pittsburgh Press, 1963). An illuminations study of the influence on Christian Biblical exegetes.

"Rashi," in *Encyclopedia Judaica*, Volume 13, pp. 1558-1565 (Jerusalem: 1972).

SHERESHEVSKY, Ezra, *Rashi, The Man and His World* (New York: Harmen Press, 1982).

ZINBERG, Israel, "Biblical Exegesis in Rashi and His Tosafists," in *A History of Jewish Literature*, pp. 3-21, translated and edited by Bernard Martin (Cleveland: Case Western University Press, 1972).

Don Isaac Abravanel

For several centuries after the death of Rashi the northern centers of Jewish life produced few outstanding Jewish personalities. The brutalities which took place at the time of the first Crusade (1096), when ten thousand Jews were killed and hundreds of communities destroyed, inaugurated a period of tragedy and repression for the Jews of Christian Europe.

While the twelfth and thirteenth centuries marked an economic and cultural revival for Christian Europe—the rise of towns, expansion of trade, growth of universities, and emergence of outstanding scholastic philosophers, for the Jew it was a period of growing insecurity and persecution which gradually isolated and segregated him from the rest of the population. The commercial supremacy he had enjoyed before the Crusades came to an end, and only moneylending and the lowest form of petty trading were permitted him.

With his economic degradation came a special political status outside the feudal system, by which the king was able to exercise the most minute control over all his activities. At the beginning of the thirteenth century the wearing of the yellow badge was imposed on Jews by Pope Innocent III, and in 1242, after a public trial, the Talmud was burned in the streets of Paris. When the bubonic plague or "black death" swept Europe in the fourteenth century, Jews were accused of having poisoned the wells and an incredible number were massacred. One by one the European states expelled the Jews from their realms—England in 1290, and France in 1394. In Germany, though no general expulsion took place, remained the classical land of Jewish martyrdom until the end of the Middle Ages.

The bitterest tragedy, however, took place in Spain, which the Christians had gradually reconquered from the Muslims during the twelfth century. At first, the Jews welcomed the Christians in place of the fanatical Almohades and were able to play an economic role in the life of the emerging nation. Indeed, for a time it looked as though Spain might be an exception to the martyrdom and exile that was the lot of their brethren in Northern Europe.

Jews rose to high positions serving as diplomats and financiers. Several outstanding scholars flourished during this period, including Moses ben Naḥman or Naḥmanides (1195-1270), commentator and rabbinic scholar; his disciple, Solomon ibn Adret (1245-1310), a prolific writer in all fields of rabbinic literature; Hasdai Crescas (1340-1410), philosopher and trenchant critic of Maimonides and of Aristotle.

Gradually, however, most of the Christian provinces began to change their policies toward the Jews. In 1391 a series of massacres spelled doom for Spanish Jewry. Roused by the preaching of a fanatic priest, a mob broke into the Jewish quarter in Seville; by the time the orgy of violence had spent itself, over fifty thousand Jews had been killed and whole communities exterminated. Thousands of Jews accepted conversion to Catholicism, including the grandfather of Isaac Abravanel (who later returned to Judaism). While Ashkenazi Jews in Northern Europe, with rare exception, had preferred a martyr's death to giving up their faith, in large segments of the Spanish community Jewish morale broke down. A large community of people, outwardly Catholic but secretly loyal to Judaism, came into being. The new generation, born and educated in the Church but still secretly Jewish, married into aristocratic Christian families and rose to high positions in the political and socal life of the country. This inevitably aroused the jealousy of the masses, who either resented their success or were genuinely dismayed at their lack of sincerity. Soon these Marranos or secret Jews were being persecuted in the same way their Jewish fathers had been.

When Isabella ascended the throne of Castille in 1474, a special tribunal for hunting out heretics was introduced. In 1480 the first auto-da-fé (act of faith) was held, and six men and six women of Jewish extraction were burned alive. Tribunals were set up all over the country with Torquemada as Inquisitor General. It is at this time that Isaac Abravanel arrived in Spain from Portugal. He was the last of a long line of thinkers and scholars who had lived on the

Iberian Peninsula and who combined vast general and Jewish learning with a dramatic public career. Abravanel represents a unique type of Jewish personality who symbolizes both the tragic end of a once powerful community and the amazing ability of the Jew to adjust to new worlds.

10 . *Don Isaac Abravanel*

[1437-1508]

JACOB S. MINKIN

D o n Isaac Abravanel was the last of a long line of brilliant
Jews of the Iberian Peninsula, a noble representative of his people at a most crucial moment in its history. He was a scholar,
thinker, and statesman who rendered service to many of the
courts of Europe. He was finance minister to the king of Portugal, high officer at the court of Ferdinand and Isabella, friend
of the king of Naples, and counselor to the Doge and the Senate of Venice. Few men carried a more massive burden of
responsibility and endured more courageously the shocks of
successive calamities. History provides no better symbol of his
people's fate and fortunes than Abravanel, alternately invited
and rejected, honored and disgraced, until, distressed and afflicted, he died as an exile in a strange land with not even his
grave clearly marked.

Abravanel was the symbol of his people in still another way
—in his love of knowledge and pursuit of learning. Despite his
arduous tasks and perpetual fears, his literary and scholarly
achievements are vast. The affairs of the states he served afforded him little leisure for writing, quiet contemplation, and
scholarship. The books on which his fame rests were written
in the midst of his duties, on stagecoaches, and in the homes of
hospitable friends when, like a driven leaf, he was fleeing for
his life from place to place and from one country to another.

Hailing from a family distinguished for Jewish leadership,
Don Isaac more than lived up to its reputation. His works are
stamped with a love for and loyalty to Jews. They were his
principal concern as he rose to power and influence in country

after country. He was their leader, guide, and spokesman—"a fortress and a shield," a "saviour of the oppressed from the hands of their enemies."

High-Ranking Family

Don Isaac Abravanel belonged to the third generation of the Abravanels who, because of their social and political position, ranked high among the Jews of the Iberian Peninsula. He was born in Lisbon, capital of Portugal, approximately in the year 1437. The exact date of his birth is not known. Likewise, little is known of his childhood. At the time of his birth, the Abravanels had already lived in Portugal a comparatively long time and acquired wealth and status. His father Don Judah and grandfather Don Samuel were friends of the royal house of Portugal and had each served their state in distinguished capacities. Except for a brief period of conversion on the part of his grandfather in 1491, the family was religious yet modern, intensely Jewish but at home in the secular environment. They created for young Isaac an atmosphere conducive to the development of the active as well as the contemplative faculties of his nature. The way for his career as a Jew and man of the world was thus prepared in his early youth.

Don Isaac's education, like that of most children of the Jewish lay aristocracy, contained what was best both in Jewish and secular culture. Religion was the foundation of that education, but it was broadened by training in the liberal arts and sciences of the day. Young Isaac's schedule of studies included the Hebrew, Latin, Portuguese, and Castilian languages, arithmetic, physics, astronomy, and logic, not counting a more than passing acquaintance with the Talmud. "Merchants and financiers, doctors and rabbis, went through the same course of literary, scientific and philosophic instruction," notes a recent writer.

Isaac later amplified what he had learned by research in the works of the Greek and Roman classics; he quoted Seneca in his commentary on *The Ethics of the Fathers,* and devoted a whole dissertation in refutation of Aristotle. He acquainted himself with the literature of Christian and Muslim scholars; he mentions Albertus Magnus and shows high regard for Thomas Aquinas. He is the first Jewish exegetical writer to take notice of Christian Bible commentators such as Jerome, Nicholas de Lyra, and even the baptized Paul of Burges, extracting from them what he found good and valuable.

Early Influences

Isaac Abravanel was quick to learn, with an absorbing and penetrating mind. He grasped everything, understood matters far beyond his years, and was of a restless, eager nature. He was endowed with an extraordinary memory, retaining everything he had ever read, heard, or learned. His later books were almost all written when the author was an exile and wanderer, with no libraries but only his memory to assist him.

After Isaac had acquired all that the elementary schools in the city of his birth could offer, his father succeeded in engaging as private tutor Joseph Chajun, Chief Rabbi of Lisbon, a man of considerable biblical and Talmudic learning. Chajun, seeking to fathom the plain meaning of the Torah, looked for the truth in the teaching of the Bible and the Talmud rather than in the dazzling and hair-splitting casuistry of the French and German scholars. This simplicity he inculcated in his pupil, who followed and later improved on his teacher's method in his own work.

Much as Isaac was impressed by his teacher, however, it was the liberal and cultural atmosphere of his parental home which proved to be the most important influence in his life. His father was both a scholar and a man of the world. His home was a meeting place for all types of men: Jews, Christians, and Mohammedans gathered there to discuss politics, philosophy, and religion. The Bible and the sacred books of Christianity and Islam were the subjects of discussion and controversy. Such diversity of personalities and views left a deep impression on the boy.

In Lisbon Don Isaac's philosophic thinking matured early. He was not long out of his teens when he surprised his friends with a philosophical essay, *Zuret ha-Yesodot*, "The Original Form of the Elements"—fire, water, air, and earth—from which, according to Aristotle, the sublunary world developed. Closely following it was a work of Jewish content, *Ateret*

Zekenim, "The Crown of the Elders," of which B. Netanyahu writes: "When he wrote this book, he had already developed the fundamentals of his world outlook. All the major themes of his writings are to be found in this brief dissertation on the concept of God and the meaning of prophecy . . . his admiration for the *Kabbalists,* 'the bearers of truth,' and his criticism of the philosophers who walk in the darkness! The only exception was Maimonides from whose influence Don Isaac could not free himself."

Commentary on the Bible

In Lisbon, too, Don Isaac's plan for a commentary on the Bible matured in his mind. The halcyon days of Bible exposition had already passed their zenith. After the work of such famous commentators as Rashi, Ibn Ezra, Naḥmanides, David Kimḥi, and Gersonides, there was seemingly little reason for him to duplicate their efforts. But Abravanel had another purpose for his commentary. He was anxious to reveal the creative and ennobling spirit of the Bible, its inner beauty and spiritual grandeur, which in his opinion had been obscured rather than clarified by some of the commentators. Abravanel felt that the correct approach to the Bible lay not in its outward form but in its inner content.

His own method was completely new, and in many respects astonishingly modern. Conservative though he was, he rejected the traditional arrangement of the books of the Bible, and classified them according to their content and the time they were written. He rearranged the chapters of several books of Scriptures, notably Joshua, Judges, Isaiah, and Jeremiah, and he contradicted the Talmudic statement that Joshua wrote his own book. He prefaced each chapter of every book with an introduction, and with questions regarding its subject matter which he carefully analyzed and answered. He quoted leading commentators, including Gentiles, whose opinion, after careful scrutiny, he either accepted or rejected.

Abravanel was also motivated in his commentary on the Bible by the practical exigencies of his times. In the hands of zealous priests and apostate Jews, the Bible had been made to serve as a weapon against Jews. With utter disregard of its meaning, texts and verses of the Bible had been twisted for the purpose of Christian propaganda. The great public disputations in which both the Bible and the Talmud suffered at the hands of their detractors were a century old when Abravanel was born, but their baneful effect continued. It was an ambitious program on which he embarked, but few men were better qualified. His knowledge of the Talmud, although not outstanding, was sufficient. His Hebrew style was fluent, elegant, and graceful. He was at ease in Latin and, as already noted, he was acquainted with the works of non-Jewish writers on the Bible. He had been a student of history, and his knowledge of statecraft afforded him an insight into the ways and habits of courts, kings, and princes. His historical and analytical faculty helped him sense the value of the time, authorship, composition, and chronology of the Holy Writ.

Business and Communal Affairs

The commentary on the Bible, which lay clearly outlined in his mind, had to be temporarily postponed in favor of the more immediate practical duties to which Abravanel was called. A student and scholar by inclination, he was a man of large business affairs by family tradition. His father and grandfather, and possibly generations of ancestors before them, had been great personages. Like them, once Don Isaac tasted the dazzle and glamour of court life, he found it exciting and invigorating. His father, a powerful courtier, but already in his sixties, instructed his son in the duties and responsibilities of the high office which, he knew, would before long fall to him. He instructed him in the intricate business of statecraft, the national budget and taxation, foreign and domestic commerce, and, above all, he conveyed to him what he knew of the temperament and disposition of the Portuguese king and his high officials.

When the student and scholar turned courtier and businessman, he flung himself into his new life with the energy and passion he had formerly given his books. Don Isaac soon won the confidence of King Alfonso and the trust and friendship of the political and financial magnates of the kingdom. His warm personality, winning manner, and practical wisdom gained him the recognition and admiration of a large circle of friends. He became associated both personally and professionally with the powerful house of Braganza, the most influential nobility in the country, especially with Duke Ferdinand, its head, who was lord of fifty towns, castles, and fortresses, and who almost rivaled the reigning monarch in prestige, wealth, and magnificence.

At the same time, Abravanel recognized his responsibility for the life and safety of his coreligionists. Unfortunately, there was great need for such protection both within and without the Portuguese kingdom. Hostile voices for the restriction of the rights of the Jews were not absent in Portugal even under the mild and tolerant rule of King Alfonso.

But life was satisfying while it lasted. "I lived," writes Abravanel in the introduction to his commentary to the Book of Joshua, "in peace in my inherited house in the renowned city of Lisbon, the capital of Portugal, where God had given me blessings, riches, and honor. I built me great houses with many rooms. My home was a meeting place of the wise and the noble. I was beloved in the palace of Alfonso, a just and mighty king, under whom the Jews enjoyed liberty and prosperity. I stood near him, and he leaned upon my hand; and so long as he lived, I went in and out of the palace." Abravanel was happy, too, in his married and domestic life. While not much is known about his wife, she presented her husband with a daughter and three sons—Judah, Joseph, and Samuel.

But the "blessings, riches, and honor" which Abravanel had enjoyed in Portugal, were short-lived; they vanished with the death of his patron, King Alfonso V, on August 18, 1482. Abravanel's trials commenced with the ascent of Jaoa to the Portuguese throne, a ruler completely different in every respect from his father. When King Jaoa came to power, Portugal was seething with discontent and rebellion. The old monarch had been mild and tolerant but not always a wise and sagacious ruler. His expansionist policy had brought ruin and disaster to the country. As against his successful campaign in North Africa, his undertaking against Sicily had ended in national disgrace and catastrophe. A disheartened and starving population was made to pay heavily in taxes for the wars they neither wanted nor could prevent. The baronial system which Alfonso had encouraged and endowed with great power and large gifts of land was another source of discontent.

Flight to Spain

The failure of Alfonso's temperate policy made King Jaoa resolve upon a sterner course. Although only twenty-nine years old upon his accession to the throne, the new king was an astute and firm ruler with definite views of government which he lost no time putting into practice. Jealous of his royal prerogatives, he allowed no interference from the feudal lords of the realm. The capital was tense with excitement and anxiety. The conflict between the king and the nobility created an atmosphere of suspense. Jaoa, set and determined, proceeded against the feudal lords with a firm hand. He struck at the head of the Braganzas first by confronting Prince Ferdinand with a charge of treason against the throne. The prince, unable to clear himself to the king's satisfaction, was summarily sent to the block. The unfortunate man's brothers escaped a like fate by fleeing to Spain.

Abravanel could hardly have expected to escape the king's purge of the Braganzas and other members of the nobility, with whom he was known to be intimately associated and identified in personal and business relations. While at a summer villa with his family, Abravanel was summoned to appear before the king. Advised by a friend to flee for his life, Abravanel lost no time in making his escape. He rode two nights and a day with his son-in-law, who was likewise charged with complicity in the so-called conspiracy, until they crossed the Portuguese border into Castile, in May 1483. It was hardly too soon, for Jaoa's armed troops were already pursuing them.

Scholars are in disagreement on Abravanel's first residence in Spain after his flight from Portugal. Graetz says it was in Toledo, where he met and struck up a friendship with Isaac Aboab, the last representative of Jewish scholarship in Castile, and Abraham Senior, collector of the king's tithes. Recent authorities, however, point to Segura, a small town with a sizeable Jewish community, which Abravanel may have chosen because of its proximity to the Portuguese border so as to keep in touch with affairs in his native country. To place himself beyond the reach of King Jaoa's agents, Abravanel changed places of residence often, spending some time at Alcala, Flascencia, and Segovia.

Thus, at the age of forty-six, Abravanel started his life again. He had managed to rescue some capital from his confiscated fortunes; by an unaccounted-for show of generosity, the Portuguese monarch permitted his wife and children to join him in his exile. The Jews of Spain, proud of the great visitor in their midst, showed him every mark of honor and respect.

Discouraged by his experience, but undaunted in spirit, Don Isaac now resumed his work on the Bible commentary. The creative urge stirred and he worked uninterruptedly day and night. Ideas surged through his mind faster than he could put them down on paper. As though fearing that he might be interrupted, he worked at a furious pace, completing his commentaries on Joshua, the Judges, and the two Books of Samuel in the unbelievably short time of two and a half months. These were significant for their social and political comments on the time in which he lived as well as for his religious and philosophical views. "It was the first and perhaps the only time," remarks Netanyahu, "that the main political part of the Bible was interpreted by a statesman."

Had Abravanel been allowed to continue his work undisturbed, he might have completed his commentary on the whole Bible. It was inevitable, however, that the reputation of his past achievement in finance and statecraft in Portugal should once more clear a path to his door. Was it Abraham Senior, collector of King Ferdinand's revenues, or the surviving members of the Braganza family, now fugitives in Spain, who spread the fame of the distinguished Jewish newcomer? At any rate, about a year after his arrival in Castile, in March, 1484, Abravanel received a summons from the Spanish sovereigns, King Ferdinand and Queen Isabella, to appear at court.

In the Service of Ferdinand and Isabella

The appointment to a high office in service of the Spanish rulers could not have been displeasing to the man who was still smarting under the humiliation of exile from the Portuguese court. What better vindication of his character and ability than to be called, as a fugitive, to serve in the greatest court in Europe, and this in spite of the laws against Jews holding public office and the protest of Pope Sixtus the Fourth? Abravanel also welcomed the appointment for a personal reason. He was essentially a man of action, accustomed from his youth to the din and clamor of large affairs and the handling of intricate matters of state.

This was a critical time in the fiscal affairs of Spain. The unremitting wars with Portugal and the protracted campaign in Granada had drained the last ounce of gold out of the Spanish treasury. The war against the Moors, though popular, was appallingly costly. No new revenues could be raised from a people already heavily burdened. The difficulty was highlighted by a renewed show of strength on the part of the stubborn Moors, and it became clear that what had promised to be a short victorious expedition was demanding a tremendous price of blood and treasure. In desperation, the royal rulers looked around for the man who would perform the miracle of pulling the country out of the mire in which it found itself; they discovered him in Abravanel who, in similar situations in Portugal, had mobilized the country's resources and supplied the armies in the field.

Abravanel advanced rapidly at the court of Ferdinand and Isabella. He was tactful and cautious, prudent and circumspect. He knew how to watch his step in the most Catholic court in Christendom. He served his masters well, building up the country's resources and, incidentally, enlarging his own fortune. Abravanel himself relates that he grew rich in the royal service and bought land and estates, and that he received great consideration and honor from the court and its highest grandees. He was impressed with the gracious attitude of his rulers: to encourage their friendship, he managed to replenish the shrinking war chest by obtaining contributions from wealthy Jews who were eager to manifest their loyal and patriotic support of the struggle against the Moors.

Rising Flames of the Inquisition

But was Abravanel unconscious of the policy of the total destruction of his people that was planned by the Spanish monarchs? Was he not aware of the expulsion of the Jews from Andalusia only three years before he received his royal commission, and their subsequent expulsion from Aragon in 1487, while he was presumably basking in the regal favor and patronage of Ferdinand and Isabella? What illusion about his own and his people's future could Abravanel have had in a country terrorized by so savage and brutal an instrument as the Inquisition? In one of his works he speaks of "the thousands and thousands of renegade Jews who were consigned to the flames by an impious and fanatical clergy, motivated not by religion but by greed, ambition and self-seeking."

Why, then, did not Abravanel try to prevent the wholesale destruction of the Jews by counselling them to emigrate to some other country, to Turkey, for instance, where Jews were free and welcomed? For what miracle could he have been waiting? Abravanel might have known that there was no future for the unbaptized Jews in Spain, and that after having finished with the Marranos, Torquemada, the evil genius of the Inquisition, would turn his bloody hand against all Jews in the kingdom, baptized and unbaptized. Abravanel sensed it in the priest's growing insolence and in his complete control over the minds of the Spanish sovereigns, who would deny him nothing, no matter how extravagant his demands. Ferdinand could not for the moment agree to his confessor's frenzied demand for the total expulsion of the Jews, for Granada had not yet capitulated, and he was badly in need of the ability and experience of his Jewish subjects in the fields of finance and taxation. But their doom was irrevocably sealed.

Still, like their brethren in Germany nearly four and a half centuries later, the Jews did not believe that the blow would fall with such crushing, annihilating force. They had faith in their leaders and influential friends at court. They had contributed mightily to the greatness and prosperity of their fatherland, and the very marriage of Ferdinand and Isabella, which joined the kingdoms of Castile and Aragon under one common rule and made possible a united Spain, was largely the work of patriotic Jewish Spaniards, especially Abraham Senior, an influential Jewish financier and statesman. Paradoxically, the king, who wrapped himself in a mantle of Christian piety and was titled by the Pope as "Ferdinand the Catholic," could not himself have withstood the scrutinizing eyes of an inquisition because of the Jewish blood in his veins, his mother having been the granddaughter of a Jewess in Toledo.

Abravanel was personally not convinced that the king, notwithstanding Torquemada's continuous urging, would carry out the total expulsion of the Jews. He was confident that the "pious" zeal of the churchman would burn itself out, that the people themselves would rise in revolt and denounce him, as the Pope had already done. He was hopeful that the sovereigns, realizing how slight were the gains from the Inquisition as compared with its power for destruction, would soon disown it together with its principal sponsor. Moreover, as Abravanel saw it, the situation of the Jews everywhere in the world was quite hopeless. If in other countries they were not treated with the same extreme violence as in Spain, they were nevertheless regarded as unwelcome strangers almost everywhere. Above all, Abravanel did not have real political power. His functions were strictly financial and administrative, and he was without influence on the political affairs of the state. When, therefore, the blow fell, he was as helpless as the other Jewish representatives at court.

Circumstances favored Torquemada's design. Ferdinand and Isabella were proceeding triumphantly through Andalusia. Scores of Moorish strongholds had fallen before the conquering Christian armies. The sovereigns now pushed forward toward Malaga, which was the prelude to the conquest of Granada, the last bulwark of Saracen dominion in Spain. This was for Torquemada the perfect moment to press for the fulfillment of the old Visigoth ideal, "one state, one faith." Torquemada snatched the opportunity, and demanded the banishment of all Jews. Neither the king nor the queen was yet prepared for so momentous a decision. But the priest pursued them relentlessly, working on their weak, yielding minds, threatening and menacing them in the name of religion and the salvation of their souls. He went so far as to acknowledge his own failure to extirpate heresy, and offered to resign his office. Terrorized by the fierceness of his onslaught, they yielded and gave him the fatal promise.

Abravanel and Torquemada

Once the royal proclamation expelling the Jews was released, the whole country seethed with excitement. The royal court became a battleground of plots and counter-plots. There were parties that were loyal in their support of Abravanel, and others that were fanatic in their zeal for Torquemada.

Abravanel himself rushed to the palace and begged for an audience with their Majesties. Fortunately, history has preserved in Abravanel's own words a record of that historic meeting:

> I pleaded with the king many times. I supplicated him thus: "Save, O king. Why do thus to thy servants? Lay on us every tribute and ransom, gold and silver, and everything that the children of Israel possess they shall willingly give to their fatherland." I sought out my friends, those who stand near the king and enjoy his confidence, and begged them to beseech and petition him to revoke the evil decree concerning our destruction and annihilation, but all in vain. Like an adder which stoppeth its ears, he remained deaf to our appeals. The queen, also, was standing by his side, but she would not listen to our plea. On the contrary, she argued in favor of carrying out the plan. I neither rested nor spared myself, yet the calamity was not averted.

Abravanel promised gold, and more gold, even greater wealth than the royal treasury of Castile had ever known. He pledged his own fortune of thirty thousand gold ducats and all the wealth of his people, the sum being sufficient to cover the entire cost of the war with Granada. Here was a treasure to whet the appetite of any monarch, even one more greedy than King Ferdinand. At the sight of so much gold, Ferdinand wavered, and although the queen remained adamant, the king was ready to accept the ransom and rescind the edict of expulsion. But Torquemada was suspicious. Not for a moment did he relax his vigilance. He had been watching outside the palace doors. When he learned what was happening, he burst into the audience chambers with the crucifix held aloft in his hand, screaming with frenzied fanatical boldness:

"Behold the crucified whom the accursed Judas Iscariot sold for thirty pieces of silver. Your Majesties are about to sell him for thirty thousand ducats. Here he is, take him and sell him. I resign my post. No one shall impute this guilt to me. You, however, shall have to answer to your God." He threw the crucifix into the faces of the monarchs and rushed out of the hall.

The priest was transported by bigoted madness, his gaunt, lean figure shaken with emotion. His voice trembled, and his deep-set eyes burned. His act decided the fate of a whole people. After this there was no doubt, no hesitation. The monarchs were stunned, and Torquemada prevailed.

On the 31st day of March, 1492, during the same year that had witnessed their triumphal entry into Granada, Ferdinand and Isabella issued in the beautiful Alhambra the proclamation ordering all Jews to depart from the Spanish dominions of Castile, Aragon, Sicily, and Sardinia. They were given four months in which to leave their homes and were to be allowed to take with them all their movable property, excepting gold, silver, and coins of any description, as well as certain goods whose export was forbidden.

Exile from Spain

The first effect of the publication of this edict was one of utter panic and desolation. Abravanel wrote: "When the Jews learned of the evil that had befallen them, they wept and mourned. Wherever the news of the king's decree was received, there was great wailing and lamentation, for no such sorrow had befallen the Jews since they had been driven out of their own land and sent into exile to live among strangers." Although they had long expected the blow, its coming found them unprepared. They could not bring themselves to believe that the measure would be so cruel, so savage. They thought of their families who would find the long weary wandering so hard to bear. They thought of their synagogues and cemeteries, their schools and institutions of learning.

But no sooner had they weathered the first shock than a strange, almost mystic, calm settled over the outcasts. They accepted their fate with patience and resignation, putting their faith in God and in the ultimate destiny of their people. "Every man," wrote Don Isaac, "said to his brother, 'Be strong and of good courage for the sake of our faith and the Law of our God. If He lets us live, we shall live. If, however, we are to die, we shall not be faithless to our covenant. Nor will we falter, but march onward in the name of our God.' "

As though to test their endurance, swarms of priests descended upon the hapless exiles in attempts to convert them. Priests met them in the streets, stopped them in the public squares, and even invaded their synagogues, propounding the doctrines of Christianity and thundering forth against Jewish "heresy" which, they pointed out, had already brought them so much misery. Though some yielded, most of the Jews followed their own rabbis and teachers, among them, the kind and generous Abravanel, who preached justice, humility, and patience. The latter passed among the unfortunate outcasts, encouraging and cheering them, rallying their spirits, strengthening their faith, and assuring them of a better and happier future. He enjoined them to be strong in the face of their present affliction. Other wealthy Jews, following Abravanel's example, assisted their poorer brethren with liberal contributions of money and clothes. All distinctions of rank and position vanished. There was boundless solidarity among the rich and the poor, the strong and the weak, as they faced together the perils of an unknown future.

Among the prominent exiles with Abravanel were Isaac Aboab, the greatest Jewish scholar in Spain and head of the *yeshiva* in Guadalajara; Jacob Habib of Salamanca, author of *Eyn Jacob*; Isaac Arama, author of *Akedat Yitzhak*, and Abraham Zacuto, the foremost mathematician in Spain, whose astronomical tables Christopher Columbus used on his expedition, and author also of the biographical dictionary, *Sefer Yuhasin*. A few outstanding Jews chose baptism rather than leave their country, including Abraham Senior, financial adviser to the crown and the most influential leader of the Jews in Spain. He was eighty years old at the time of the expulsion, and yielded to the king's strong inducement to become a Christian.

An attempt was made to prevent the departures of Don Isaac Abravanel and his son Judah, a talented surgeon who had been the personal physician to the king and queen. Ferdinand, anxious to retain their services, secretly arranged to seize Judah's year-old son, hoping thereby to force both the Abravanels to remain in Spain. His plot, however, miscarried. Judah Abravanel learned of the scheme and quickly sent the child to Portugal with a nurse, intending to join them later.

On the second day of August, 1492, after a respite of two days, three hundred thousand Jews sorrowfully departed from their native Spain. By a strange coincidence, the day happened to be the Ninth of *Av*, on which, fourteen hundred and twenty-two years before, their forefathers had lost their national independence through the fall of Jerusalem. It was also the same day on which Columbus set out on the historic voyage which was to result in the discovery of the new continent.

Joseph Ya'abetz, a contemporary writer, while censuring those Jews who were tempted into baptism rather than leave their great fortunes, had only high praise and admiration for the courage and heroism of Abravanel. Don Isaac asked for no immunity for himself or his family. To him it was unthinkable to preserve his fortune by disloyalty to his suffering brethren. He not only shared their hardships but was among the first to go into exile. What little he managed to save from his wrecked fortune he distributed among the poor and distressed.

It was a miserable and wretched army of fugitives that left the country in which Jews had lived happily and creatively for centuries. To quote Abravanel: "The expulsion was accompanied by pillage on land and piracy on sea. Amongst those who were stricken and sorrowful was I. All rose against our congregation, expelling rich and poor, men and women, fathers and sons of the children of Zion. Several abandoned their religion, fearing that their blood would be shed like water, or that they might be sold into slavery. For men and women, young and old, were carried away in ships without pity for their lamentations, and compelled to abandon the Law in their captivity."

According to Abravanel, of the three hundred thousand Jews —a Spanish historian claims as many as eight hundred thousand—who left Spain, scarcely more than ten thousand survived. And their wealth, which at the time of their departure from Spain amounted to the considerable sum of thirty million ducats, was now entirely gone.

Naples: From Refugee to Courtier

After a long and dangerous voyage lasting many months, Abravanel arrived with his family in Naples, a beautiful city on the Mediterranean whose climate was much like that of his once beloved Spain. Naples was one of the few areas of western Europe which was open to the Jewish victims of the expulsion, and where, under King Ferdinand, they were actually welcomed. Like the rest of his stricken brethren, Abravanel was a poor and penniless exile, and a greatly changed man. The experiences of the past few years had left their mark. He was no longer as strong nor as energetic and ambitious as he had once been. He had suffered much, having witnessed not only the loss of his own career and fortune but also the ruin and desolation of his people. He had beheld perhaps the greatest catastrophe that had befallen the Jews since the destruction of the Temple, and had seen Zion clad again in mourning, her glory gone, her pride humbled, and her children dispersed over the whole world.

At fifty-five Abravanel felt himself an old man, broken in spirit and courage. Although the Jewish community of Naples welcomed him warmly, showing him every mark of honor and respect, Abravanel felt himself a stranger in a country whose habits, customs, and language he did not understand. Gloomy and despondent, this man who had so often cheered others was himself now in need of encouragement.

Abravanel might have turned again to his books and his studies. But minds are sharpened by contact with other minds, and Naples lacked the atmosphere congenial to scholarship. The Jews there were traders rather than thinkers; business was their chief occupation. Until the arrival of Abravanel, Naples was devoid of the barest essentials of a Jewish community. It had neither rabbis nor teachers, schools nor scholars. To a man like Abravanel, however, the cultural poverty of his new home constituted a serious challenge. With every ounce of his remaining energy he set about to raise the spiritual level of his environment. He installed a rabbi, trained teachers, and created facilities for the religious education of the young.

Attracted by his presence, other Jewish scholars came to Naples and settled there. The Jewish community of the city was no longer as desolate as Abravanel had found it. Though seared by his experiences, he wanted to resume his work. There were many things which, in the stress and hurry of his active life, had remained undone. There were manuscripts to be completed, more commentaries to be written, but, above all, there was the despairing, anguished spirit of his stricken people to be strengthened and comforted. As a result of their suffering, the faith of many Jews was crumbling. Their exile and martyrdom had engendered all sorts of religious doubts and uncertainties, and missionary priests were taking advantage of their breach of faith. It was a situation that Abravanel could not ignore. In this connection, he began a program of writing that would require many years to complete.

But as had happened before in Portugal and in Spain, he was again "betrayed" by his fame and reputation. His renown as a statesman had followed him into exile, and he was again to be deprived of leisure for scholarly work.

King Ferdinand of Naples, in striking contrast to his royal namesake in Spain, was an enlightened and humane ruler. Although historians have recorded a different impression of Ferdinand and his son, Alfonso, attributing to them all kinds of vices and cruelties, Abravanel called them "princes of mercy and righteousness." It was probably not disinterested kindness alone which prompted the king's generosity. At the time of Abravanel's arrival, the political situation of the country was fraught with difficulties. Its diplomatic relations with the French court were strained. The young and ambitious King of France was threatening war, a challenge that Ferdinand was not prepared to accept. The king of Naples knew of Abravanel's services to their Spanish Majesties and of his reputation as financier and statesman; he attempted to attract the refugee statesman to his court by extending every kindness and courtesy to the Jews.

Thus, for the third time Abravanel joined the court of a reigning monarch and lived in the familiar splendor of kings and princes. Though he had arrived in Naples a stranger and all but a beggar, one among thousands of stranded refugees, he was sought out and entrusted with the duties of a high officer in less than a year. Abravanel served his royal patron well, and when Ferdinand died and was succeeded by his son, Alfonso II, he continued at court. Simultaneously, Abravanel managed to complete his commentary on the two Books of Kings, in which, besides carefully elucidating the text in its historic setting, he commented upon the Spanish exile, the suffering of the Jews in the Diaspora, and the disastrous effect upon their faith.

But fate pursued Abravanel relentlessly, robbing him of lasting peace. The dangerous war with France, which Naples was now unable to avert, resulted in its capture by the armies of King Charles VIII. The French ruthlessly destroyed whatever came their way, including Don Isaac's priceless library. His account of what then befell him is brief: "I amongst the exiles came to Naples, where, however, likewise I had no rest, for King Charles VIII of France ruined us. His soldiers plundered all my possessions. The French were masters of the city, the very inhabitants having abandoned the government."

Corfu and Monopoli: Literary Labors Resumed

Abravanel followed his unhappy monarch into exile. When all other courtiers and counselors forsook their sovereign, Don Isaac remained loyally with Alfonso, soothing and comforting him in his misfortune. Together they went to Sicily, where he could not remain as a professing Jew. After the death of Alfonso, he therefore fled to Corfu for refuge. Abravanel's frequent change of residence caused him considerable fatigue and hardship, and would have proved well-nigh unbearable were it not for the fact that in Corfu he discovered the manuscript copy of his commentary to Deuteronomy which had been lost during his travels. In Abravanel's own words, "I embarked on board a ship, and by God's mercy, came to the island of Corfu, and whilst there, got hold of what I had before written on this book (Deuteronomy), and joyfully resolved to enlarge it."

While in Corfu, Abravanel also wrote the major portion of his commentary on Isaiah, although it was not to be completed until three years later. It is a curious work with its lengthy introductions entirely devoted to the belief in resurrection, a subject much discussed in those days. Since life offered the Jews so little, their thoughts frequently turned to the contemplation of death and life after death.

Abravanel then set out for Monopoli, a small seaport near Naples, where he was to spend the next seven years, from 1496 to 1503, the period of his greatest literary activity. His family had scattered. "My wife and my sons," he wrote, "are away from me and in another country, and I am left by myself alone, an alien in a strange land." One must marvel at his sheer power of endurance. Freed from the political activities which had hitherto absorbed him, he surrendered himself to his literary labors with zeal and enthusiasm. In his work he found solace and comfort. He felt compensated for all the sorrow and suffering he had endured. His frequent migrations had seemingly not interrupted the flow of his thought and the grace of his style. Books covering a variety of subjects issued in rapid succession.

Driven by a mighty desire to bring a measure of hope and comfort to the exiles, Abravanel turned to the Messianic prophecies of the Bible in an attempt to restore the waning faith of his people. Under the horrors of their wretched existence, a mood of defeatism had seized the fugitives. Many Jews, even the most loyal and faithful, despaired of the future and were ready material for the missionizing church. Abravanel was critical of Jewish philosophers who treated the Messiah allegorically, deploring and rejecting the tendency among them to rationalize the Messiah out of existence and create instead a kind of nebulous, mythical figure without relation to the physical and spiritual needs of Jews. The times, he insisted, demanded a real and living Messiah able to redeem and to save. Much as Abravanel admired Maimonides in other respects, he could not accept the Rambam's statement that there will be no difference between the present and the Messianic era save in Israel's subjection to the nations of the earth.

Abravanel presented his own conception of the Messiah and the Messianic era in three books which demolished both the Jewish rationalist view and the Christian Messiahship of Jesus. In order of composition, these were: *Mayone Yeshua* (Wells of Salvation, 1496); *Yeshuat Mesiḥo* (The Salvation of His Anointed, 1497); *Mashmia Yeshua* (Announcement of Salvation, 1498)—the latter a collection of passages in the Bible relating to the Messiah. Besides these, Abravanel wrote *Rosh Emunah* (The Pinnacle of Faith), and, at the request of his son Samuel, a commentary on *Avot* under the title, *Naḥlat Avot* (Inheritance of the Fathers, 1505), and *Zebah Pesaḥ* (The Passover Sacrifice), on the tales relating to Israel's first redemption. Abravanel's treatises were widely read and have survived to this day as classics of Messianic literature.

Moved by the wretchedness and hopelessness of his people following their expulsion from Spain, Abravanel had not only tried to strengthen their despondent mood by preaching to them the belief in the Messiah but he actually predicted the very time of the latter's advent. Regarding himself as a descendant of the Davidic dynasty Abravanel entertained the idea that the promised redeemer would come from his house, and that his own eyes would behold his appearance. Supported by vague allusions in the Book of Daniel and passages in the Talmud, he set the date 1503, that is, in his own lifetime, for the coming of the Messiah. Abravanel must have smarted under the pain of his disillusion, but the intensity of his belief in the immediacy of redemption spread a feeling of hope and comfort among the exiles.

Pure and holy as were Abravanel's intentions, it was natural that his faith in the speedy end of his people's suffering through the coming of the Messiah should have fired the imagination of a host of deluded dreamers and visionaries who presented themselves as the hoped-for redeemer. In the East and in the West they appeared, in Christian and Muslim countries, bearing the glad tidings of the Messiah, influenced by, if not verbally repeating, Abravanel's fervid eloquence. Messianic pretenders like Asher Laemmelein, Diego Piros, or as he later called himself Solomon Melko, David Reubeni, an adventurer from Khibar, Central Asia, and the notorious Sabbatai Zevi, were either acquainted with Abravanel's Messianic writings themselves or knew of them by reputation. In either case, to quote Netanyahu: "We find his (Abravanel's) ideas reverberating in all the Messianic movements that stirred Jewry down to the end of the seventeenth century."

Last Years in Venice

Venice provided the last setting for the career of the aged statesman-philosopher. At the age of sixty-six, the wanderer took up his staff once again to spend the remaining years of his life in the classical city of democracy, popularly known as the "Queen of the Adriatic." In an age of almost universal intolerance Jews had had their occasional difficulties in the Venetian Republic; they had nevertheless established in its capital city an active community life with rabbis, scholars, and schools of learning. Jews all along the Dalmatian coast made Venice their trading center. But with them came also merchants of another kind, men who carried with them spiritual goods which they dispensed freely for the religious and cultural enlightenment of their Venetian coreligionists.

Abravanel was happy in his new home, where, for the first time in his life, he could maintain cultural relations with Jews of other lands. He was reunited with his two sons, Judah and Joseph—Samuel was studying in Salonica. Not a small part of his happiness was that, for the moment, free from the burden of state business, he would be able to complete the work he had left unfinished in Monopoli.

If, however, Don Isaac had planned to pass his days in Venice incognito, with no other responsibility than the one he owed to his work, he was doomed to disappointment. The year 1508 was a critical one for the Venetian Republic, close to war with Portugal on account of their conflicting maritime trade interests. Whether Abravanel offered his services or was invited to appear before the Venetian Senate, he was commissioned to negotiate a trade treaty with Portugal, which only twenty years before, in 1485, had passed the death sentence upon him. Though the treaty did not come through, he was long remembered for his ability, tact, and personality.

With the last act of Abravanel's diplomatic career over, he could devote himself undisturbed to his literary work. Notwithstanding his burden of years, he presented his ideas with clarity and precision, and his material was well balanced. He completed his commentary on the entire Bible with the exception of the Hagiographa; he finished the commentary on the *Guide*, and wrote other books besides.

Abravanel's fame was by now universal. He was known in the East as well as in the West, in middle Europe as well as in southern Europe. Letters came to him from every country where Jews resided, asking for his counsel and guidance in all sorts of matters. Some of these inquiries were of a learned nature. Thus, when Saul Ashkenazi, a learned rabbi of Candia, wrote to him about certain obscure passages in Maimonides' *Guide for the Perplexed*, Abravanel's reply is particularly valuable for the information it contained about his own life and writings: "These books," he wrote, referring to his enormous literary output, "were written after I left my country. Before then, all the time I spent at the courts and palaces of kings was given to royal service. I had no leisure for study, and knew no books but spent my days in vanity and my years in trouble, achieving only riches and honor. And now these very riches have perished, and the glory is departed from Israel. It is only after I had been a fugitive and a wanderer on earth from one kingdom to another, and without money, that I sought out the Book of the Lord, according to the words of him who says in the Talmud, 'He is madly in want, and therefore he studies.' "

Abravanel regretted the hours spent on what he called "unsatisfying knowledge," as he wrote to Ashkenazi: "I confess my guilt that in the vanity of my youth, I spent much time on the natural sciences and on philosophy. Now, however, that I have become an old man and seen much affliction, I say to myself, 'Why devote so much attention to Greek literature and other such matters foreign to me?' Therefore, I have limited myself to the contemplation of the *Guide for the Perplexed* and to the exposition of the books of the Bible. These are the sources of all knowledge, and in their wisdom all doubts and perplexities are dissolved."

Though advanced age had impaired his physical powers, his mental faculties remained intact, and he might still have considered new tasks. What embittered Abravanel and made his closing days dismal, however, was that, instead of witnessing the redemption of his people as he had hoped and predicted, he saw fate cruelly harden against them. There were clouds on the horizon threatening Jews in Italy. The unexampled ferocity with which Ferdinand had stamped out Jews and Judaism in his country he was now directing against them in the Italian provinces under Spanish rule. Fortunately, Abravanel did not live to see the full impact of the events, for he died on November 25, 1508, according to some authorities, at the age of seventy-two, and according to other sources on January 13, 1509.

Since under the laws of Venice, the burial of Jews was not allowed in the city, the body was taken for interment to Padua. Fate, however, willed it that the man who had enjoyed little rest during his life should find no greater repose in death. Not long after Abravanel was laid to rest, the Venetian Republic, to which Padua at the time belonged, was involved in a war with Maximilian, Emperor of Germany, and in the course of fighting, Venice was sacked and destroyed and so too was the old Jewish cemetery of Padua. The slabs and tombstones were demolished and every mark of identification of Abravanel's grave was obliterated. It was not until 467 years after his death, in 1904, that the Jews of Padua erected a monument, in the center of the cemetery, to the memory of Don Isaac Abravanel. An inscription in Hebrew and Italian, a quotation from his son, Judah Abravanel, pays a final tribute.

FOR FURTHER READING

"Isaac Abravanel Ben Judah," in *Encyclopedia Judaica*, Volume 2, pp. 103–109 (Jerusalem: 1972).

REINES, Alvin, *Maimonides and Abravenel on Prophecy* (Cincinnati: Hebrew Union College Press, 1970).

ZINBERG, Israel, "Don Isaac Abravanel," in *A History of Jewish Literature*, translated and edited by Bernard Martin, pp. 281–289 (Cleveland: Case Western University Press, 1973).

"The Baal Shem Tov"

The expulsion of the Jews from Spain in 1492 and the consequent search for havens of refuge led to the gradual establishment of new centers of Jewish life and the revitalizing of several old ones. Tens of thousands of refugees settled in North Africa, particularly in Morocco, where despite many restrictions and occasional outbreaks against them they were tolerated and some attained influence as financial agents, diplomats, and physicians. The greatest number of exiles settled in Constantinople and Salonica, where individual Jews began to play an important part in international politics. These included Donna Gracia, the most benevolent and adored Jewish woman of her day, and her nephew Joseph Nasi, who achieved greater power than any Jew since the days of Hasdai ibn Shaprut in tenth-century Spain.

A new center also grew up in Palestine, where several scholars with a mystical turn of mind settled in Safed, in upper Galilee. Among them was Joseph Karo (1488-1575), author of the *Shulkhan Arukh*, which was adopted as the definitive code of Jewish law. After the expulsion from Spain Karo's family had gone to Bulgaria where Joseph was educated. They then moved to Adrianople where he served as head of an academy and began to compose his *Beth Yoseph* (The House of Joseph), a systematic arrangement of the immense material of Talmudic law. Joseph Karo spent twenty-five years on this work, which he finally finished in Safed. The *Shulkhan Arukh* (The Set Table) is a digest of his larger work, which soon became the most popular code among Sephardic Jews, and later the code of entire Jewry.

Among the mystics who lived in Safed was Isaac Luria (1534-1572), known as Ari, who exerted great influence through his teachings of *Kabbalah*. Taken as a young child from Jerusalem to Egypt, Luria was raised by a wealthy uncle. Becoming engrossed in the study of the *Zohar*, he adopted the life of a hermit, and lived in isolation in a small hut on the banks of the Nile. Meeting with little encouragement in Egypt, he settled in Safed, and immediately gained a following, such men as Joseph Karo accepting him as their master. Luria's mystical ideas on God and man, on prayer, the fate and destiny of the human soul, his emphasis on inwardness in religion, and the example of his upright moral life won for him disciples all over the Jewish world.

But the major center of Jewish life during the sixteenth and seventeenth centuries was in Poland. Just as Babylonia had replaced Palestine as the center of Jewish life in the third century and Spain had become the center after the decline of Babylonian Jewry, so now East European Jewry took over the mantle of Jewish leadership.

Jews had begun to migrate to Poland from Germany after the Crusades, and continued to come in increasing numbers during the fourteenth century as a result of further persecutions and expulsions. The Polish kings gave these German Jewish refugees a ready welcome for they were anxious to have a middle class to build up trade after the devastations of the Tartar invasions. Boleslav, the Pious, granted them a charter of liberties in 1264, and Casimir the Great, one of the noblest of Polish kings (1333-1370), ratified and extended the provisions granting the Jews every opportunity to live and carry on their business activities. While recurrent attacks and petty persecutions took place in Posen, Cracow and other cities in southern Poland during the sixteenth century, by comparison with West European countries, conditions were quite tolerable.

Polish Jewry attained its zenith from 1501 to 1648. During this century and a half the Jewish population grew from fifty thousand to more than half a million. The Jews lived in self-contained communities, spoke their own vernacular (Yiddish), which they had brought from Germany, and enjoyed a remarkable degree of self-government. From the middle of the sixteenth century, Polish Jewry possessed a central organization—the Council of Four Lands —which met regularly like a parliament, and passed laws regulating Jewish civil and religious affairs. This council apportioned taxes, enforced royal decrees, tried to prevent undue economic competition among Jews, enforced regulations such as moderation in dress, supervised education, and helped foster among the Jews of Poland a spirit of discipline and obedience to law. Though legally restricted to Poland, its decisions carried great weight throughout Ashkenazic (German-Polish) Jewry.

This era was rich in scholars who left their mark on Talmudic learning. There were two who were particularly outstanding. Moses Isserles (1520-1572) in his many notes or additions to the *Shulkhan Arukh* set forth the Ashkenazic views of Jewish law, which differed somewhat from Karo's Sephardic tradition. These additions made Karo's code complete, and it was gradually accepted as the final authoritative code of Jewish law. Solomon Luria (1510-1573), Lithuanian rabbi, known for his independence of mind and great learning, authored one of the most famous collections of Responsa.

The unique feature of Polish Jewry during this period, however, consisted not so much in its scholars as in its networks of *ḥeders* and *yeshivas*, which extended throughout most of the cities of the land. While, from the modern point of view, Polish-Jewish education was somewhat narrow, restricted primarily to the Talmud, with an over-emphasis on *pilpul*, with its useless and futile discussions and display of cleverness, in no country was the pursuit of learning so wide-spread.

In the middle of the seventeenth century, however, this comparative security and preoccupation with learning were shattered by a succession of massacres which threatened to destroy Polish Jewry both physically and spiritually. Bogdan Khmelnitzki, leader of the Ukrainian Cossacks, a man with a murderous temperament and a personal grudge against Jews, entered into an alliance with the Tartars and revolted against the Polish nobles. The Cossacks hated not only the Poles, who had treated them like a conquered province, but also their tax agents and the supervisors of their estates, who happened to be Jews. These Jewish supervisors, who lived in isolation on the Polish estates with no one to turn to for help, were therefore the first to be slaughtered. In the towns many Jews fought side by side with the Poles, but were often betrayed by their fellow townsmen. Later, Khmelnitzki made an alliance with the Russian czar, and this new invasion led to further exterminations. The Jews could have saved themselves by accepting baptism, but with very few exceptions they preferred to die as martyrs. The campaign which the Swedes undertook against Poland made the lot of the Polish Jews still more sad. When the bloody decade was over (1648-1658), and Poland had managed to expel the invaders, more than one hundred thousand Jews had been killed, seven hundred communities affected, thousands sold into slavery, and those that remained completely impoverished.

The Polish kings in the period following the massacres tried to help the Jews rehabilitate themselves by relieving them of some of their taxes and by confirming their ancient privileges. But these acts could not avert the terrible economic crisis and the impoverishment of the masses which, by the middle of the eighteenth century, became almost catastrophic. Also, a frenzy of ritual murder libels took place from which the Polish kings were unable to protect the Jews, as in earlier times, for their influence had begun to wane as the nobles and clergy gained increasing power and Poland headed for dissolution.

Poland still remained the major center of Jewry, but the old vitality and recuperative powers seemed to be gone.

Mysticism, which through the centuries had been a minor stream in Jewish tradition, began to rival the Talmud as an object of study. The writings of Isaac Luria, with their emphasis on asceticism, were circulated in Poland in manuscript form, and copies went from hand to hand. The sufferings of the people made them ripe for all sorts of dreams and delusions. Both Christians as well as Jews at this time believed that the world was on the eve of some great change and that their sufferings were the prelude to the coming of the Messiah. According to *Kabbalistic* reckonings this was to take place in 1648 (Christians predicted the year to be 1666). Thus, when Sabbatai Zevi proclaimed himself in Smyrna as the Messiah (1665), this made a deep impression on the masses. Many abandoned their homes, stopped working, and prepared themselves to go to Palestine. The subsequent conversion of the pseudo-Messiah to Islam inevitably had a deep and paralyzing effect. A sense of gloom and hopelessness settled over the people.

Talmudic learning could not appeal to the many simple unlearned Jews in the villages of southern Poland nor furnish them with the spiritual sustenance they needed. In Galicia, Podolia, and Volynia, the southern provinces of Poland, Talmudic learning was at a low ebb. Religion began to deteriorate into superstition as Jews resorted to magicians and sorcerers to cast out the evil spirits or get rid of demons which filled them with fear. These men, called *Baalei Shem*, wrote amulets, and by their manipulation of the letters which spelled the Ineffable Name, were believed to exercise power over the spirits.

Asceticism of all kinds became prevalent during the century following the Khmelnitzki massacres. Self-flagellation, fasting, self-imposed wanderings from place to place, refusing food and drink even when faint from hunger, were resorted to in order to torment the soul and hasten the coming of the Messiah. It is in this atmosphere of gloomy asceticism, fear, and superstition that the Baal Shem Tov was born. His life and the new religious orientation he taught helped to fill the spiritual needs of Polish Jewry during the declining years of the Polish Kingdom and to insure the survival of Polish Jewry for another two centuries.

11 . *"The Baal Shem Tov"*

[1700-1760]

LOUIS I. NEWMAN

I s r a e l ben Eliezer, better known as the Baal Shem Tov or
Besht ("Master of the Good Name"), is, without doubt, one
of the world's greatest spiritual leaders. A warm, sympathetic,
and colorful personality, he made a great impact on his own
and subsequent generations. The movement he founded, which
came to be known as *Ḥasidism*, effected a veritable spiritual
revolution in the life of the Jewish people in Eastern Europe of
the eighteenth century. In recent years, not only the personality
but also the message of the Besht have won increasing recognition.

Israel ben Eliezer was born about 1700 in Okup, near
Kamenatz-Podosk on the old Polish-Turkish boundary, in a region known as Podolia. Early in his childhood, Israel lost both
parents; his father's last words, urging him to fear nothing
since God would be with him, made an indelible impression on
the boy. Okup's community leaders took him under their protection, but in the *ḥeder* he proved to be a free-roaming, imaginative lad, constantly breaking school regulations to go his
own way into the woods. No amount of ordinary discipline
served to control the boy, and finally the authorities permitted
him to express his own remarkable nature and temperament as
he saw fit. Israel became assistant to the schoolmaster at the
age of twelve, escorting the pupils to and from school and singing joyfully all the way. Later he became a *shamash* or synagogue attendant, who seemed to sleep during the day, but in
the stillness of the night devoted himself to his studies, chiefly
the *Kabbalah*. At eighteen he was married, but his young wife

died immediately after the ceremony. Young Israel left Okup; he served as a helper and assistant teacher in various communities of Galicia, and then settled in Tlust near Brody as a teacher in the ḥeder.

In Tlust his magnetic personality and keen human insight won him many friends, and intricate human problems were constantly laid before him for judgment. Ephraim, an affluent and learned resident of Kuty, impressed with Israel's wisdom, promised him his daughter in marriage. But Ephraim died before the betrothal, and his son, the proud aristocratic Rabbi Abraham Gershom, sought to prevent his sister's marriage to Israel. The latter was pretending to be a shabby, ignorant peasant, a disguise which he assumed, in part, as a protest against the ostentation of some rabbinic leaders. Hannah insisted on the marriage, however, not only in fulfillment of her late father's wish, but because she had fallen in love with Israel. Indignant at his sister's act, Rabbi Gershom compelled the couple to leave Brody, their only possessions a horse and wagon he had given them. The exiled pair settled in a Carpathian village between Kuty and Kassov, earning their livelihood, chiefly through Hannah's industry, by the sale of a weekly wagonload of lime from nearby quarries. Israel continued to be a *luftmensch* (Yiddish for "rootless person"), spending most of his time in a forest hut, communing with animals, flowers, and trees in the Carpathian mountains.

Teacher and Healer

Later Israel accepted a post as *shoḥet* in Koshilowitz, near Jaslowitz. Rabbi Gershom, the brother-in-law, repenting for his harshness toward his sister and her husband, purchased a tavern for the pair, which Hannah competently managed while her extraordinary husband continued his hermit's life in the forest. Through his friendship with the peasants, non-Jews as well as Jews, Israel acquired the secrets of herbs, plants, and roots for medicinal purposes. By reason of his congenial and magnetic nature, he soon became a beloved counselor, and was sought out by the wealthy and learned as well as the lowly. After seven years, he established himself in Tlust as a teacher and healer, where he "revealed" himself, winning the title "Baal

Shem Tov" or "Good (Kind) Master of the Name" (The Ineffable Name of God).* From his Tlust headquarters he visited neighboring communities in Galicia, Podolia, Volynia, and the region adjoining Kiev; once he journeyed as far as Slutsk in Lithuania on a "healing" mission.

In 1740 he established himself in Medziboz, a strategic center on the frontiers of a number of important areas of Poland, the Ukraine, and Lithuania. Without doubt his migration from Tlust to Medziboz was motivated in part by the Besht's desire to shed his reputation as a miracle-worker, and to extend his renown as an ethical and religious mentor. But it must be admitted he wrote amulets and gave advice to his followers for monetary payment (very much like a contemporary psychiatrist) to such an extent that his livelihood was assured. The Besht was always generous in his charities, his resources being so abundant in his later years that even if the house was without food and money, fresh supplies always seemed to arrive in time.

At Medziboz, where the Besht was active the rest of his days, he attracted from all walks of life disciples who, as his fame increased, were able to free him from the financial anxieties which had so long plagued him. So manifold were the requests made to the Besht from all parts of the Ukraine that in his later years he was compelled to engage the services of a second secretary to answer letters and transmit advice. Multitudes of disciples were drawn to the Besht because of the charm and animal vitality of his nature. He persuaded many doubters, among them Rabbi Yehiel, later the "Maggid of Zlotchov." Whenever a disciple was in doubt he traveled to the Master; one such was Pinchas of Koretz, who found the Besht expounding the verse (Exodus 17:11) which tells that the hands of Moses were "held up in the hour of the struggle with Amalek." "The influence of a leader," said the Besht, "is likened in the Talmud (*Ethics* 2:15) to a burning coal. Do not hold yourself aloof from the Master; you will remain cold. Do not approach him too closely; you may be burned. This applies also to your re-

---

* The "Name" thus used was believed to possess supernatural powers both in Christian and Jewish life, both in the domain of thought and of practical healing. The addition of the adjective *Tov* or "Good" set Israel ben Eliezer apart from the professional and less gifted aspirants to the title.

lationship with your friends." We can "cleave unto the wise," the Besht explained, "by searching out those gracious traits which are common" to a vulgarian and a sage. In order to win the tempestuous Rabbi Jacob Joseph of Polonnoye as an adherent, the Besht told the story of the rabbi who impatiently struck a water-carrier, and who later repented his anger. "If he should come to me," said the Besht, "I could indicate to him a path of repentance." The Polonnoye rabbi, of course, became one of the Besht's most ardent disciples.

The Besht instituted a "fellowship" at Medziboz, which included great throngs of disciples and adherents. Out of the multitude arose certain eminent personalities; among them, in addition to Rabbi Jacob Joseph, were Rabbi Dov Baer of Mezeritz, known as "The Great Maggid"; Rabbi Pinchas of Koretz; Rabbi Yehiel Mikhal of Zlotchov, and numerous others, who, in turn, raised up disciples, followed by later generations of Zaddikim.* The Besht ordained a number of pupils who became preachers, rabbis, shohetim, cantors, and leaders of prayer in numerous smaller communities; in this way the influence and message of their master and patron were disseminated. Hosts of unnamed lay visitors served as advocates of the Besht's teachings. Thus the Hasidic movement gained ever-increasing popularity among the East European masses, and served as an effective antidote to the arid rationalism and pilpulism which had impeded the flow of creative religious thought and action.

The Besht as a healer and an alleged wonder-worker provoked hostility among the more rationalistic Jews of his time, but among his devout followers, many of them non-Jewish peasants and Polish nobles, he was greatly revered. He became adept in prescribing homeopathic folk remedies based on knowledge gained from peasants and from his own extensive study of the curative powers of herbs, roots, and plants, many of which serve as the basis for drugs used by physicians today.

---

* The title Zaddik was applied not only to the "righteous man" in general, but also to the particular leader who gained the loyalty and adherence of the Hasidim or "Pious Disciples" who gathered about him. With the Zaddik as their leader, they formed a community or society in the spirit of the Master, the Besht, and in accordance with the special teaching or emphasis of the religious leader they had chosen to follow. Many of these Zaddikim were known by the names of the towns where they taught, thus, the Berditschever, the Lubliner, the Ladier.

Often he cured his devotees by fervent prayer, profound ec-
stasies, gesticulations, and other seemingly magical means; it is
said that he also revealed secrets and foretold the future. But he
was no ordinary Baal Shem who employed conjuring, incanta-
tions, and amulets. "To his credit, be it said that he was far
from practicing the quackery of his fellows in the craft. In
treating, for instance, those who suffered from melancholy, or
the insane, he sought to influence their minds." [1]

His Psychological Insight

The Besht was clearly a penetrating student of individual
and group psychology; he understood the people with whom
he dealt, and wished ardently to communicate with them in a
language and by methods which, in the light of the current culture, they could understand. The "miracles" attributed to him
can be explained in psychological terms. That some of the ailments apparently "cured" by the Besht were of a psychosomatic
character is illustrated by a number of tales. For example, Rabbi
Nahum of Tchernobil, a hypochondriac, felt the pain leave his
limbs when the Besht himself read aloud from the Scriptures
the passage of reproof on "The Sabbath of Blessings." Once
the Besht refused to pray for a *Zaddik*'s recovery, but the latter's pain left him a few days later when a band of brigands
was captured by the police. The Besht explained that the *Zaddik*'s pains had served to delay the brigands until they could be
discovered. "The sufferings of a *Zaddik* act as a shield," he said.
If a man believes he can dispel his tribulations by moving to
another place, he is like an invalid who imagines his illness will
similarly depart if he moves. The real cure, said the Besht, is
obtained by repentance, by prayer from the heart, and by petitions for God's mercies.

The psychological effect of the Besht's influence can be seen
in the story of the rabbi whose grandfather had been a disciple
of the Besht. In pursuance of the dictum that "a story must
be told in such a way that it constitutes help in itself," he narrated: "My grandfather was lame. Once they asked him to tell
a story about his Master, the Besht. And he related how the
holy Baal Shem used to hop and dance while he prayed. My
grandfather rose as he spoke, and he was so swept away by his

story that he himself began to hop and dance, to show how the Master had done. From that hour on, he was cured of his lameness. That's the way to tell a story." Such an example of auto-suggestion would have gladdened the heart of Émile Coué, the faith-healer of Nancy, France, in the 1920's.

Did the Besht himself believe in the healing powers attributed to him? If neurasthenic or psychotic persons seemed "possessed by spirits," the Besht, following the folk-beliefs and folkways of the time would engage in the exorcism of these *Dybbukim*.[2] Perhaps the very nature of the Besht prompted him to travel, in his mind, between the natural and the divine, between the physical and the metaphysical, between empirical reality and a "miracle of God." [3] The Besht is quoted as saying: "If a man clings closely to the *Shekhinah* and thinks of himself in such a circumstance in the Higher World, he is in an instant transplanted into the Higher World, for where a man thinks himself to be, there he is, and if he were not in the Higher World, his thinking could not attain to it." [4] Apparently the Besht was convinced that the sincere, spiritual devotion of a righteous man could achieve changes in the Higher World, but God did not always alter His decrees according to the wishes of the pious; on one occasion, a wonder would occur; on another, the divine decree remained unalterable; sometimes the prophecies of the righteous were fulfilled; at other times, they came to naught. *Hasidic* legend itself tells that the Besht once realized he could not restore a wealthy man's son to health. Observing that the parents were about to castigate the Besht, the latter disappeared with phenomenal speed lest "this incident harm his reputation elsewhere."

If the Besht was unable to cure a person who was either physically or psychologically ill, he would sometimes explain to the patient's kinsfolk that Satan had intruded and interrupted his efforts; on other occasions he would affirm he had heard a voice from heaven announcing that an irrevocable judgment had been decreed against the afflicted one's recovery. The Besht seems to have been careful to avoid families that resorted to either physicians or to gypsies who practiced magic. Once when a non-Jewish physician inquired whence the Besht had derived his skill, he replied with sincerity: "The Lord, praised be He, was my teacher."

Like other *Baalei Shem*, the Besht would take a metal container, insert a slip of parchment inscribed with the Secret Names of God, and place it beneath the garments of a sick person. Such amulets were said to be efficacious for women giving birth, or in other extremities that required the warding off of evil spirits. Associated with these amulets was the gift of money for the "Redemption of the Soul" (*Pidyon ha-Nefesh*), usually in the amount (in small or large coins) of the numerical value of the Hebrew word *ḥay*, or eighteen.

The resort to amulets naturally brought the Besht into disfavor in Talmudic and medical circles.[5] On one occasion, Rabbi Yitzhak of Drohobycz queried the Besht regarding his use of them. The Master opened one of the amulets and showed the doubter that on the parchment nothing was inscribed but his own name and that of his mother, namely, "Israel ben Sarah." In other words, the amulet itself did not possess magical power and was nothing "but a sign and pledge of the personal bond between the helper and the one who is given help, a bond based on trust . . . The amulet is the permanent symbol of his direct influence at the given moment. It contains his name and thus represents him. And through this pledge of personal connection, the soul of the recipient is 'lifted.' " [6]

In spite of this contemporary rationalization of the Besht's practices, the fact remains that he was "a man of his age," and, with respect to his activity as a healer, he deserves no more tolerant treatment than Jewish and non-Jewish practitioners of the nineteenth and twentieth centuries. The Besht as a "wonder rabbi" exemplified the tendencies of his particular period, and we must no more condemn him than we do the physicians who employed leeches and blood-letting (as the Besht likewise did) in conformity with the medical knowledge prevalent during the eighteenth century.

In 1752 the Besht undertook a journey with his daughter and Rabbi Hersch (Zevi), his secretary, to the Holy Land. Though they reached Stamboul, numerous vicissitudes compelled them, to their disappointment, to return without reaching their goal.

Seven years later, in 1759, the Besht was one of three Talmudist delegates to the disputation with the followers of Jacob Frank, a pseudo-Messiah who later converted to Christianity.

The Master fell ill from overexertion and died on the fifth day of *Shavuot*, 1760.

Character of His Message

In what way did the Besht transcend the function of the ordinary Baal Shem? What was it that made him the leader of the great movement which in his lifetime and thereafter exerted so profound and widespread an influence? The answer lies in a description of the many-sided teachings of the Besht which went far beyond his profession as a "faith-healer." The character, message, and institutions of the movement known as *Hasidism* are the Besht's true monument in history. From the first moment of his career as a teacher throughout the years of his ever-mounting fame and in the years of his fruition as a Master of hosts of disciples, he acted upon the central theme of his mission, namely, that communion with God is not confined to a select and aristocratic few, but is the possession of all of His creatures. The motivating idea and the very name of the *Hasidic* movement is derived from the rabbinic statement attributed to Hillel: "an ignorant man cannot be pious." In order to provide an antidote for the arrogance and aloofness among many scholars of his day, the Besht encouraged the commoners to believe in their faculty for authentic religious feeling. His very masquerade in his youth as an *am ha-aretz* was undertaken to bring him closer to the ordinary folk of the villages, farms, and cities—the teamsters, water-carriers, tailors, bakers, peasants, carpenters, servants, storekeepers—so that they might realize they were not excluded from fellowship with the All-Compassionate, All-Loving, Omnipresent, Universal Father on High.

Thus, the shepherd boy blows his whistle at *Neilah* services in a mood of spiritual fervor, to the delight of the Besht; another lad recites the letters of the alphabet as a prayer, having forgotten the words of the prayer book. When a pious man deplores his failure to attain improvement, the Besht solaces him by the reminder that to recognize his lack of worth is an accomplishment. A stocking-maker, accustomed to recite the psalms while at work, was praised for thus laying "the cornerstone which will uphold the Temple until Messiah comes." A man so busy that he must recite his prayers in a by-street is very dear to the Lord, and his "prayer pierces the firmament." Said the Besht: "The lowest of the low you can think of is dearer to me than your only son is to you."

Scholarship as such was not condemned by the Besht, but he believed that excessive concentration on Talmudic texts often proved a barrier to genuine inwardness (*Kavanah*). He once remarked of a famous sage: "I envy him his scholarship. But what am I to do? I have no time to study because I am under the compulsion to serve my Maker." While the Besht did not specialize in rabbinic learning, nevertheless he had a genius for illustrating his ethical and spiritual lessons with items which ordinary folk could comprehend and appreciate. In a parable concerning two petitioners, he declared: "Even if we do not behold the king face to face, we may view his treasures in his palace; namely, we may study God's Torah and thereby at least be near His presence." Using a simile of the maiden who declined a prince's admiration until he had developed an affection for learning, the Besht remarked that the Lord instils within us a desire for a long life, but He tells us we may not enjoy it until we have learned Torah. He defended the minority in Torah interpretations, saying they were the "kindlers of the lamps." Later the *Zaddikim* (righteous ones), among them the Mezeritzer and Rabbi Schneour Zalman of Ladi, sought to achieve a synthesis between Rabbinism and *Hasidism*, but the pristine emphasis upon simplicity in learning and in piety remained. Thus, the fable, the anecdote, and the parable drawn from the daily experience of his adherents always engaged the Besht. He quoted Psalm 14:15: "The simple believeth every word"; and Psalm 116:16: "The Lord preserveth the simple." He declared that just as coarse food proves as helpful as fine food to the defenders when a castle is besieged, "likewise, my friends, store in your memory those common tales I narrate to you, as well as the teachings which seem to you profound. In your work among the people, everything will prove useful." Sometimes a man feels remote from God, even as a child, learning to walk, is sometimes left alone by his father so that he may walk unaided. Just as a father takes delight in the stumbling words of his child, so God does not object if a man misunderstands what he is studying, provided he aspires to learn.

Role of Joy in Ḥasidism

Joy and good cheer were heartily recommended by the Besht and became a leitmotif of *Ḥasidism*. Asceticism and mortification of the flesh were abhorrent to the Master. He believed such practices led to melancholy and depression. "Only where there is joy do God's dictates prevail. For it has been explicitly commanded: 'Thou shalt not hide thyself from thine own flesh.'" "Asceticism," he said, "should be practiced only at the commencement of a man's self-discipline, until his evil inclinations are subdued. Later he should conduct himself in a normal way and be in communication with his comrades. Otherwise he will fall into pride." "The strength thou wert willing to lose through fasting devote to the Torah and to worship," he counselled. Once the Besht answered some disputants, saying: "It is the aim and essence of my pilgrimage on earth to show my brethren by living demonstration how one may serve God with merriment and rejoicing. For he who is full of joy is full of love for men and his fellow-creatures."

Once a Jew in great tribulation asked the Besht: "How many days have I to fast, to make atonement for a grievous sin?" The Besht replied: "Not through fasting is the ire of God averted, but through the joy of which the psalms are harbingers. Say the psalms with inward rejoicing and you will be quit of your sin." Again he said: "Weeping is evil indeed, for man should serve God with joy. But if one weeps from joy, tears are commendable." He cordially praised a rabbi who read the *Yom Kippur* prayers in most cheerful tones, comparing him to a royal servant who sings a merry song while he sweeps the forecourt free of dirt, "for he does what he is doing to gladden the king."

In the way of life recommended by the Besht he gave a practical application of his ideals. He emphasized again and again the importance of good health and normal activity, saying: "Do not consider the time you spend for eating and sleeping wasted. The soul within you is rested during these intervals, and is enabled to renew its holy work with fresh enthusiasm . . . You may be free from sin, but if your body is not strong, your soul will be too weak to serve God aright. Maintain your health and preserve your strength." He laid great stress upon the ritual bath and immersion. Music played a decisive role in the community life which the Besht helped fashion. The drinking of wine, adding merriment and gaiety to the *Ḥasidic* way of life, was approved by the Besht though it later brought the *Ḥasidim* under strenuous rabbinical reproof. In speaking of the beauty of womankind, the Besht said: "When you admire beauty in a woman, remember that her beauty is but a reflection of the Supreme Source of Beauty—the Lord." The Besht explained the *Shalosh Seudah* as follows: "The *Ḥasidic* custom of eating the Third Sabbath Meal in company with comrades is founded upon the following reason: among good Jews it is eminently desirable that a man offer up his soul in the presence of ten Jews. At the conclusion of the last Sabbath meal, we offer up our Super-Soul (*Neshemah Yeteiarah*) received by us on the Sabbath. We desire to do this in congenial company."

The dance, of course, was a major interest of the *Ḥasidim* in their effort to express joy in worship. Once on *Simḥat Torah*, the Besht danced with his disciples. "He took the scroll of the Torah in his hand and danced with it. Then he laid the scroll aside and danced without it. At this moment one of his disciples who was intimately acquainted with his gestures, said to his companions: 'Now our Master has laid aside the visible dimensional teachings and has taken the spiritual teachings unto himself.' " Out of the *Ḥasidic* dances intricate and decorative art forms have developed which have found their way into the theaters of the nations.

Religious Ideas

The religious system enunciated by the Besht revolves, of course, about the concept of God. The Besht's interpretation of God was in strongly pantheistic terms, even so-called evil itself existing in the nature of the deity. Cleaving to the Lord (*Deveikut*) was a paramount virtue in the eyes of the Besht. "Thou art righteous," he said, "only when thou feelest more joy in cleaving unto the Lord than in any material pleasure." On another occasion he said: "Some seek God as if He were far removed from us, and surrounded by many walls . . . Had they been wise, however, they would have known that 'no space is free of Him.' They can find Him in everything and everywhere, and they should understand that 'one who attaches himself to any part of God is as if he were attached to the All in All.' "

Concentration (*Kavanah*) in the endeavor to cleave unto God is essential. "When it is desired to solder a piece of silver to a silver vessel, the edge of the piece must be cleansed so that no foreign substance may intervene. Likewise when a man wishes to cleave to God, he must purify himself of every foreign thought beforehand." "Most tribulations," the Besht said, "come to those who are wavering in their beliefs and resolutions, whether they concern matters of substance or spirit." Not only is concentration required in work for pleasure or wealth, but also in labor which will bring you into "communion with the Lord and His holiness." In another parable the Besht contrasted two farmers, one indolent, the other diligent, to illustrate the point that one man collects many *mitzvot* without proper attention to his prayers; another performs fewer *mitzvot* but displays concentration and sincerity. "It is desirable that a man should frequently interrupt his occupation, sacred as well as secular, for a moment, whatever it may be, and concentrate his mind upon the fear of the Lord." "Mind," said the Besht, "is the foundation of man. If the foundation is solid, the building is secure. By the same token, if a man's mind is filled with holy thoughts, his action will be sound. But if his mind is occupied with selfish thoughts, even his good actions are unsound, being built on a weak foundation."

The love of God and its counterpart, the fear of God or reverence before Him, are linked with concentration or inwardness in worship of the divine. Once when the spirit of the Besht was so downcast that it seemed to him he would have no share in the world-to-come, he said to himself: "What need have I of a world-to-come, if I truly love God? . . . Our love of God should be more like the love between brother and sister, or between a mother and her child, than the love between man and wife or between lovers. The first may show their love both in private and public, whereas the latter may do so in private only. We should not imitate those who say that our love of God should be demonstrated only in the synagogue or the home, but should not be shown on the street or in public places."

In the spiritual system of the Besht, the concept of the fear of God was associated with the idea of repentance and also of attachment or cleaving to God (*Deveikut*). While he underscored the love of God, the Besht appreciated the value of *Yir'ah*, namely, reverence or fear before God. To him there were two kinds of fear of the Lord, one outer, the other inner. "The outer is fear of punishment, and induces a man to repent. The penitent may then gain the inner fear, namely, the fear of displeasing his beloved Father in Heaven, and thus he will have no further need of the outer fear."

In accordance with his humane and tender attitude toward mankind and the world, the Besht declined to believe in "absolute evil," saying: "When the good man perceives evil-doers, he rejoices in goodness." In speaking of the "sediment of evil inclinations," the Besht remarked: "When a man squeezes wine-grapes into a vessel, he must first use a sieve with large holes to strain it; later he uses a cheese cloth. But no matter how many times he strains it, some sediment still remains. It is the same with the *Zaddik*. He must rid himself of his evil inclinations and continue to do so his entire life. But there are always a few dregs left over." Thus while the Besht was mindful of the unceasing struggle for moral perfection, at the same time he recognized man's capacity to enthrone goodness in his soul.

One of his best-known parables called "The Bird's Nest" describes the effort by the king's strong men to capture a migratory bird of rare beauty. To do so the courtiers formed a human ladder; but when one weakened, the entire structure crumbled to the ground. In the same way, he said, the man of holiness depends on the support of lesser and even lowlier men; but when one man weakens, the structure totters and falls, and even the *Zaddik* must begin anew.

Though the Besht was venerated by his contemporaries, he tolerated no deification of himself, nor did he pretend to the Messianic role. He shared in the traditional Hebraic concept of the Messiah and the Messianic age, emphasizing the individual Jew's responsibility to usher in the redeemer's reign. In this connection he speaks of the "pangs of the Messiah," saying: "before the coming of the Messiah there will be a period of prosperity and Jews will become wealthy. They will grow accustomed to extravagant living and forget all their habits of frugality. Later, a terrible depression will arise, and the means of livelihood will be scarce. Poverty will descend upon those who no longer know how to live sparingly." Not only did the Besht oppose the Messianic pretensions of Jacob Frank, but he also commented in a derogatory way on Sabbatai Zevi, the pseudo-Messiah of Smyrna: "Many have trodden the same steep path, and have attained the same fortunate goal. He, too, had a holy spark in his being; he fell, however, into the net of Samuel, the false deceiver, who thrust him into the role of a redeemer. This overtook him only because of his arrogance." The Besht's insistence upon the virtue of humility served as a safeguard against any overweening ambitions within himself.

Importance of Love

Filled with a love of man, the Besht was strongly opposed to sermons which excoriated sinners. Once he said to a *Zaddik*, accustomed to vituperative, castigating discourses: "What do you know about admonishing? You yourself have remained unacquainted with sin all the days of your life, and you have had nothing to do with the people around you. How should you know what sinning is?" On another occasion he said:

A prince was banished from his father's realm. Two servants were assigned to him, commissioned to report on his conduct. One servant made a dry report of facts unfavorable to the prince. The other made the same report, but added that the youth's misconduct resulted from his exile, and his sense of disgrace and melancholy. The father took compassion upon his son, restored him to the palace, and rewarded the loyal servant. In the same fashion, when a sage or a preacher reproves Israel, let him always employ the method of the second servant. It is in this way that he will surely please the Father in heaven.

In recommending loving rebuke, the Besht said:

One who sees faults in another and dislikes him for them is surely possessed of some of these very faults in his own person. The pure and good man can see only the goodness in others. We read (Leviticus 19:17): "Thou shalt not hate thy brother in thy heart; thou shalt surely rebuke thy neighbor, and not bear sin because of him." This teaches us: rebuke thyself first for seeing faults, and thus being to a degree impure; then thou shalt not hate thy brother, but feel love towards him. If thou rebukest him, it will be in the spirit of love. He will become attached to thee, joining the goodness within him to thine own goodness, and all his faults will disappear. If he should refuse to listen to thee, and to admit his fault and abuse thee, he shall lose thereby his goodness to thee, and remain wholly evil. Thus through a loving rebuke, either of these two courses is open: both of ye shall join in love, and both of ye shall attain improvement. Or if there is hatred left, it shall be in his heart, not thine.

Love, in the judgment of the Besht, is the cardinal thing. When asked: "What is the chief point in service to the Lord if it be true that fasting and self-chastisement are sinful?" he replied: "The main thing is to encompass oneself in the love of God, the love of Israel, and the love of the Torah. A man may attain this if he secures enough nourishment to preserve his health, and if he makes use of his strength to battle against evil inclinations."

The Master's love of Israel is illustrated by his words of comfort to a stricken mother who had lost her only child at the age of two. He narrated to her the tale of the prince who had become a Jew and whose soul had entered the mother's beloved child for its two years on earth. From the commandment to love one's fellow man as oneself he learned the Talmudic commandment to judge one's fellow man on the scale of merit. "Since thou always findest excuses for thine own misdeeds, make excuses also for thy fellow man." When a Jew was exposed as a thief, the Besht said to him: "God pardons and helps. But you must promise me never to commit another transgression of this kind in the future." A few years later when the same Jew came to Rabbi Jacob Joseph of Polonnoye to complain of business difficulties, Rabbi Jacob exclaimed: "Do penance!" The Jew exclaimed: "Alas, would that the Holy Baal Shem Tov were still living . . . He knew that I was a receiver of stolen goods and yet he spoke to me with kindness. You, however, address me angrily and demand penance from me, before I have stolen anything at all."

The love which the Besht displayed toward God and the universe expressed itself also in his love for God's dumb creatures, the domain of nature, and human beings in their arduous social relationships. For example, when a father complained that his son had forsaken God, and asked what he should do, the Besht answered: "Love him more than ever!" On every side there is evidence of the keen psychological and human insight which the Besht displayed throughout his entire life.

The Master always sought to make repentance easily accessible if the offender were sincere in his appeal for pardon. "If a man sins purposely, how can he know whether his intentional repentance can overcome his intentional sin? The remedy lies in maintaining his mood of repentance for a long time until he is confident his sins have been forgiven." "The chief joy of the Satan," said the Besht, "is when he succeeds in persuading a man that an evil deed is a *mitzvah*. For when a man is weak and commits an offense, knowing it to be a sin, he is likely to repent of it. But when he believes it to be a good deed, does it stand to reason that he will repent of performing a *mitzvah?*"

The Besht compared the tactics of the evil impulse to those of a man who secured permission to drive a nail into the wall of a householder, and ended up by marring the entire wall. In his recommendation of self-discipline, the Master showed his disciples an acrobat at a fair walking a high tightrope. He commented: "I reflected that if men would submit their soul to such discipline as that to which he has submitted his body, what deep abysses might they not cross upon the tenuous cord of life!"

Ethical Virtues

Sincere humility contrasted with pride and hypocritical self-abasement engaged the Besht's attention among his disciples. He declared that a man who serves God has no leisure for pride, and the world's respect or disrespect does not concern him. "He is then able to perform any good deed without feeling pride in doing it." In an eloquent parable the Besht said: "A king was told that a man of humility is endowed with a long life. He attired himself in old garments, took up his residence in a small hut, and forbade anyone to show reverence before him. But when he honestly examined himself, the king found himself to be prouder of his seeming humility than ever before. A philosopher thereupon remarked to him: 'Dress like a king; live like a king; allow the people to show due respect to you. But be humble in your inmost heart.'" The Besht affirmed that a gifted man is inclined to attain to pride before he is aware of it; he is like a traveler who falls asleep in a stagecoach while it ascends to the summit of a hill; only when a descent is made, after a smooth ride downhill, does he realize how high he has been. The Besht also told of a man who studied humility so earnestly that when someone failed to show him deference, he became incensed and cried out: "Don't you know that since I have learned humility, I am a man of perfect character?" He believed that God was even with the sinner who considers himself base, for He "dwelleth with him in the midst of their uncleanness" (Leviticus 16:16); from the Gemarah, however, we learn concerning the man who prides himself that he is unburdened by sin: "There is not enough room in the world for myself and him."

Needless to say, the Besht lost no opportunity to convey to others his disdain for luxury and ostentation. He once taught his little son concerning the silver objects of a well-to-do scholar: "The silver truly stands in the wrong place, but not because it is not ours. It should rather be given away as charity, instead of glittering here as futile ornaments." In describing the four dispositions with reference to charity, the Master remarked: "The uncharitable man is the chair upon which the charitable sits." In speaking of ethical virtues in everyday living, the Besht declared that a boy before he becomes thirteen cultivates a taste for *mitzvot* without the necessity of battling the evil impulse. "It is like a man who enters a new confectionery store and is offered a free sample of a new condiment. If he finds it sweet and wishes more of it, he is asked to pay. The adult may taste the sweetness of the *mitzvot* only after he has triumphed over his inclinations."

Role of Zaddik

The Besht recognized the important role of the *Zaddik* or righteous man, described in the Book of Proverbs as "the foundation of the universe." Though he believed the wealth of the world exists because sometimes the *Zaddik* may find comfort in it, nevertheless the Master always urged that a man rely upon his own personal efforts to secure moral improvement. The verse (Psalm 52:13), "Also unto Thee, O Lord, belongeth mercy; for Thou renderest to every man according to his work," was applied by the Besht to teach that God makes it possible for man to perform good deeds. "Man's work is of slight merit, yet He rewards man as if he achieved it by his own unaided efforts."

In similar vein the Master taught:

> The lion became enraged at his subjects, the animals of the forest. They asked the fox to placate the king of beasts by relating to him an appropriate fable. The fox replied, however, that fear had caused him to forget his fables. Hence the beasts were compelled to wait on the lion themselves. In the same fashion, on the Awesome Days, the people of the congregation should not depend upon their rabbi to pray in their behalf. Each man should do so by and for himself.

The Legacy of Ḥasidism

The Besht's message has been transmitted not by his own writings but by those of his disciples and their followers.*

* The first of the Besht's disciples to present his words in print was Rabbi Jacob Joseph of Polonnoye. The Polonnoyer, as he came to be known, was first a vehement opponent of the Besht; but once he came under the spell of the Besht's personality and influence, he was thereafter a devout exponent of the Master's ideals. Because of his disposition, however, the Besht did not select him as his successor. He issued, however, three books within twenty years after the Master's demise, namely, *Toledot Yaakob Yoseph*, *Ben Porat Yoseph*, and *Zaphnat Paaneaoh* (1780-82). These include short utterances of the Besht which the disciple had himself heard, or which he recorded from the recollections of his friends. Sentences of the latter type the Polonnoyer designated by the introductory words: "I have heard in the name of my Teacher."

Rabbi Aaron ben Zevi Kohen of Opatow issued at Zolkiev, in 1784, a collection of the Besht's utterances under the title *Keter Shem Tov* (The Crown of a Good Name). About the same time two other books appeared: *Maggid Devarav le-Yaakob* (Koretz, 1784 and 1787; Zolkiev, 1792 and 1797), with several other editions into the nineteenth century; the *Zawaat ha-Ribasch*, set down by Rabbi Yeshayah of Janow, out of the mouth of the Maggid Dov Baer of Mezeritz, 1793 and later, was a purported "Testament of Israel ben Eliezer," and has been accepted as a probable expression of the Besht's pattern of teachings without necessarily being an exact reproduction. Later works on the Besht's sayings appeared, but these are more in the spirit than the letter of the Master's utterances. The *Degel Maḥaneh Ephrayim* (The Banner of the Camp of Ephraim) was issued by Rabbi Moses Chaim Ephraim of Sudilkov, the grandson of the Besht, between 1780 and 1785; other editions appeared in Koretz in 1811, and in Josefover in 1833.

Though the Master's activity covered a period of more than twenty-five years, his literary work consists of only a few letters. He did not write down his doctrines, but communicated them by word of mouth to his pupils and friends. He was accustomed to write special prayers which are preserved in a *Siddur*, regarded as a veritable Holy Gospel by the Besht's followers. In recent years scholars have occupied themselves with a new Genizah or "hidden collection" of the letters of the Besht and his disciples. Many of these letters are palpable falsifications, and though considerable effort has been expended to distinguish the authentic from the apocryphal material, the reliability of some of the documents has not yet been determined.

The *Shivhei ha-Besht*, namely "The Legends (Praises) of the Baal Shem Tov," was published in Kopyss in 1815 by Israel Joffe; in the same year another edition appeared in Berditschev under the name of the author, Dov Baer ben R. Samuel, *shohet* of the community in Linetz, and son-in-law of the Besht's secretary, Alexander.* This is regarded by the *Hasidim* as a holy book, the teachings of which bring healing to the body and soul. A considerable number of similar works, intended for distribution among the masses, finally moulded the personality and work of the Besht into a monumental entity, based partly on truth, but chiefly on psychologically correct legends.†

The *Hasidic* movement, evolving in many forms and tendencies, gained immense popularity, in spite of the hostility of the *Mitnagdim* or the "Opponents." During the nineteenth century, it crystallized into a distinctive system and became institutionalized. Unfortunately, the veneration shown the *Zaddikim* in their respective communities and areas of influence encouraged the

---

* New editions appeared in 1816 and 1817 in Hrubiesczow, Lasczow, and Ostrog, the best being given in the Yiddish dialect. This work, edited and placed in a new arrangement, with an introduction and notes, was published by S. A. Horodetzky, Berlin, 1922. In this new edition, based on the Kopyss edition of 1815, the material is placed in new divisions, fashioned into chapters, and given a stylistic revision. Horodetzky is recognized as one of the foremost European authorities on *Hasidism* and its personalities, their career and message.

† Wherever a statement is mentioned as an authentic tradition transmitted from the Master, or from his immediate disciples who knew him face to face, historical literary importance can be attached to it. But if the material in the various volumes written about the Besht is clearly of an apocryphal or legendary character, the reader must look upon it with caution and discrimination.

very ostentation and pride which the Master had opposed. Some of them became selfish potentates, and their gullible adherents only encouraged their regrettable ways.*

The Nazi catastrophe during World War II resulted in the annihilation of communities where Hasidism had flourished. But a few Zaddikim with some of their followers found refuge outside of Eastern Europe, including the United States.

In recent years, as a consequence of the activity of Chaim Bloch, Martin Buber, Simon Dubnow, S. A. Horodetzky and others in Europe; and of Jacob S. Minkin, Maurice S. Friedman and others in the United States, Hasidic literature has enjoyed an extensive vogue. There is a close affinity between the direct, simple approach of Hasidism and the ideals of modern Judaism as expressed in the United States. The parables, folk-tales and biblical interpretations of the Besht and his disciples have proved helpful to contemporary preachers, both Jewish and Christian. The literature on Hasidism is steadily increasing, and the contemporary world seems to be discovering in the teachings of the Besht and his disciples a warmth, an enthusiasm, and a vitality which the ultra-rationalistic philosophic and religious systems are believed to lack.

The legacy of the Besht for the modern world cannot be easily appraised. Without doubt, his reliance upon seemingly magical methods of healing, while deserving of study by persons interested in the power of mind over body, cannot be approved by the advocates of medicine, surgery, and psychiatry. We must go beyond this phase of the Besht's activity, and understand him in the role he sought most to fulfill, namely, that of an ethical and religious teacher and mentor. The concern of searching men and women today for an interpretation of the universe and of society in terms of "dialogue," of a close relationship to God, leads them, as it has Martin Buber, to a preoccupation with Hasidism and with the Besht, its progenitor and supreme exponent.

* I. J. Singer in Yoshe Kalb has presented a vivid picture of the Zaddik who tended to give Hasidism a negative reputation in many quarters of Jewish life.

FOR FURTHER READING

BEN-AMOS, Dan, and Jeremy R. Mintz, translators and editors, *In Praise of the Baal Shem Tov* (Bloomington: Indiana University Press, 1970). The earliest collection of legends about the founder of Hasidism.

BUBER, Martin, *The Origin and Meaning of Hasidism*, translated and edited by Maurice Friedman (New York: Harper & Row, 1960). An enthusiastic personalized approach.

DRESNER, Samuel, *The Zaddik: The Doctrine of the Zaddik According to the Writings of Rabbi Yoakov Josef of Polnoy* (New York: Schocken, 1974). The best account of the major disciple and transmittor of the teachings of The Baal Shem Tov.

GREEN, Arthur, "Teachings of the Hasidic Masters," in *Back to the Sources* — Reading the Classic Text, edited by Barry W. Holtz (New York: Summit Books, 1984).

HESCHEL, Abraham, J., *The Circle of the Baal Shem Tov*, edited by Samuel Dresner (Chicago: University of Chicago Press, 1985). A collection of scholarly studies.

SCHOCHET, Jacob, Immanuel, *Rabbi Israel Baal Shem Tov* (Toronto, 1961).

Vilna Gaon

After the death of the Baal Shem Tov, *Ḥasidism* spread with great rapidity through Galicia, Podolia, and the provinces of southern Poland, and before long began to move northward. The Besht's successor, Dov Baer, known as the *Maggid* or preacher of Meseritz, was a Talmudic scholar, and soon the movement began to attract some of the learned. A union of learning and *Ḥasidism* was achieved by Shneour Zalman of Ladi, who became the leader of a group that called itself *Ḥabad.** While the movement made a clean sweep of southern Poland and managed to establish a few secret groups in Vilna and other cities to the north, it met on the whole with fierce resistance in Lithuania. While belonging to the same cultural milieu and owing loyalty to a common government (Poland and Lithuania were joined in 1569 in the Union of Lublin and had a common legislature and government), the Jews of the two countries differed from one another in their mental and spiritual outlook, and gradually in speech, mannerisms and traditions. In Poland *Kabbalah* and superstition were rampant, but in Lithuania Talmudic scholarship continued to flourish.

The first Jewish settlers were probably brought as captives from the Crimea at the end of the fourteenth century when Lithuania was a vast empire stretching from the Baltic to the Black Sea. Later, Jews began to migrate from Germany, and soon established themselves in a number of important communities such as Brest, Grodno, and Lutzk. They enjoyed a considerable degree of tolerance in the early days owing largely to the late introduction of Christianity there (1388), and the length of time it took for the fanaticism of the Polish clergy to penetrate this region.

Under Grand Duke Witold (1388-1430), they were granted a charter of rights similar in content to that granted by Boleslav and

---

* A name derived from the first letters of the words *Hakhmah, Binah,* and *Deah,* meaning wisdom, understanding, and knowledge.

Casimir in Poland. They enjoyed autonomy in religious affairs, carried on various forms of business and trade, and benefited from the protection of the Grand Duke. They were suddenly expelled in 1495 but after eight years were allowed to return from Poland, where they had sought refuge and were completely rehabilitated. Sigismund I (1506-1548), King of Poland and Grand Duke of Lithuania, being less handicapped by the nobles in Lithuania than in Poland, made Michael Yosefovich his financier, appointed him "Senior" of all Lithuanian Jews, and invested him with far-reaching power (1514).

Unfortunately the union of Lithuania and Poland in 1569 had a detrimental effect on the status of the Jews for they now became subject to the reactionary and hostile influences exercised by the church and the nobility. Likewise, with the termination of the hereditary system of sovereignty, the power of the king, whose interest lay in protecting the Jews, was considerably weakened. In the following century, therefore, periodic acts of persecution and violence occurred.

Regardless of the political and economic conditions, however, Lithuanian Jewry was free to carry on its own spiritual and cultural life. As in Poland, a *kahal*, or council, exercised supervision over communal life. Until 1623 the Lithuanian *kahal* was part of the Council of Four Lands, but in that year the Lithuanians withdrew and established a provincial organization of their own.

The Khmelnitzki massacres, which devastated the Ukraine and brought about the decline of Polish Jewish life, did not spare Lithuania, though far less destruction took place than in the southern provinces. Russian and Cossack troops occupied the city of Vilna, where Jews had settled in the middle of the sixteenth century, and the Jews were forced to flee in terror. Those who did not were slaughtered by the invaders without pity, and the Jewish quarter and other sections of the city burned. The municipality took advantage of the Russian occupation to petition the czar that Jews be forbidden in the city. But when the Poles recovered Vilna, the Jews were allowed to return and rebuild their homes.

Despite these events, the Lithuanian Jews were spared the disintegration of Jewish morale which followed the Khmelnitzki uprisings in Poland and, therefore, unlike their brethren in the south, did not turn from rabbinic study to mysticism. The tradition of Talmudic learning continued without interruption for almost three centuries. To be a "native of Vilna" in eighteenth and nineteenth-century Europe was considered a mark of prestige because of this tradition. In the *Bet Hamidrash* near the courtyard of the great synagogue, around which clustered the many buildings and institutions that made up the intensive Jewish life of the city of Vilna, the "sages of Vilna" maintained the high level of Talmudic scholarship of the previous centuries. Vilna boasted of no more than five thousand Jewish adults in the eighteenth century, but it produced a long line of rabbis and sages who set the scholarly tone for the community. These included among others Moshe ben Isaac Lima (1648-1655) who presided over the *Bet Din* (rabbinical court) and wrote a commentary on the *Shulkhan Arukh;* Shabbetai ben Meir Hakohen, the most outstanding of Vilna scholars who at the age of twenty-six published a commentary on the *Yoreh Deah*, the second section of the *Shulkhan Arukh*, known as the *Shakhk*, in which he decided between the opinions of Joseph Karo and Moses Isserles and defended both from attack; Rabbi Moses Rivkes (d. 1671), also author of a commentary on the code of Karo and Isserles which he composed in Amsterdam while a refugee during the Khmelnitzki attack on Vilna.

It is in this cultural environment in what later came to be called the "Jerusalem of Lithuania" that Elijah was born. In a sense, he is both the last of the great medieval rabbis and the first of the modern. In his life and approach to Judaism he represents a vivid contrast to the Baal Shem Tov. While the latter stressed emotion in religion, the Gaon put great emphasis on the role of learning. The Baal Shem Tov was a mystic, but the Gaon was in many ways a rationalist. One was a teacher who went out to the people; the other withdrew from society to write and study. But each in his own way raised the tone of spiritual life and helped restore balance to Jewish life in Eastern Europe.

12 . *Vilna Gaon*

[1720-1797]

MEYER WAXMAN

E L I J A H, Gaon of Vilna, was a modest retiring man who held no public office, rarely took part in communal affairs, and who published very few books in his lifetime. Yet he was acknowledged as the outstanding teacher and rabbinic authority of his time by the tacit consent of Jewish scholars the world over. Though his generation abounded in scholars, he was the only one to be called Gaon,* a title which had been bestowed earlier upon the heads of the two academies of Babylonia. Not only was he called Gaon but "The Gaon," an honor comparable to that offered by medieval philosophers to Aristotle when they spoke of him as "The Philosopher." When Rabbi Elijah received the crown of Gaonite from the scholarly elite of his generation, he was only thirty-three. Since then down to our own times the Vilna Gaon has been the symbol of great Jewish learning and equally great personal piety.

Hayim Volozhin, founder of the famous Volozhin *Yeshiva*, said of the Vilna Gaon, "God in His mercy sent a light to our generation, the angelic and holy man and teacher, Rabbi Elijah." [1] An eyewitness relates that "whenever the Gaon appeared on the streets of Vilna crowds surrounded him seeking to do him homage and feast their eyes upon the light that emanated from his saintly face." [2] Though they saw him daily, they sensed intuitively that a saintly personality walked in their midst.

* See Saadia Gaon, chapter 6. The scholars held no convocations for conferring such an honor. It was done tacitly by addressing him thus in letters, or mentioning his name with the title in Responsa. Gradually it became known to the people at large.

Life Devoted to Study

Elijah was born in a little town near Vilna. His father, a noted scholar and descendant of a leading Jewish family, was the boy's first teacher, but the abilities of the young Elijah were so extraordinary that at the age of six he was able to continue his studies in rabbinics practically unaided. At the age of seven, he delivered in the great synagogue of Vilna a Talmudic discourse which attracted the attention of leading scholars of that and other cities who were present. One of the latter, Abraham Katzenelenbogen, rabbi of Brest-Litovsk, received from Elijah's parents permission to supervise the boy's education. He sent him to his own father, the rabbi of Kaidan, a town where the young student spent several years. He benefited greatly by his contact with the leading scholars of his day, among whom was Rabbi Moses Margolis, a noted commentator, who introduced him to the study of the Palestinian Talmud, a subject which was not pursued by most Talmudists of the day.

Elijah's thirst for knowledge was unbounded. At the age of eight, after he had mastered the entire *Halakhic* literature, he turned his attention to the *Aggadah* and Bible. A year later, he began to delve into the mysteries of the *Kabbalah*, and at the age of ten he was attracted by science. He studied astronomy, mathematics, and anatomy. He wanted to study medicine at the university but was prevented by his father from carrying this out for fear that the youth might forsake his study of Torah.

Elijah refused to submit to any yoke other than that of the Torah. His marriage was a mere incident in his life and was not allowed to interrupt his studies. He never accepted a rabbinical position nor any other communal office. In his youth Elijah, like the Besht, in accordance with the custom of the very pious of the day, "went into exile," that is, he spent a number of years wandering incognito through the Jewish communities of Poland and Germany. At the age of twenty-eight, he returned to Vilna, where he settled permanently, studying and teaching the Torah for half a century.

The community granted him a small pension from a fund left by one of his ancestors, Rabbi Moses Rivkes, for the support of indigent scholars. The small weekly sum was, of course, hardly enough for the support of his family, but Elijah was satisfied to live in poverty as long as he was independent and not forced to interrupt his studies.

For the same reason, he refused to act as judge (*dayan*) in a Jewish court or participate in other communal activities. Thus, when he was approached to state his view in the controversy which raged between Rabbi Jonathan Eybeschütz and Rabbi Jacob Emden, which aroused the Jews of Germany and Poland, he refused to intercede. "Oh that I had wings like a dove, then would I fly to restore peace and quench the strange fire, that fire of contention," he wrote. "But who am I that people should listen to me? If the words of the rabbis, the heads of the holy congregations, are not listened to, who would care about the opinions of a young man hidden in his study?" Until the end of his life the position that Rabbi Elijah occupied in Vilna was that of a private individual.

Study of Torah was to him the very breath of his life; he never interrupted his studies for more than half an hour, and those interruptions were few. His son Abraham testified that little interested him except study. He even restrained his love for his children and spoke little to them so as not to take time from his books. He closed the shutters during the day and read by candlelight in order to eliminate the noises of the street.[3] Study to him was a form of prayer, and those who were privileged to see him while he worked thought that he was praying. Only after he was forty did he begin to teach, selecting a small circle of scholars and teaching them according to his own outlook. He brought to them new interpretations of the Talmud codes, Responsa, proper readings of texts, explanations of difficult passages in the Bible, and remarks on certain phases of Hebrew grammar. He was the ideal teacher in the Talmudic sense for he made his learning "neither a crown with which to decorate himself, nor a spade with which to dig."

Lithuania: Haven of Traditional Judaism

To understand the vastness of Rabbi Elijah's achievement as a scholar, it is necessary to know something of the Lithuania of his day. It was there that traditional Judaism, which consisted in love of Torah, observance of its precepts, and high ethical conduct, found its complete and full expression. The other European centers which had flourished in earlier times had begun gradually to deteriorate. In Germany Judaism had already shown signs of decline in the middle of the seventeenth century. Even in Poland, a fortress of Jewish life for centuries, the massacres by the Cossack hordes of Bogdan Chmelnitzki in 1648 and 1649 had shattered the spiritual life of hundreds of Jewish communities in Podolia, the Ukraine, Eastern Galicia, and in central Poland. Untouched by these persecutions, Lithuania remained undisturbed in its spiritual and intellectual life. There were many men of learning in every city and town, and even in the smallest communities every rabbi was a master of Talmud and the Codes. And Vilna, a relatively large city, could boast of a great scholar on every street.

In consequence, among Lithuanian Jews of all social strata, scholarship, piety, and ethical conduct were considered essential qualifications for membership in community councils and participation in public activity. In spite of the honored place learning held in Jewish life, however, the range and conception of that learning was often quite limited. Most rabbis confined their scholarship to mastery of the Babylonian Talmud, its commentaries, and the Codes. Only a few studied the Palestinian Talmud, and very few the extensive *Halakhic* works like the *Tosefta, Tannaitic* Midrashim, and Gaonic writings. The Bible, except for the weekly portion read on the Sabbath, was likewise little studied. Those who delved into *Kabbalah* did not usually excel in *Halakhic* studies.

New Concept of Scholarship

With Rabbi Elijah, a new concept of scholarship was introduced into Jewish life. In his assiduous studies, he sought to acquire a thorough knowledge of the Babylonian and Palestinian Talmuds, and various other rabbinic classics which most Talmudists of his time entirely neglected. In addition, he studied physics, mathematics, astronomy, metaphysics, and music, so far as those branches of learning were accessible to him.

The Gaon's main claim to fame rests in his breaking new paths in the study of Torah, which influenced his generation and indirectly widened the concept of Jewish education and the total spiritual horizon of European Jewry. The Bible was of course holy to Lithuanian Jewry; it was read publicly in the synagogue on the Sabbath, Holy Days, and week days, but its study was neglected, and so too were many earlier *Halakhic* works.

Approach to the Bible

The Gaon looked upon the vast Jewish literature of the ages, from the Pentateuch to contemporary works, as one grand circle possessing numerous radii dividing it into sections, with the Scriptures at the very center. It followed then that one who did not master the center fully was bound to lose his way. Since the Scriptures were divine, every word possessed great importance. But words were not isolated; they combined into sentences, and their meanings changed according to their punctuation, accent, and the rules of syntax. Accordingly, one could not master the Scriptures without mastering the Hebrew language and its grammar; he literally knew the exact number of letters in each section[4] and penetrated deeply into the meanings of the texts.

Such an approach to Scriptures, new in those days, changed the Gaon's own scholarly activity as well as the general thinking of the generation. First, he insisted on interpreting the Bible in accordance with the *peshat*, i.e., according to the logical and grammatical meaning. He was, of course, aware of the hundreds of interpretations found in Jewish literature, and at times employed them himself because everything was holy to him. But he never lost sight of the *peshat*, which meant more to him than the understanding of the words as such.

In addition to laws, the Gaon held that it was necessary to master concepts of nature and human life included in the Bible, and much about the history and land of Palestine, which required knowledge of geography and map reading. Nor could the period of the Judges be comprehended without fixing the time of each judge. Geographical knowledge was also necessary to understand the last eight chapters of Ezekiel in which the future division of the land is outlined. Many laws expounded in the Talmud, such as those relating to the calendar and determining the holy days, could not be mastered without knowledge of mathematics and astronomy.

The Gaon undertook a thorough study of all these sciences, and his mastery of them is evident from his commentaries, espe-

cially the one on Joshua, which contains a map which he drew
of Palestine as it was divided among the tribes. To his commentary on the Books of Judges, Kings, and Chronicles, he appended
chronological tables of the periods of the Judges and the Kings
of both Judea and the Northern Kingdom. His historical knowledge is also displayed in his notes on the *Tannaitic* historical
book, *Seder Olam Rabba*, written by Rabbi Jose, a disciple of
Akiba, which corrects many dates and erroneous facts. The
Gaon's scientific works include *Ail Meshulach*, a book on trig-
onometry, and the *Sefer ha-Tekunnah* on astronomy. He also
wrote a text on Hebrew grammar, *Dikduk Eliyahu.*

Scientific Approach to Oral Law

To arouse Jewish scholars to follow these studies the Gaon
repeatedly emphasized, as Maimonides had done, the need to
study the sciences in order to understand the Torah more completely. He encouraged the translation of scientific books into
Hebrew. Such work, he said, would not only bring about a
better understanding but would also raise the esteem of the people of Israel. "Other nations often chide us and ask where is your
wisdom and knowledge and thus the name of the God of Israel
is desecrated." This attitude planted the seeds of the intellectual
movement known as the Vilna type of *Haskalah* (Enlightenment), which was to flower in the next generation.

The Gaon also applied the "scientific" attitude to the literature of Oral Law, which engaged his attention for many years.
Here, too, he attempted to penetrate to the essential meaning
beneath various layers of interpretations by generations of
scholars. To chart a path in the vast expanse of rabbinic literature he searched for early sources, corrected faulty copying and
printing, and wrote commentaries on numerous tractates of the
Mishnah and the Talmud. His emendations in the texts of
Halakhic works, embracing Talmudic literature from the early
Halakhic Midrashim to the smallest tractate of the Palestinian
and Babylonian Talmud, are of inestimable value, especially for
texts not included in the Talmud such as the *Tannaitic* and
Aggadic Midrashim and the *Tosefta*. Unlike the Babylonian
Talmud, the text of which had, on the whole, been carefully
guarded through the ages, the other works had been entirely

neglected and abounded in errors and misprints before the Gaon's emendations. Of special interest are his corrections of the *Tannaitic* historical work, *Seder Olam* (The Order of the World), to which most Talmudists had hitherto paid no attention.

The Gaon also turned to the ramified literature of the Codes, quoting the sources on which decisions were based, correcting errors, and appending comments to difficult passages. At times, his corrections led him to arrive at a decision different from that of the original codifiers.

In spite of the cryptic style of the Gaon's comments and emendations, scholars from his day to the present have acclaimed them for throwing light on thousands of difficult passages. Moreover, his method stimulated the scientific study of Talmudic and post-Talmudic literature by western scholars, many of whom were able to publish corrected and scientific editions of important works like the *Tosefta*, the *Tannaitic* Midrashim, *Mekilta* (on the Book of Exodus), and the *Sifre* (on Numbers and Deuteronomy).

Interested in Kabbalah

Nor did this vast work exhaust the Gaon's concept of what Torah encompassed. *Kabbalah* also claimed his attention, and there is hardly a mystical book which he did not emend or comment upon, and memorize. Hayim of Volozhin, his disciple, once asked the Gaon the meaning of the word *hesed* (kindness) in a certain passage of the *Zohar*, which seemed out of place and unrelated to the preceding or following words. Without consulting the text, the Gaon informed him that several lines were missing. The copyist had found the passage unintelligible, and had written on the margin *hasar* ("missing"). The printer mistook the last letter, the *resh*, for a *dalet*, and the word became *hesed*.

Religious Outlook[5]

Though the Gaon did not develop a systematic theological view of Judaism, it is possible from various remarks in his works, especially in his comments on the Bible, to arrive at his religious outlook. On the whole, he did not depart from the traditional theology of the ages, but broadened and deepened it in many instances. Like most traditional theologians, he believed that the goal to which a Jew should strive all his life is the perfection of his soul through Torah, observation of its precepts, and ethical conduct. The Torah, the basis of this perfection, should be the constant companion of man through life, and its study pursued intensively. Since every *mitzvah* has a definite time and manner for its performance, observance of the precepts alone is not sufficient for a good life. Torah is the spiritual bread of life, without which a man remains hungry; it also guards him against straying into unethical conduct.[6] Like the rain which comes down from heaven, the effect to Torah study is conditioned by the state of its receiver. When rain falls upon ground sown with wheat or other grain, it makes it grow and ripen, but if the ground is covered with poisonous weeds, its effect will only be to increase the latter. The rain is always good, and the evil that it may cause is entirely due to the imperfections of the ground which receives it. Likewise, the Torah must be received by a man with a good heart if it is to bring out the best in him. In order to be really affected by his study, man must prepare himself by acquiring virtues and doing good deeds.

The Gaon laid special emphasis upon ethical conduct in both its positive and negative aspects, namely, the acquisition of virtue and the avoidance of vices, especially greed and lust. Aware of the difficulty in taming those desires, he believed that man could best acquire virtue through its habitual practice. Man, said the Gaon, must develop his ethical self gradually and must not strive to attain perfection immediately; nor must he overlook his individuality, for all men are not alike in character.[7] Furthermore, this distinctiveness of character must also be observed in the education of children, as the Bible indicates: "train up a child in the way he should go" (Proverbs 22:6), namely, train him according to his individual nature. Once this is done, "even when he is old, he will not depart from it." But if his individual nature is disregarded, he may later turn away from the training he received in his childhood.

The Gaon's view of life and Judaism, though based on the traditional approach, reflects his own personal enlightenment and liberalism. On the other hand, a number of stories told by contemporaries, as well as certain passages in his works, reveal that the Gaon was at times intolerant and at other times inclined to asceticism. This manifestation of dualism is also evident in his attitudes toward philosophy. For example, several passages in the Gaon's commentary on the code of Joseph Karo (*Shulkhan Arukh*) contain harsh words against philosophy and its students, not excluding Maimonides.[8] There is also testimony from several disciples, however, that these remarks may never have been uttered by the Gaon, but were rather inserted by an editor of the manuscript. The same sources also reveal that the Gaon spoke with reverence of Maimonides and even of Gersonides, the most radical Jewish philosopher.[9] Indeed, it is hardly possible for the Gaon, who mastered the entire range of Jewish literature, was versed in medieval Jewish philosophy, and certainly studied Bahya's *Duties of the Heart*, a work which contains both philosophy and deep religiosity, not to have been influenced by some of its views. Numerous passages in his biblical commentaries, especially on the Proverbs, employ philosophical terms and concepts and at times express views which do not seem to harmonize with his otherwise typically traditional religious outlook.

The reconciliation of the two contradictory traits in the outlook of the Gaon can be explained by the conflict in his soul between reason and unbounded loyalty to tradition. As a logical thinker he undoubtedly valued reason but feared lest it overstep its boundary. The fact that he knew so much of the Torah by heart and had a reverence for the tradition perhaps unconsciously repressed all rational questioning. Though fearless in contradicting authorities in matters of legal interpretation, in questions relating to rational conceptions he refrained from deviating from the path of his predecessors.

Struggle against Ḥasidism

This reverence of tradition and fear of deviation were responsible for the Gaon's struggle against *Ḥasidism* in a severe and violent manner not compatible with his usually gentle and humble character. Though *Ḥasidism* did not introduce new principles into Judaism, it did initiate differences in the mode of worship, in the attitude toward Jewish ideals of intellectuality and reverence in learning, and also in certain religious customs. The

Ḥasidim began to change the accepted version of the prayers in accordance with readings and emendations of the *Kabbalah* of Isaac Luria known as the *Ari*. Prayers were carried on in a loud voice and with gesticulations. These mannerisms stemmed from the demand that prayer be offered with enthusiasm and with signs of inner emotion. In general, *Ḥasidism* laid more emphasis on emotion and religious enthusiasm than it did on study of Torah.

These deviations and changes aroused opposition, especially after the movement penetrated into Lithuania, which was then the center of learning and Jewish intellectualism. The Gaon, heading a group of rabbis and leaders, was afraid of what might result from a movement in which unbridled religious emotion held sway. They decided to take steps to check the spread of *Ḥasidism*, and in the year 1772, when a *Ḥasidic* congregation was established in Vilna, it was banned with the consent of the Gaon, excluding members of the sect from the activities of the Jewish community. Other communities followed by issuing bans against *Ḥasidism* and its followers. Several *Ḥasidic* leaders, including Shneour Zalman of Ladi and Menahem Mendel of Vitebsk, made attempts to meet the Gaon in order to refute the charges against *Ḥasidism*, but he refused to see them.

In 1780 the first classic book on *Ḥasidism*, *Toledot Yaakob Yoseph* by Jacob Joseph of Polonnoye, a disciple of the Besht, was published. Besides presenting the principles of the movement, this book contained much polemic matter, expressed disregard for learning and scholarship, and spoke disparagingly of the rabbis and intellectual leaders. When the book reached Vilna, the struggle broke out anew, this time with greater force. A new ban was endorsed by the Gaon, and he urged its enforcement in a personal letter to the Lithuanian Jewish communities. In the same letter he spoke in harsh terms of the *Ḥasidim*, demanding their exclusion from the Jewish communities and even asking for some form of persecution in the form of economic boycott rather than physical violence.

The Gaon sensed the danger of a serious schism in Judaism in the attitude of the *Ḥasidim* toward life, as expressed in their mode of hilarious conduct at public gatherings, in their noisy manner of prayer, and primarily in their minimization of the value of Torah study. Possibly he and his colleagues also suspected that the *Hasidim* were in contact with the remnants of the Sabbatians and Frankists, followers of those false Messiahs still in existence in the southern provinces of Poland. The conflict lasted for several decades and resulted in regrettable episodes. After the death of the Gaon in the year 1798, opponents informed the government authorities against the *Hasidim*, charging them with heresy and political sedition. The leader of the *Habad* branch, Shneour Zalman of Ladi, was arrested twice, but later liberated. The Gaon did not advise such type of persecution and were he alive would have undoubtedly protested against such action.

Personal Saintliness

Aside from his scholarly contributions the Vilna Gaon made his mark on his generation through his personal piety and saintliness. He observed every precept of the codes of Jewish law in its minutest severity, and also additional practices which most codifiers had allowed to fall into disuse because of changed conditions of life. The mere fact that they were mentioned in the Talmud was for the Gaon sufficient reason for their observance. As for ethical conduct, he often went to extremes. Indeed, according to his son, he interrupted his study only to obtain support for the poor. If he did not succeed in collecting the necessary sum, he gave away his last meal or even his furniture. He also was instrumental in marrying off daughters of the poor and providing them with dowries and wedding expenses.

He led an ascetic life which he also taught his family to follow. But the discipline he imposed was primarily ethical, and did not include physical asceticism. On the contrary, the Gaon repeatedly asserted that one must enjoy whatever is needed for physical well-being. His insistence on ethical conduct consisted primarily in extreme care in avoiding certain vices, especially slander, envy, and immodest conduct by women. In a letter sent his wife when he was on his way to Palestine, he warned her against indulging in gossip or slander. He asked her to isolate herself at home, avoid the company of women even at the stores, and to do her marketing through a messenger even though it would be costlier. He also asked his daughters not to go to services in the synagogue but to stay at home, for at the synagogue they might see other girls wearing finer clothes than theirs, and as a result they would envy them and ultimately commit the sin of slander. He said, "Man must not indulge in fasting or in any asceticism, but take care to restrain his mouth from gossip and slander, and tame his passions all his life." He also urged his wife to be strict in the training of the children and to assure peace and harmony among them. He insisted that the Sabbath be spent in meditation and study, with a minimum of conversation and frivolity.

The Gaon was exceptional also in his desire to spare others the slightest humiliation, directly or indirectly. For example, it happened that a dishonest *shamash* (synagogue attendant) kept for himself over a long period of time the weekly stipend which the Gaon received from the community for his support. Yet Rabbi Elijah refused, despite the vigorous protests of his wife, to inform the communal officers of this dishonesty. He chose hunger for himself and his family rather than to accuse a fellow man of theft. The perfidious act became known only when the clerk confessed the crime on his deathbed.[10] Because of this same consideration, the Gaon never mentioned in writing or orally the name of any scholar whose view or decision he opposed in order not to cause him shame or grief.

Influence of the Gaon

Unlike the Besht, the Gaon did not create a movement or a distinct party; yet his influence lasted for generations. Many of the scholars in Lithuania considered themselves his disciples, and there was a smaller circle of men who were really close to him. This group adopted his method of studying the Talmud, introduced the study of the Bible and Hebrew grammar into Jewish circles where hitherto it had been neglected, cultivated the sciences, and created a new scientific literature in Hebrew.

One such disciple was Joshua Zeitlin of Shklow, a scholar who also carried on extensive business transactions with the Russian government, and was in close contact with General Grigori Potemkin, a Russian politician and great favorite of Empress Catherine II. A man of wealth, he used his money to encourage learning and scholarship, both Talmudic and secular. He supported a number of scholars and writers on his estate at Shklow. It was there that another disciple of the Gaon, Baruch of Shklow, translated Euclid's geometry into Hebrew and busied himself with the study of natural sciences to the extent of making chemical experiments in a laboratory provided by his patron. Members of the Gaon's family also contributed to widening the horizon of Jewish studies. His brother, Isaachar Baer, composed an excellent commentary on the Pentateuch and a short Aramaic dictionary. The son of the Gaon, Abraham, collected and edited a number of smaller Midrashim with a critical introduction which laid the foundation for future critical studies of the *Aggadah*. He also wrote a geography in Hebrew.

The favorite disciples of the Gaon were Rabbi Hayim of Volozhin and his brother Shlomo Zalman. Both were exceptionally learned in all branches of Torah studies and were considered by the Gaon as younger colleagues. Shlomo Zalman excelled his brother in keenness of mind and mastery of the extensive Torah literature. Like the Gaon himself, he knew by heart both the Palestinian as well as the Babylonian Talmuds as well as the Codes. His early death undoubtedly deprived Jewish scholarship of many important works.

Rabbi Hayim left a number of works, among them a commentary on the ethical tractate of the Mishnah, *The Sayings of the Fathers*, and a religious philosophy entitled *Nefesh ha-Hayyim* (*The Soul of Life*). Most of his Responsa and a number of *Halakhic* works were burned in a fire in 1815. His greatness consists not so much in his works as in his personality and activity in spreading the word of Torah. He was the founder of the Volozhin *Yeshiva*, which for over one hundred years was the leading center of Torah and scholarship in Eastern Europe. Generations of rabbis, scholars, and leaders in Israel were raised in its halls. Many great men, who enriched Jewish literature and contributed to the amelioration of Jewish life, were nurtured there in love of Torah and the Jewish people. The leading Hebrew poet of our day, Chaim Nahman Bialik, was a student at Volozhin, where he imbibed the love of Torah and Israel which he later expressed in many poems, notably *Ha-Matmid* (The Diligent Student).

The influence of the Gaon reached not only his followers

but also his opponents. In J. L. Maimon's biography of the Gaon, a story is told about the famous *Ḥasidic* rabbi Levi Yitzhak, who was forced to leave the city of Pinsk, where he held his first rabbinical position, because of the Gaon's opposition to *Ḥasidism*. Yet, according to *Ḥasidic* tradition, after hearing of the Gaon's death, he said to his followers; "When Rabbi Elijah died, and his soul ascended to heaven, the heavenly court found it pure and righteous, but there was one spot on it, his opposition to *Ḥasidism*. After much discussion, it was decided that he must go to hear one discourse by Rabbi Nahum of Chernobel, a disciple of the Besht, which he delivers from time to time before a group of *Zaddikim*. Then he will be led directly to paradise. But if he refuses he will be led to paradise by passing the doors of *Gehinnom* (hell). The Gaon answered, 'I will rather pass by the door of the *Gehinnom* than hear a *Ḥasidic* discourse.' Then something wonderful happened. Thousands upon thousands of pages of the Talmud, which Elijah had studied so often, so intensely and devotedly, came and arranged themselves in an enormous mass and closed the door of the *Gehinnom*. The angels were then forced to lead him directly to paradise." [11] The fact that the legend was current among the *Ḥasidim* demonstrates the admiration in which the Gaon was held even among those he strongly opposed.

Great and fundamental changes have taken place since the death of the Gaon, and the world of Eastern European Jewry which produced the Gaon has been completely shattered. Yet his influence continues, and his example still inspires those who endeavor to devote their lives to the realization of Jewish ideals, though under changed conditions and in a different form.

FOR FURTHER READING

"Elijah Ben Solomon Zalman" (The Vilna Gaon or Elijah Gaon) in *Encyclopedia Judaica,* Volume 6, pp. 651–658 (Jerusalem: 1972).

GINZBERG, Louis, *Students, Scholars and Saints* (Philadelphia: Jewish Publication Society, 1928).

MENES, Abraham, "Patterns of Jewish Scholarship in Eastern Europe," in *The Jews: Their History, Culture and Religion,* 3rd ed., edited by Louis Finkelstein, (Philadelphia: Jewish Publication Society, 1960).

Schechter, Solomon, *Studies of Judaism,* (Philadelphia: Jewish Publication Society, 1938).

YOSHER, Moses, "Eliyahu of Vilna," in *Jewish Leaders,* edited by Leo Jung (New York: Bloch, 1953).

A Concluding Word

"The hero," wrote Carlyle, "can be prophet, poet, king or priest or what you will, according to the kind of world he finds himself born into." Jewish heroes, born into many different worlds, each with its own unique challenges, have included a variety of types: the king, prophet, teacher, sage, philosopher, statesman, mystic, and scholar. Several things stand out about these personalities that we have studied. They demonstrated, first of all, an unusual ability to adjust to diverse civilizations such as the Canaanite, Greek, Roman, Persian, Muslim, and Christian, and to live in such contrasting milieux as Palestine, Hellenistic Egypt, Babylonia, Spain, Northern and Eastern Europe. Philo spoke Greek, Akiba used Aramaic, while Saadia, Halevi, and Maimonides wrote in Arabic. Rashi often explained a Hebrew or Aramaic term in French. They had to cope with antagonistic and alien philosophies which seemed to put their ancestral faith on the defensive. Yet they managed to harmonize Judaism with the prevailing philosophies of their time.

They were able (as was true of the Jewish people as a whole) to overcome persecutions of various kinds and to transform adversity into a blessing. Few of them enjoyed quiet and tranquil lives. During the days of all of them except Saadia and the Gaon of Vilna, there occurred anti-Jewish outbreaks of various kinds and serious threats to the physical security of the Jew. Thus, both Philo and Akiba had to interrupt their work to go to Rome and intercede with the emperor on behalf of the Jews. Rashi's last years were clouded by the massacres which took place at the time of the Crusades, Maimonides and his family had to flee from their native land, and Abravanel was several times a refugee in search of a home. Their lives are thus dramatic illustrations of the perennial miracle of Jewish survival which, despite all sociological explanations, remains a mystery.

We may note, secondly, how unbroken has been the process of Jewish creativity. There are those who think of Jewish spiritual productivity as limited primarily to the Bible. These biographies make amply clear that at no time did Judaism exhaust its capacity to evolve new and vital contributions to the religion of mankind and to the moral foundations of society. In ancient times, the development of the Oral Law, the Apocrypha, Hellenistic literature, the Mishnah, Talmud, and Midrash all represented milestones in a long pattern of growth. Nor did medieval Jewry lack in cultural output. Indeed, as we have seen, in Muslim lands Jews made contributions to poetry, philosophy, science, medicine, and other fields. In Christian lands, in spite of all the restrictions and oppression, there arose commentators, codifiers, philosophers, and mystics, each of whom made a significant contribution to the chain of tradition.

Finally, these biographical accounts indicate how relevant are the teachings of past Jewish thinkers. Of course, not everything they wrote is still meaningful to us of the modern world. Many of the allegorical interpretations of Philo, the theological ideas of the medieval philosophers, or the explanations of Rashi, to cite some examples, are not acceptable to a person brought up in the spirit of twentieth-century science and philosophy. But much remains in the works of these personalities that can be of value. Certainly Jeremiah's emphasis on the personal side of the covenant relationship with God, the primacy of morality, and his faith in the eternity of Israel, or Akiba's defense of the economically and socially oppressed, and of the rights of women as well as his opposition to superstition can be appreciated by us. Saadia's rational approach to religion, his keen analysis of the factors causing disbelief such as mental laziness, the spirit of acquisitiveness, and pride, as well as some of his comments on the art of living, all have a contemporary ring. Much of the ethical teachings of Maimonides, and his use of reason to solve religious problems, can still inspire us. And whether one is inclined to mysticism or not, some of the psychological insights of the Baal Shem

Tov, his approach to prayer, and the democratic spirit of the *Hasidic* community are particularly relevant for our time. These are but a few examples of the abiding value of many of the teachings that have come to us from these great figures of our past.

We must, of course, not attribute a greater role to these men than is due them. Except for Moses and in a limited sense Abravanel, they were not statesmen who determined the actual course of history. Economic and social forces were as crucial a factor in Jewish history as the impact of these heroes. But there is little doubt that they left a lasting impression on the development of Judaism. The accounts of their lives should give us inspiration and encouragement in our own struggle for a creative Jewish survival, and lead us to a renewed faith in Judaism and the Jewish people.

Notes

Editor's Introduction to Ancient Times

1. Max L. Margolis, *The Hebrew Scriptures in the Making*, Chapter 2.
2. Harry M. Orlinsky, *Ancient Israel*, p. 6.
3. Quoted in Charles Francis Potter, *Great Religious Leaders*, Chapter 4.
4. Nelson Glueck, *Rivers in the Desert*, p. 31.
5. Werner Keller, *The Bible as History*, Chapter II.
6. *Ibid.*, Chapter V.
7. Cyrus H. Gordon, *Introduction to the Old Testament*, Chapter 6.
8. James B. Pritchard, *Archaeology and the Old Testament*, p. 75ff.
9. *Ibid.*, pp. 206-215.
10. W. F. Albright, "The Biblical Period" in *The Jews*, edited by Louis Finkelstein, Vol. I, p. 6.
11. *Ibid.*, p. 12.
12. André Parrot, *Babylon and the Old Testament*.

Moses

1. A recent historian, J. A. Wilson, has designated the first two chapters of his study *The Burden of Egypt* (Univ. of Chicago Press, 1951), "The Black Land" and "Out of the Mud." This excellent work has now appeared in a Phoenix paperback edition, under the title *The Culture of Egypt* (1956).
2. From H. M. Orlinsky, *Ancient Israel*, pp. 31-34. Wilson, *op. cit.*, has described this period in Chapter VII as "The Great Humiliation."
3. Cf. G. E. Wright, *Biblical Archaeology* (Westminster Press, Phila., 1957), Chapter IV, "Sojourners in Egypt," pp. 53-68.
4. The Midrash waxes eloquent in its imaginative tales of the birth of Moses, his rescue from the water, and the like. See Louis Ginzberg's wonderful collection of *The Legends of the Jews* (7 volumes, of which 1-4 are the Legends, 5-6 the Notes, and 7 the Index), Vol. II, pp. 262ff. See one-volume abridgment, *Legends of the Bible* (1956), "Moses," pp. 277-506.
5. "The Legend of Sargon," translated by E. A. Speiser, *Ancient Near Eastern Texts Relating to the Old Testament* (edited by J. B. Pritchard), p. 119; the technical notes and signs have here been deleted.

6. By G. Steindorff and K. C. Seele (Univ. of Chicago Press, 1942). Or Wilson, *op. cit.*, Chapter VIII, "Far Frontiers," pp. 166-205.

7. The best treatment of this phenomenon is to be found in Wilson, *op. cit.*, Chapter IX, "Irrepressible Conflict," pp. 206-235; the quotations in this section derive from Wilson. See also J. H. Breasted, *Cambridge Ancient History*, Vol. II (1924), pp. 109 ff.

8. See J. H. Breasted, *The Dawn of Conscience* (New York, 1933).

9. See note 7 above. See also R. J. Williams, "The Hymn to Aten" (pp. 142-150 in *Documents from Old Testament Times* (Nelson and Sons, 1958), edited by D. Winton Thomas).

10. From Orlinsky, *op. cit.*, pp. 27-9, 41-2.

11. See Wilson in *Ancient Near Eastern Texts*, pp. 376 ff.; or Williams, in *Documents from Old Testament Times*, pp. 137-41.

12. In general, see Wright, *op. cit.*, pp. 58-60 ("With Moses and the Exodus"). More details may be found in M. Noth, *The History of Israel*, pp. 109-119 ("The Deliverance from Egypt"); Y. Kaufmann, "The Biblical Age" (in *Great Ages and Ideas of the Jewish People*, edited by L. W. Schwarz (Random House, 1956), pp. 14ff.

13. *When Egypt Ruled the East*, in the "Outline of Egyptian History," p. 275. Wilson, *op. cit.*, states (p. 247): "The fact remains that the arrogant bellowing of victory comes as an insincere ostentation similar to the bloated bulk of Rameses II's monuments or to his shameless appropriation of the monuments of his ancestors. Blatant advertising was used to cover up the failure to attain past glories."

14. Biblical scholarship has long accepted the Documentary Theory, according to which the Pentateuch is made up, in the main, of four distinct Documents (or, sources), designated *J*, *E*, *D*, and *P*, deriving from about 10th-9th (J and E), 7th (D) and 6th (P) centuries B.C.E. Before World War I, scholars tended to regard much of these Documents as fictitious. But archeology since World War I and closer analysis have reversed this attitude sharply; these sources are now generally regarded as substantially historical, preserving much that the careful and objective scholar may use with discreet confidence. See S. R. Driver, *Introduction to the Literature of the Old Testament* (1913; now reprinted as a Meridian paperback); or the excellent "Introduction" in the revised edition of his *Westminster Commentary on Genesis*.

15. See, e.g., "Passover," Chapter VII, pp. 173-218 in J. H. Greenstone, *Jewish Feasts and Fasts* (Phila., 1945), or H. Schauss (Union of American Hebrew Congregations, 1938), *The Jewish Festivals*, "Pesach," Chapters V-IX, pp. 38-85.

16. F. S. Bodenheimer, "The Manna of Sinai," *Biblical Archaeologist*, X (1947), pp. 1-6.

17. On the route to the Red Sea and Mount Sinai, see Wright-Filson, *Westminster Historical Atlas to the Bible*, pp. 38-9; or Wright, *Biblical Archaeology*, pp. 60 ff.

18. See Orlinsky, *op. cit.*, pp. 27-8.

19. See G. E. Mendenhall, "Covenant Forms in Israelite Tradition," *Biblical Archaeologist*, XVII (1954), pp. 50-76; Wright, *Biblical Archaeology*, pp. 98-100.

20. See T. J. Meek, *Hebrew Origins*, Chapter II, "The Origin of Hebrew Law," pp. 49-81; the chapters by E. A. Speiser and I. Mendelsohn on Mesopotamia (pp. 8-15) and Canaan-Israel (pp. 25-33) respectively in *Authority*

and Law in the Ancient Orient (*Supplement* to the *Journal of the American Oriental Society*, No. 17, 1954); G. E. Mendenhall, "Ancient Oriental and Biblical Law," *Biblical Archaeologist*, XVII, pp. 26-46; *The Ancient Near East*, pp. 133-170.

21. See Wilson's chapter on "Ancient Egypt" in the above cited *Supplement*, pp. 1-7.
22. From Orlinsky, *op. cit.*, p. 38, with reference to F. M. Cross, Jr., "The Tabernacle," in *Biblical Archaeologist*, X (1947), pp. 45-68; Wright, *Biblical Archaeology*, pp. 65-67.
23. See Driver, *International Critical Commentary on Deuteronomy* (1896), pp. 26-28.

David the King

1. *Baba Bathra*, 14 b.; H. M. Orlinsky, *Ancient Israel*, pp. 76-77.
2. Louis Ginzbeg, *Legends of the Bible* (1956), p. 533.
3. *Ibid.*, p 534.
4. Nelson Glueck, *Rivers in the Desert*, p. 23.
5. Bernard W. Anderson, *Understanding the Old Testament*, p. 134.
6. Glueck, *op. cit.*, pp. 95, 106.
7. Orlinsky, *op. cit.*, p. 70. Also Anderson, *op. cit.*, p. 134.
8. W. F. Albright, in *The Jews*, edited by Louis Finkelstein, Volume I, pp. 24 f. Also, Anderson, *op. cit.*, pp. 132-133.
9. Orlinsky, *op. cit.*, pp. 72 ff.
10. Anderson, *op. cit.*, pp. 122 ff.
11. Ginzberg, *op. cit.*, p. 530.
12. Orlinsky, *op. cit.*, p. 75.
13. Albright, *op. cit.*, p. 26. Also Orlinsky, *op. cit.*, p. 70.
14. Albright, *op. cit.*, pp. 24 ff.
15. Glueck, *op. cit.*, p. 123, and elsewhere.
16. W. F. Albright, *Archaeology and the Religion of Israel*, pp. 123 ff.
17. Albright, *The Jews*, Volume I, p. 22. See also Orlinsky, *op. cit.*, p. 70.
18. Robert H. Pfeiffer, *Introduction to the Old Testament*, p. 798.
19. Orlinsky, *op. cit.*, p. 75.
20. Anderson, *op. cit.*, pp. 139 ff.
21. Albright, *The Jews*, Volume I, p. 25.
22. *Ibid.* See also Albright, *Archaeology and the Religion of Israel*, p. 121.
23. Anderson, *op. cit.*, p. 141.
24. Ginzberg, *op. cit.*, p. 551.

Jeremiah

1. John Skinner, *Prophecy and Religion*, p. 19.
2. Cyrus Gordon, *Introduction to Old Testament Times*, p. 239.
3. *Cambridge Ancient History*, Volume III, Chapter IV. See also Will Durant, *Our Oriental Civilization*, Chapter X.
4. On the problem of the "foe from the north," see Adam C. Welch, *Jeremiah: His Time and His Works*, Chapter V, and Skinner, *op. cit.*, Chapter III.
5. Durant, *op. cit.*, p. 284.
6. *Ibid.*, p. 225.
7. André Parrot, *Babylon and the Old Testament*.

8. Robert Pfeiffer, *Introduction to the Old Testament*, p. 723. See also Julius Bewer, *Literature of the Old Testament*, pp. 189, 191.
9. Gordon, *op. cit.*, p. 255.
10. This aspect of Jeremiah's thought is discussed in Joseph Klausner, *The Messianic Idea in Israel*, pp. 94, 95.
11. Quoted in *Jeremiah* (Soncino Books of the Bible), edited by Harry Friedman, Introduction, p. xii.
12. Beryl Cohen, *The Prophets: Their Personalities and Teachings*.
13. Heinrich Graetz, *History of the Jews*.
14. For detailed bibliography of legends on Jeremiah, see Louis Ginzberg, *Legends of the Jews*, Volume VII, Index, pp. 253-4.
15. Ahad Ha'am, *Essays* (East and West Library), edited by Leon Simon, pp. 105-6.

Editor's Introduction to Medieval Times

1. Jacob Marcus, *The Jew in the Medieval World*, p. ix. For various interpretations of the concept of the Middle Ages in general history see H. E. Barnes, *History of Western Civilization*, Volume I, pp. 347-350.
2. Meyer Waxman, *A History of Jewish Literature*, Volume II, Chapters III-V.
3. Louis Finkelstein, editor, *Rab Saadia Gaon*, p. 9.
4. Will Durant, *The Age of Faith*, Chapter XII.
5. Salo W. Baron, *A Social and Religious History of the Jews*, Volume VIII.
6. Abraham Halkin, "The Judeo-Islamic Age" in *Great Ages and Ideas of the Jewish People*, Leo Schwarz, editor.
7. Baron, *op. cit.* See also article on Karaites by Leon Nemoy in *Universal Jewish Encyclopedia*, Volume VI.

Rashi

1. *The Social Life of the Jews of Northern France in the Twelfth-Fourteenth Centuries*, p. 237.
2. Smalley, Beryl, *The Study of the Bible in the Middle Ages*, p. 55.
3. Zeitlin, Solomon, *J.O.R.*, Vol. XXXI, No. 1.
4. Smalley, *op. cit.*, XVI, XII.
5. Yahudah, A. S., *Bitzaron*, Vol. VI, p. 488.
6. Avinery, Isaac, *Hechal Rashi*, 1940, p. 13.

Baal Shem Tov

1. Louis Ginzberg, article on "Baal Shem Tov," *Jewish Encyclopedia*, Vol. II, p. 384.
2. S. Ansky's *The Dybbuk* is a famous play portraying an instance of Ḥasidic expulsion of a Cleaving Spirit.
3. See Simon Dubnow's section in *Geschichte Des Chassidismus*, Vol. I, pp. 89-90.
4. *Zawaat ha-Ribasch*, 1793, p. 16.
5. The recommendation of amulets or "remembrances" by at least one contemporary non-Jewish preacher-psychologist has brought him under severe fire in present-day America.
6. Martin Buber, *Tales of the Ḥasidim*, Vol. I, pp. 12-13, where the role of

the Besht as healer is discussed at length, together with a consideration of his healing methods, including the use of amulets. See also Dubnow, *op. cit.*, pp. 84-87.

Vilna Gaon

1. Rabbi Hayim of Volozhin, Introduction to the Gaon's commentary on the order *Zeraim* of the Palestinian Talmud.
2. *Aliath Eliyahu*, p. 14.
3. *Ibid.*, p. 65.
4. *Ibid.*, p. 74.
5. *Saarat Eliyahu, a Treatise on the Life of the Gaon* by his son Abraham, p. 45.
6. Commentary on Proverbs, 9:5.
7. *Ibid.*, 12:6.
8. Commentary on *Yoreh Deah*, Ch. 179, 6.
9. S. J. Finn, *Kirya Neamanah*, p. 152.
10. *Saarat Eliyahu*, p. 27.
11. *Toldot Nagid*, Biography, the Gaon Rabbi Elijah, p. 35.

Aggadah:
> The imaginative and poetic part of the Talmud, which consists of stories, legends, chronicles, speculations, proverbs, and epigrams. Complements the *Halakhah* of the Talmud, which deals with the regulation of religious practice.

am ha-aretz (Hebrew, "people of the land"):
> The masses of the people (as distinct from certain aristocratic classes). Applied in Talmudic times to the common people who did not adhere to the rabbinic regulations as regards the laws of purity, etc. Ultimately became a derogatory phrase meaning "ignoramus," or one not educated in Jewish matters.

anthropomorphism:
> The ascribing to God of human form and characteristics: for example, biblical phraseology referring to God's hands, fingers, etc.

antinomian:
> Opposed to law; in Hellenistic period, used to describe opposition to traditional Jewish law (particularly to the practical commandments in Leviticus).

Bar Kokhba Rebellion (c. 132-135 C.E.):
> The last great rebellion of the Jews against the Romans under Hadrian. Led by Simeon Bar Kokhba, it became a symbol of the Jewish struggle for independence.

B.C.E.:
> Before the Common Era, the designation used by Jews to identify the period before the advent of Jesus and Christianity.

Code (s):
> Another term for the Talmud, which is regarded as the legal code book for the regulation of Jewish life. Various compila-

tions or codes of Talmudic law have been handed down, among which the most important is the *Shulkhan Arukh* of Joseph Karo.

C.E.:

Common Era, the term used by Jews to designate the period following the advent of Jesus and Christianity.

dayan (Hebrew, "judge"):

The title for a judge of a rabbinical court, who was qualified to legislate not only on religious matters but also on problems of civil law.

Decalogue:

The Ten Commandments.

Ethics (or *Sayings*) *of the Fathers* (Hebrew, *Pirke Avot*):

Tractate of the Mishnah containing collection of ethical and religious precepts of the rabbinic sages, which has been incorporated into the Jewish prayer book.

Frankists:

Followers of Jacob Frank (1726-1791), a false Messiah, who claimed to be the successor of Sabbatai Zevi. He and his disciples publicly embraced Christianity.

Gemarah ("completion" of the teaching):

A commentary by later scholars on the Mishnah, and the most extensive portion of the Talmud. The Mishnah is the earliest basic part of the Talmud, consisting mainly of the interpretations of the biblical law.

Hagiographa (Greek, "holy writings": in Hebrew, *ketuvim*, "writings"):

Third and last section of the Bible (after Pentateuch and Prophets) containing eleven books: Psalms, Proverbs, Job, Song of Songs, Ruth, Lamentations, Ecclesiastes, Esther, Daniel, Ezra and Nehemiah, and Chronicles.

Halakhah (Hebrew, "law"):

The legal part of Talmudic and later Jewish literature, as contrasted with *Aggadah*, the homiletical and narrative portions.

Ḥasidism:

Religious and social movement founded in the eighteenth century by Israel Baal Shem Tov. In contrast with the stress on scholarship and study of the Talmud, *Ḥasidism* emphasized personal prayer and joyous faith in God. See Chapter 11 on the Baal Shem Tov.

Haskalah:

Refers to the enlightenment movement among the Jews of Europe during the eighteenth and nineteenth centuries. In Germany it attempted at first to bring into the ghetto the best thought of the day in Hebrew, but later took the form of modernized Jewish scholarship in the vernacular. In Russia the emphasis was on the introduction of secular literature to Jewish circles through the medium of Hebrew.

Hellenism:
Amalgam of Greek and Oriental civilization which flourished in the ancient world after Alexander the Great. The conflict that developed between it and Judaism came to a head with the Maccabean revolt (165 B.C.E.), which checked the spread of Hellenism in Judea.

Hillel (c. 1st century B.C.E.):
President of the Sanhedrin and Talmudic scholar famed for his liberal interpretations of the law and his concern for the welfare of the common people. The school which he founded differed in its liberalism from that of Shammai.

Johanan ben Zakkai (1st century C.E.):
Religious leader. Disciple of Hillel and teacher of Akiba. According to legend, during the siege of Jerusalem, he was carried out of the city in a coffin, and opened the Talmudic academy at Yavneh.

Josephus, Flavius (c. 38-c. 100 C.E.)
Historian and military leader of the Jews in Palestine when they revolted against Romans. After the fall of Jerusalem, he accompanied the Roman Emperor Titus to Rome. Josephus' historical writings—which include *The Jewish War*, *The Antiquities of the Jews*, *Autobiography*, and *Against Apion*—are the principal source for knowledge of Jewish history of that period.

Judah the Prince (ha-Nasi) (135-222 C.E.):
Editor and compiler of the Mishnah, and seventh president of the Sanhedrin, the highest court of Jewish law, which made him the religious and political head of the Jewish community in Palestine.

Kabbalah (Hebrew, "the tradition"):
The system of Jewish philosophical mysticism which began about 1200 and expressed itself in various movements up to modern times. The *Zohar*, a mystical commentary on the Bible of the thirteenth century, is its great classic, and Isaac Luria (1534-1572) of the Safed Brotherhood one of its major teachers. It also exerted a profound influence on *Ḥasidism*.

Karaites:
A religious sect founded in Babylonia by Anan ben David about 767, which rejected the authority of Talmudic law, and based

its religious life on a literal interpretation of the Five Books of Moses. It encouraged freedom and individual inquiry in the explanation of Scripture.

Law, Oral:

The tradition of interpretation and analysis of the Written Law, which was handed down orally from generation to generation. Its importance was based on the tradition that it was likewise given to Moses on Sinai and represented an amplification of the Written Law. Though it was not accepted by some sects, in its development it became the whole body of Talmudic legislation and hence the core of Jewish practice.

Law, Written:

Term referring to the Law received by Moses in written form. Strictly speaking, this is limited to the Pentateuch; but by extension it is also used for certain books of the Hagiographa, which are also recorded in written form.

Mekilta:

Term applied to certain Midrashic works; sometimes used as a synonym for a tractate of the Mishnah or Talmud.

Midrash (Hebrew, "exposition"):

Books of Talmudic and post-Talmudic times that deal with the homiletic exegesis of Scripture. Made up of illustrative parables, stories, and similes which were used by the ancient rabbis to teach the people the meaning of certain biblical passages.

Mishnah:

See Gemarah and Talmud.

mitzvah (Hebrew, "commandment"):

The name given to the 613 affirmative and prohibitive obligations or duties arranged by Maimonides. It was traditionally regarded as a means of expressing the immeasurable love of the Jews for God. A person is said to have "earned a *mitzvah*" by performing a good deed.

Oral Law:

See Law, Oral.

Pentateuch:

Greek term (meaning "fivefold") for the Five Books of Moses, or what Jews traditionally call *Ḥumash*.

Pharisees (Hebrew, *Perushim*, probably meaning "set apart," avoiding contact with others for reasons of ritual purity):

One of the three religious and political parties during the period of the Second Temple, which was responsible for the foundation of Jewish law as it exists today. The New Testament speaks of them disparagingly as hypocrites, adhering to the letter rather than the spirit of the law, but this is a falsification of history. Their views were accepted by the overwhelming majority of the Jewish people so that, in a certain sense, Judaism and Pharisaism were identical at that time.

pilpul:

An analytic method used in Talmud study, which explored all sides of an argument, and which was often used excessively. It came to be associated with hairsplitting and unproductive argumentation.

pogrom (Russian, "destruction"):

Term used to describe any organized massacre or attempt to annihilate any group of people. Originally applied to attacks against Jews in Russia.

Prophets:

The second section of the Bible. The First or Former Prophets include Joshua, Judges, Samuel I and II, Kings I and II. The Later Prophets, which contain the great body of prophetic teachings, refer to Isaiah, Jeremiah, and Ezekiel, the Major Prophets; and the twelve Minor Prophets—Hosea, Joel, Amos, Obadiah, Jonah, Micah, Naḥum, Habakkuk, Haggai, Zephaniah, Zechariah, and Malachi.

Rabbinism and Rabbinites:

Name given by Karaites to their opponents who accepted the precepts of Jewish law contained in the Mishnah and Talmud. Rabbinism came to mean the acceptance of the authority of Oral Law. It is synonymous with normative traditional Judaism.

Revelation:

The act of communication from God to man and the content of that communication. In traditional Jewish belief, man's knowledge of the existence of God came originally from God Himself. Thus, the Mosaic revelation on Mt. Sinai provided Israel with a Written and an Oral Law. The relationship between knowledge obtained by revelation (Torah) and knowledge obtained through human reason alone has been discussed by philosophers and theologians down through the ages.

Sabbatai Zevi (1626-1676):

A false Messiah and *Kabbalist* of magnetic personality who won a great following among Jews and whose fame spread to all corners of the world.

Sadducees:

Second largest religious and political party during the Second Temple period in Palestine. Opposed to the Pharisees, who represented the aristocracy of wealth and power. They were formed originally as the party which acknowledged the leadership of the priests and took the Torah as their religious foundation. They were conservative in spirit and practice.

Sanhedrin:
A Greek term meaning "assembly," and referring to the trial courts of the Second Temple. There were two types: smaller Sanhedrins of twenty-three to deal with capital cases, and the Great Sanhedrin of seventy-one, a court at the peak of the entire judiciary system. The latter interpreted the Jewish law and enacted decrees for religious observance. Its president was called *nasi* and his deputy *ab bet din.*

Shammaites:
Disciples of Shammai, Talmudic scholar of the first century B.C.E., who, unlike the disciples of Hillel, interpreted the laws rigidly.

Shekhinah (Hebrew, "divine presence"):
Expresses idea of God's omnipresence and often used as a synonym for God. Implying radiance, it has assumed a mystical meaning.

Shema Yisrael (Hebrew, "Hear, O Israel," from Deuteronomy 6:4):
Basic Jewish prayer which declares faith in unity of God, traditionally recited mornings and evenings.

Shulkhan Arukh ("The Set Table"):
Standard code of Jewish laws, based on Talmudic sources and later opinions or decisions of the great rabbis, compiled by Joseph Karo (1564-5). Still regarded by Orthodox Jews as the standard code.

Sifra:
Midrash to Leviticus.

Sifre:
Midrash to Numbers and Deuteronomy.

Talmud:
Name applied to each of two major compendia (completed at the end of the fifth century) of the records of discussion, administration, and interpretation of Jewish laws by generations of scholars and jurists in many academies and countries. Containing both *Halakhah* and *Aggadah,* law and legendary lore, the Talmud is made up of two basic divisions: the Mishnah or interpretations of biblical law, and Gemarah or later commentaries. There are two Talmuds: the *Palestinian* and the *Babylonian;* both were written in Aramaic for the most part, but the latter is three times as large and wider in scope, covering the religious, communal, and social life of Jews for many

centuries. The Talmud is the authoritative source for Judaism, second only to the Torah.

Tannaim (Aramaic, "to teach"):

Teachers and scholars of first two centuries C.E. who taught the Oral Law. Johanan ben Zakkai, Akiba, and Meir were three of the outstanding figures among nearly three hundred *Tannaim*.

Temple, First and Second:

The central edifice for divine worship in the Holy Land until 70 C.E., situated on Mt. Moriah, in Jerusalem. The First Temple, planned by King David and erected by King Solomon, was destroyed by Nebuchadnezzar, king of Babylonia, in 586 B.C.E. The Second Temple, completed seventy years later, was destroyed by Titus and the Romans in 70 C.E.

Torah (Hebrew, "teaching"):

Generic term used to cover the Bible, the Talmud, and all later commentaries. Specifically, it refers to the Five Books of Moses.

Tosaphot (Hebrew, "additions"):

Supplements to the commentary of Rashi by a school of twelfth-century European Talmudic scholars, headed by Rabbenu Tam, who were called *Tosafists*. They analyzed critically conflicting opinions in the Talmud, and rendered important legal decisions on problems arising in their own day.

Tosefta (meaning "additions"):

An elaboration of the Mishnah, containing discussion of the laws compiled by the *Tannaim*. Its systems and arrangement correspond to those of the Mishnah.

Written Law:

See Law, Written.

yeshiva:

Traditional Jewish school devoted primarily to study of the Talmud and rabbinic literature.

Zohar:

Important and influential book of the *Kabbalah*, published in the thirteenth century, compiled by Moses de Leon but attributed to Rabbi Simeon ben Yohai of the second century. Deals with the mystery of creation, and explains stories and events of the Bible in a symbolic manner.

*About the Contributors

SALO W. BARON, Ph.D., Pol.Sc.D., Jur.D., occupies the Chair of Jewish History, Literature and Institutions of the Miller Foundation at Columbia University. Since 1939 he has served as editor of *Jewish Social Studies*. His books and studies number more than 200, and some have appeared in German, French, and Hebrew. Among his works are three volumes on *The Jewish Community, Its History and Structure*, and *A Social and Religious History of the Jews*, eight volumes of which have appeared thus far. He is also editor of *Essays on Maimonides, an Octocentennial Volume*.

SAMUEL M. BLUMENFIELD, Ph.D., is Director of the Department of Education and Culture of the Jewish Agency for Israel, and was formerly a member of the faculty of the New School for Social Research. He is the author of *Master of Troyes*, *Maimonides the Educator*, and *John Dewey and Jewish Education*.

MORTIMER J. COHEN, Ph.D., is rabbi of Congregation Beth Shalom in Philadelphia, Pa., and has for the past six years served as editor-in-chief of *In Jewish Bookland*, and for the last two years as editor of the *Jewish Book Annual*. He is author of *Pathways Through the Bible*, *Jacob Emden: A Man of Controversy*, and co-author of *Counterattack: Scapegoats or Solutions*.

LOUIS FINKELSTEIN, Ph.D., D.Litt., S.T.D., is Chancellor of the Jewish Theological Seminary of America, author of *Akiba*, *The Pharisees*, *The Beliefs and Practices of Judaism*, and editor of *Rab Saadia Gaon: Studies in His Honor*, and the four-volume work *The Jews: Their History, Culture, Religion*.

ERWIN R. GOODENOUGH, Ph.D., is Professor of the History of Religion at Yale University. He is author of *Jewish Symbols in the Greco-Roman Period*, and several works on Philo, among them *An Introduction to Philo Judaeus* and *The Politics of Philo Judaeus*.

*The contributors are identified by their occupations at the time of the writing of the essays

JACOB S. MINKIN, M.A., D.H.L., is the author of *The Romance of Hassidism, Herod: A Biography, Abarbanel and the Expulsion of the Jews from Spain, The World of Moses Maimonides*, and contributor to many Anglo-Jewish publications.

LOUIS I. NEWMAN, Ph.D., has been rabbi of Congregation Rodeph Sholom since 1930. He is author of *Jewish Influence on Christian Reform Movements, The Jewish People, Faith and Life, Biting on Granite*, and other works. He is co-author of *Studies in Biblical Parallelism*, and co-compiler of *The Hasidic Anthology* and *The Talmudic Anthology*.

SIMON NOVECK, M.H.L., Ph.D., is National Director of the Department of Adult Jewish Education of B'nai B'rith. From 1950 until the fall of 1956, he served as rabbi of the Park Avenue Synagogue in New York, and has taught political and social sciences at the College of the City of New York. He is also editor of *Judaism and Psychiatry*, author of *Adult Jewish Education in the Modern Synagogue*, and editor of the quarterly journal *Jewish Heritage*.

HARRY M. ORLINSKY, Ph.D., is Professor of Bible at Hebrew Union College-Jewish Institute of Religion in New York, author of *Ancient Israel*, and editor-in-chief of the committee of scholars producing the new English translation of the Hebrew Bible for the Jewish Publication Society of America. In 1959, he received the National Jewish Welfare Board Frank L. Weil Award for "distinguished contribution to the development of American Jewish culture."

MEYER WAXMAN, M.A., Ph.D., is Professor Emeritus of Jewish Literature and Philosophy of the Hebrew Theological College in Chicago. In addition to his five books in Hebrew, his published works include: *The Philosophy of Don Hasdai Crescas;* a translation of Moses Hess' Zionist classic, *Rome and Jerusalem; Judaism: Religion and Ethics;* and the five-volume *A History of Jewish Literature*.

TRUDE WEISS-ROSMARIN, Ph.D., is editor of *Jewish Spectator*, and author of *Jewish Survival, Judaism and Christianity: The Differences, Religion of Reason, Jerusalem, Highlights of Jewish History, Jewish Women Through the Ages*, and other works. She is well known throughout the American Jewish community as a lecturer and platform speaker.

Index